Peter Kaiser

Whole-Body Affordances for Humanoid Robots

A Computational Approach

Karlsruhe Series on Humanoid Robotics

Edited by Prof. Dr.-Ing. Tamim Asfour

Vol. 04

Whole-Body Affordances for Humanoid Robots

A Computational Approach

by

Peter Kaiser

KIT Scientific Publishing

Dissertation, Karlsruher Institut für Technologie
KIT-Fakultät für Informatik

Tag der mündlichen Prüfung: 21. Dezember 2017
Referenten: Prof. Dr.-Ing. Tamim Asfour, Prof. Dr. Justus Piater

Impressum

KIT Scientific Publishing

Karlsruher Institut für Technologie (KIT)
KIT Scientific Publishing
Straße am Forum 2
D-76131 Karlsruhe

KIT Scientific Publishing is a registered trademark
of Karlsruhe Institute of Technology.
Reprint using the book cover is not allowed.

www.ksp.kit.edu

Print on Demand 2018 – Gedruckt auf FSC-zertifiziertem Papier

ISSN 2512-0875
ISBN 978-3-7315-0798-7
DOI 10.5445/KSP/1000083165

Whole-Body Affordances for Humanoid Robots: A Computational Approach

Zur Erlangung des akademischen Grades eines

Doktors der Ingenieurwissenschaften

der KIT-Fakultät für Informatik
des Karlsruher Instituts für Technologie (KIT)

genehmigte

Dissertation

von

Dipl.-Inform. Peter Kaiser

aus Aachen

Tag der mündlichen Prüfung:	21. Dezember 2017
Referent:	Prof. Dr.-Ing. Tamim Asfour
Korreferent:	Prof. Dr. Justus Piater

Zusammenfassung

Die humanoide Robotik beschäftigt sich mit der Konzeption von Robotiksystemen mit anthropomorpher Struktur, die in für Menschen geschaffenen Umgebungen operieren sollen. Ein autonomer oder teilautonomer humanoider Roboter muss in solchen unstrukturierten und teilweise unbekannten Umgebungen selbstständig Interaktionsmöglichkeiten mit der Umgebung und den darin enthaltenen Objekten erkennen und in seine Aktionsplanung bzw. -ausführung einbeziehen können. Zur Beschreibung der menschlichen Wahrnehmung von Interaktionsmöglichkeiten mit Umgebungsobjekten wurde die Theorie der *Affordanzen* durch den amerikanischen Kognitionspsychologen James J. Gibson aufgestellt. Diese Theorie besagt, dass Umgebungsobjekte einem Agenten, das könnte ein Mensch oder ein humanoider Roboter sein, Interaktionsmöglichkeiten anbieten. Dabei entstehen Affordanzen in Abhängigkeit von den Objekteigenschaften und den spezifischen Fähigkeiten des Agenten. Ein Stuhl bietet beispielsweise die Affordanz *Sitzen* an, sofern der wahrnehmende Agent über entsprechende Fähigkeiten und Körpermaße verfügt. Die Theorie der Affordanzen ist in der Kognitionspsychologie weit verbreitet und in Ansätzen anhand des menschlichen Gehirns bzw. der menschlichen Sensorik biologisch begründet. Auch in der Robotik sind affordanzbasierte Ansätze zur Perzeption verbreitet.

Ziel dieser Dissertation ist es, basierend auf Gibsons Theorie der Affordanzen, ein Konzept für das perzeptiv-kognitive System eines humanoiden Roboters zu entwickeln und zu implementieren, das insbesondere in unbekannten und unstrukturierten Umgebungen wichtige Informationen zur Aktionsplanung und -ausführung liefern kann. Dabei liegt der Fokus auf Affordanzen für Ganzkörperaktionen zur stabilen Lokomotion oder Manipulation, sogenannten *Loko-Manipulationsaktionen*, beispielsweise für das *Abstützen* oder *Festhalten* an Umgebungsobjekten. Das System ermöglicht zusammen mit einer Pilotschnittstelle die teilautonome Steuerung eines humanoiden Roboters und wird anhand verschiedener realistischer Szenarien in Simulation und auf realen humanoiden Robotern evaluiert. Die Einzelbeiträge der Arbeit bestehen dabei in der Formalisierung eines berechenbaren Modells des Affordanzbegriffs, der Definition eines hierarchischen Systems zur Propagierung von affordanzbasierter Evidenz, der Konzipierung und Implementierung einer affordanzbasierten Pilotschnittstelle für die teilautonome Steuerung eines humanoiden Roboters und der Evaluation des Gesamtsystems in simulierten Szenarien, sowie mit realen humanoiden Robotern. Im Folgenden werden die Einzelbeiträge der Arbeit im Detail besprochen.

Formalisierung von Affordanzen Der grundlegendste Beitrag dieser Arbeit ist die geeignete Formalisierung des Begriffs der *Aktionsmöglichkeit*, basierend auf der psychologischen Theorie der Affordanzen. Das Ergebnis soll ein berechenbares Modell für Affordanzen sein, welches im Kontext realer Robotikanwendungen eingesetzt werden kann. Dieses Modell wird im Hinblick auf Affordanzen für Ganzkörper-Loko-Manipulationsaktionen entwickelt und repräsentiert Affordanzen als Evidenzfunktionen über dem Raum der Endeffektor-Posen. Neben der effizienten Auswertbarkeit ermöglicht diese Wahl der Repräsentation die direkte Parameterisierung von Aktionen. Zur Repräsentation und Kombination von affordanzbezogenen Evidenzen werden die *Evidenztheorie von Dempster und Shafer* und die *Theorie der subjektiven Logik* verwendet. Diese liefern das theoretische Rahmenwerk, um affordanzbezogene Evidenzen effektiv miteinander zu verrechnen.

Hierarchie von Ganzkörper-Affordanzen Die Formalisierung von Affordanzen als Evidenzfunktionen ermöglicht die hierarchische Definition von Affordanzen höherer Ebene als Kompositionen von Evidenzfunktionen niederer Ebene unter Einbeziehung von körper- bzw. umgebungsbezogenen Parametern. Durch die hierarchische Definition von Affordanzen wird implizit ein Modell vorgegeben, nach dem affordanzbasierte Evidenz in den Hierarchieebenen weiterpropagiert wird. Dieses Modell kann direkt für die visuelle Wahrnehmung von Affordanzen in unbekannten Umgebungen und für die physische Validierung der erkannten Affordanzen eingesetzt werden. Evidenz aus verschiedenen Quellen bezogen auf Affordanzen in verschiedenen Hierarchieebenen kann konsistent zu einem Gesamtbild der affordanzbezogenen Evidenz verrechnet werden. Die Menge der definierten Affordanzen ist ausreichend groß, um komplexe Aufgaben aus dem Bereich der einhändigen und zweihändigen Loko-Manipulation in unbekannten Umgebungen zu bewältigen. Dies wird anhand von simulierten Szenarien und in Experimenten mit realen humanoiden Robotern evaluiert.

Affordanzbasierte Autonomie und Teilautonomie Die Formalisierung des Affordanzbegriffs und die darauf aufbauende Hierarchie von Ganzkörper-Affordanzen ermöglichen die Implementierung eines Systems für die Wahrnehmung von Interaktionsmöglichkeiten in unbekannten Umgebungen durch humanoide Roboter. In einem weiteren Beitrag der Arbeit wird die Anwendung dieses Affordanzsystems für die autonome und teilautonome Steuerung von humanoiden Robotern untersucht. Dazu muss eine zuverlässige Verbindung zwischen wahrgenommenen Affordanzen und bekannten Aktionsprimitiven des Roboters hergestellt werden, die dann für autonome Komponenten zur Aufgaben- und Aktionsplanung verwendet werden können. In Anlehnung an aktuelle Entwicklungen in der humanoiden Robotik liegt der Fokus dieser Arbeit auf der teilautonomen Steuerung eines humanoiden Roboters, in der ein menschlicher Pilot über eine geeignete Schnittstelle mit dem Roboter interagiert und die Aufgaben übernimmt, die durch den Roboter nicht autonom zu bewältigen sind. Dazu wird eine Pilotschnittstelle entwickelt, die dem menschlichen Piloten eine Visualisierung der Umgebungswahrnehmung des Roboters zur Verfügung stellt, inklusive erkannter Affordanzen. Der Pilot übernimmt die abstrakte Aufgabenplanung und steuert den Roboter, indem er aus autonom erkannten Affordanzen und den damit verbundenen Aktionsprimitiven des Roboters auswählt und automatische Vorschläge zur Aktionsparameterisierung überwacht. Wenn nötig kann der Pilot den Roboter jederzeit auch teleoperativ steuern.

Evaluation des Affordanzsystems Das entwickelte perzeptiv-kognitive System und die damit verbundenen Strategien zur autonomen und teilautonomen Steuerung von humanoiden Robotern zielt auf die reale Anwendung in unbekannten Umgebungen ab. Neben der individuellen Evaluation verschiedener Teilaspekte der Arbeit, werden systemweite Evaluationen in komplexen Simulationsumgebungen sowie auf den realen humanoiden Robotern ARMAR-III und WALK-MAN durchgeführt. Die Anwendung auf realen humanoiden Robotern unterstreicht die Realisierbarkeit von affordanzbasierter Autonomie und insbesondere von affordanzbasierter Teilautonomie in anwendungsnahen Szenarien.

Acknowledgment

This thesis is the result of my work at the High Performance Humanoid Technologies Lab (H^2T) of the Institute for Anthropomatics and Robotics (IAR), Karlsruhe Institute of Technology (KIT) and was partly funded by the EU research project WALK-MAN.

First of all, I would like to thank my doctoral supervisor Prof. Tamim Asfour for giving me the opportunity to work in the rapidly evolving and equally fascinating field of humanoid robotics. I am particularly grateful for the continuous and valuable support that I received and for the fruitful discussions I had with him. I would like to extend my thanks to Prof. Justus Piater who kindly agreed to co-supervise my thesis.

The Humanoids group at KIT has always been a great environment with great colleagues and friends. I would like to thank all past and present humanoids, including Eren Aksoy, Graziella Barbaro, Michael Bechtel, Diana Becker, Jonas Beil, Christian Böge, Júlia Borràs Sol, Christine Brand, Martin Do, Isabel Ehrenberger, David González-Aguirre, Raphael Grimm, Markus Grotz, Hans Haubert, Paul Holz, Lukas Kaul, Manfred Kröhnert, Christian Mandery, Pascal Meißner, Michael Neaga, Simon Ottenhaus, Ekaterina Ovchinnikova, Fabian Paus, Markus Przybylski, Samuel Rader, David Schiebener, Julian Schill, Fabian Schültje, Sebastian Schulz, Dmitriy Shingarey, Julia Starke, Sandra Tartarelli, Ömer Terlemez, Stefan Ulbrich, Nikolaus Vahrenkamp, Mirko Wächter, Isabelle Wappler, Pascal Weiner, Kai Welke, Natsuki Yamanobe and You Zhou. Furthermore, the students Matthias Hadlich, Veith Röthlingshoefer, Jan Nouruzi-Pur, Fabian Paus and

Andreas Boltres contributed to this thesis in different ways which I gratefully appreciate.
I would like to particularly thank Nikolaus Vahrenkamp for his continuous support and advise, Mirko Wächter for his tireless work on ArmarX, as well as David González-Aguirre, Markus Grotz, Lukas Kaul, Manfred Kröhnert, Simon Ottenhaus, Samuel Rader, David Schiebener, Ramin Shirazi-Nejad and Mirko Wächter for the enjoyable times abroad on conferences and holidays. I further thank my friends Eva Grotelüschen and Ramin Shirazi-Nejad for their continuous support and in particular Johannes Ernesti for his friendship and for the endless and curious times we spent together working on different projects and ideas, many of which are hopefully still to follow.
Most importantly, I want to thank my parents Ulrich and Angelika, my brother Klaus and my sister Anne for their continuous support and valuable feedback that reaches far beyond the period of this thesis, and last but not least, my girlfriend Naila for her ability to make even the most stressful phases pleasurable.

Karlsruhe, December 2017 *Peter Kaiser*

Contents

1 Introduction

In the most general sense, a *robot* is a programmable machine designed for automatically performing sequences of actions in order to complete a defined task. Robots can roughly be categorized into *industrial robots* and *service robots*. Industrial robots are traditionally employed in well-defined production environments, like automated assembly lines, physically separated from human workers. Service robots on the other end are expected to perform their tasks in less structured environments, like public areas or households in close co-existence and cooperation with humans. Service robots are designed to perform tasks that are considered *dirty*, *dull* or *dangerous* for humans, either in professional or private environments. Recent studies investigating the dimensions of the global robotics market reveal that there exists a total of about 1.6 million operational industrial robots in 2015. Similar studies concentrating on service robots differ between about 300,000 sold units for professional use and about 5.4 million sold units for personal and domestic use, both until 2015 (International Federation of Robotics 2016a,b). Common examples for service robots with domestic application include autonomous vacuum cleaners and lawn mowers.

A *humanoid robot* is a particular type of service robot that is designed to at least partially resemble the shape, the behavior, the sensory-motor skills and the cognitive capabilities of human beings. While specialized robotic solutions are sufficient for many relevant applications, humanoid robots are commonly regarded as a perspective solution for general-purpose robots that are as flexibly applicable as human workers. Humanoid robots are kinematically and dynamically complex machines and their conception and construction combines several challenging problems from various areas of mechanical engineering, electrical engineering and computer science. These challenges make *humanoid robotics* an active field of fundamental research.

Figure 1.1: The humanoid robot ARMAR-III (Asfour et al. 2006) in a kitchen. Such human-centered environments impose high challenges on the perceptive-cognitive skills of a humanoid robot.

The human-centered environments that humanoid robots are intended to be employed in, see e. g. the kitchen environment in Figure 1.1, are typically *unknown*, *arbitrary*, *cluttered* and to a certain degree *unstructured*. For successful operation under these circumstances, humanoid robots need to demonstrate sophisticated capabilities in perceiving and understanding such environments, although not having previously been exposed to the particular scenes. Based on the scene perception, the robot needs to reason about possible ways of interaction afforded by available objects and the environment. In the context of humanoid robotics, possible ways of interaction include actions that incorporate the whole body of the robot for combined locomotion and manipulation (see Figure 1.2). These *whole-body loco-manipulation actions* are particularly important, as multi-contact stabilization for locomotion, e. g. by *supporting* on or *leaning* against suitable surfaces, and whole-body manipulation, e. g. *pushing* or *pulling* of large objects or opening of doors, are considered essential capabilities. Despite impressive advances in the field, general-purpose solutions to the problem of scene understanding and the perception of action possibilities are a challenging area of active research and the robust applicability of available approaches lies beyond the state-of-the-art, which has recently been demonstrated at the *DARPA Robotic Challenge* (DRC). The DRC was an international competition for humanoid robots held in 2015, in which the participating teams had to perform various challenging tasks in the context of a disaster response scenario. The robots employed during the DRC were operated in a *shared autonomous* control mode which allows the autonomous operation of a humanoid robot to the degree that is robust and reliable. Behaviors that exceed the autonomous capabilities of the state-of-the-art are leveraged to a human pilot which is remotely connected to the robot through a *pilot interface*.

Figure 1.2: Examples for whole-body loco-manipulation actions: *Pulling* and *pushing* of large and heavy objects and *climbing* of staircases or ladders.

1.1 Problem Statement and Contributions

This thesis approaches the problem of developing a perceptive-cognitive system for autonomous humanoid robots that allows the perception of action possibilities in unknown and unstructured environments by consistently integrating information from the visual and haptic sensory systems of the robot. In line with the incorporated theoretical backgrounds, action possibilities are called *affordances* in this work. The primary focus is the detection of whole-body action possibilities or *whole-body affordances*, particularly with respect to loco-manipulation tasks (see Figure 1.2), but the developed mechanisms are not necessarily constrained to those. The individual contributions of this thesis consist of the computational formalization of the concept of *action possibility* based on the psychological *theory of affordances*, the definition of a hierarchical framework for the detection of whole-body affordances in unknown environments, the implementation of an affordance detection and validation system for autonomous and shared autonomous control of humanoid robots and the evaluation of the developed methods in multiple realistic scenarios in simulation and on real robotic platforms. In the following, the individual contributions of the thesis are described in further detail.

Computational Formalization of Affordances The first contribution of this thesis is a novel computational formalization of the concept of *action possibility* based on the psychological theory of *affordances*. This formalization is based on the ideas that actions are fundamentally defined by end-effector contact and that the process of affordance detection can be understood as a continuous process of evidence fusion. Affordances are represented as *affordance belief functions*, i. e. *Dempster-Shafer belief functions* over the space of end-effector poses. This allows the consistent fusion of affordance-related evidence from various possible sources, e. g. visual perception or haptic validation, into a joint system belief. Affordance belief functions allow the integration of environmental properties, e. g. object sizes, and body-scaled parameters, e. g. hand dimensions, into the process of affordance detection. Furthermore, the *theory of subjective logic* is applied to formulate logic operations on affordance belief functions which eventually allows the hierarchical composition of affordance belief functions.

Hierarchy of Whole-Body Affordances The second contribution of this thesis is the application of the affordance concept to the perception of whole-body action possibilities which forms a novel approach to action possibility perception in humanoid robotics. Based on the idea that action possibilities, i. e. affordances, are an inherently hierarchical concept, a hierarchy of whole-body affordances is defined based on the computational formalization of affordance belief functions. The benefits of the hierarchical definition of affordance belief functions is the effective incorporation of evidence from different sources, e. g. affordance validation experiments, at different hierarchical layers. The defined affordance hierarchy can directly be used for visual affordance detection based on simplified environmental representations in terms of geometric primitives. The proposed whole-body affordance hierarchy contains a selected set of whole-body affordances, reasonably sufficient for performing actions of locomotion, unimanual manipulation and bimanual manipulation. Although the choice of affordances represented in the hierarchy is justified based on the aspired evaluation scenarios, the hierarchy is subject to extension.

Affordance-Based Autonomous and Shared-Autonomous Control
The computational model for affordances developed in this thesis can be employed for the operation of humanoid robots on different levels of autonomy. Methods for affordance-based robot control are developed for fully autonomous operation of humanoid robots and for shared autonomous operation which is closer to real applications. In affordance-based shared autonomy, a human pilot is connected to the robot via a *pilot interface* which shows the pilot a visualization of the robot's environmental perception and a selection of available affordances. While switching to traditional low-level teleoperation is possible at any time, the pilot interface aims at providing the pilot with the possibility to control the robot based on detected affordances. Fundamental parameterization for action execution is automatically proposed based on information from the affordance belief

functions, particularly end-effector poses, and can be adjusted by the pilot. The developed affordance-based pilot interface allows the pilot to abstract from the detailed low-level control of a complex humanoid robot to a more task-centered control scheme, focusing on the selection of affordances that lead to successful task execution.

Figure 1.3: The humanoid robots ARMAR-III (*left*), ARMAR-4 (*middle*) and WALK-MAN (*right*) which are used throughout this thesis.

Evaluation of the Affordance System In this thesis, a computational model for whole-body affordances for humanoid robots is developed and implemented, aiming at the application in autonomous and shared-autonomous control modes. While multiple aspects of the system are evaluated individually, the central idea is to perform a system evaluation that demonstrates the effectiveness of the proposed methods for affordance detection and validation as a whole in a simulated evaluation environment. Furthermore, the affordance system is implemented and evaluated on three humanoid robotic platforms, ARMAR-III (Asfour et al. 2006), ARMAR-4 (Asfour et al. 2013) and WALK-MAN (Tsagarakis et al. 2017), in different challenging evaluation scenarios, demonstrating the feasibility of the concept in combination with real robot hardware and real sensor data. See Figure 1.3 for a visualization of the employed humanoid robots.

1.2 Structure of the Thesis

This thesis is structured into eight chapters which consecutively introduce, discuss and evaluate the approach taken towards an affordance system that satisfies the requirements for the contributions outlined in Section 1.1:

Chapter 2 introduces and discusses fundamentals and related work. This includes the psychological theory of *affordances* as one of the foundations of this work, as well as various approaches to the formalization of this concept and to the implementation of affordance-based approaches in robotics. One central body of related work is provided by the *DARPA Robotics Challenge* (DRC), a successful competition for humanoid robots held in 2015. The chapter concludes with an introduction into the concepts of *autonomy* and *shared autonomy* which are central for understanding the proposed ideas of affordance-based autonomy.

Chapter 3 introduces the frameworks which are necessary for the concepts proposed and developed in the following chapters. This includes the H^2T *perception pipeline* for the extraction of geometric primitives in unknown environments, as well as the concept of *Object-Action Complexes* (OACs) as a conceptual framework for the representation of sensorimotor experience with a strong connection to symbolic planning and affordance detection. The chapter concludes with a brief introduction into *ArmarX*, the robot development environment used within this thesis.

Chapter 4 describes the *computational model for whole-body affordances* in humanoid robotics as the first contribution of this thesis. Affordances are represented as *affordance belief functions*, expressing *Dempster-Shafer* belief values over the space of end-effector poses. The chapter introduces these concepts and formalizes the proposed computational model. It further formalizes methods for incorporating properties of embodiment and environment, for evidence fusion, for inference on affordance belief functions and for representing *bimanual affordances*. The chapter concludes with a discussion of *discretization* of the continuous formalism of affordance belief functions.

Chapter 5 bases upon the formal methods developed in Chapter 4 for creating a *hierarchy of whole-body affordances*. This hierarchy is based on fundamental power-grasp affordances for *prismatic grasping* and *platform grasping* and successively formulates higher-level affordances by combining lower-level affordances with properties of the environment or the robot embodiment. The developed affordance hierarchy represents unimanual affordances as well as bimanual affordances.

Chapter 6 introduces the concepts of *affordance-based autonomy* and *affordance-based shared autonomy* as fundamental control modes for humanoid robots. As full autonomy in humanoid robotics lies beyond the state-of-the-art, *shared autonomy* is proposed as a viable approach for the successful control of complex humanoid robots by human pilots. In the proposed cognitive architecture, affordances are seen as explicit preconditions for the instantiation of OACs. This approach provides a functional link between detected affordances, action execution skills and symbolic planning domains. A pilot interface is introduced which allows the affordance-based control of a humanoid robot based on the concept of affordances. In practical applications, the robot supports the pilot by suggesting possible ways of interaction with the unknown environment based on detected affordances.

Chapter 7 evaluates and validates different aspects of the proposed concepts. First, fundamental aspects of the formalization from Chapter 3 are evaluated, particularly the definition of affordance belief functions and its suitability to the fusion of affordance-related evidence. In a simulated experiment, the concepts of autonomous affordance detection and validation based on the hierarchy of whole-body affordances are evaluated. Furthermore, the utilization of detected affordances for multi-contact pose sequence planning is reviewed. Before concluding the chapter with a discussion of system performance, multiple experiments on real humanoid robots are reviewed, demonstrating the applicability of the proposed concepts to real robots in real environments based on the concept of affordance-based shared autonomy.

Chapter 8 summarizes the contributions of the thesis and the obtained results. It further discusses strengths and weaknesses of the proposed approach, as well as possible aspects of extension and future work.

2 Fundamentals and Related Work

The goal of this thesis is the conception and development of an affordance system for action possibility detection in unknown environments and the application of these methods in the context of autonomous robot control. This chapter introduces and discusses fundamental concepts that will be of central use throughout this thesis, particularly focusing on the *theory of affordances* which provides the conceptual framework for the proposed approach.

The psychological theory of affordances is systematically introduced and discussed in Section 2.1. Subsequently, Section 2.2 discusses existing, pioneering approaches to the computational formalization of the affordance concept, aiming at applications in artificial intelligence and autonomous robotics. Although affordance-based approaches in these areas share a common motivation and terminology, the available formalizations vary substantially. Section 2.3 gives a broad overview over affordance-based approaches in autonomous robotics and reviews the differences to the concept of whole-body affordances as proposed in this thesis. In Section 2.4, an overview over autonomous control modes in humanoid robotics is presented with a focus on *shared autonomous* control modes in which a human pilot controls a humanoid robot in collaboration with autonomous capabilities of the robot itself. Finally, Section 2.5 concludes the chapter with a summary of the insights obtained from the reviewed approaches.

2.1 The Psychological Theory of Affordance

The American psychologist James J. Gibson[1] initially introduced the concept of *affordances* as an approach to explaining the visual perceptual process in humans and animals (J. J. Gibson 1966). With his influential work, Gibson founded a psychological school, commonly referred to as *Ecological Psychology* or *Gibsonian Psychology*[2]. Affordances are typically defined as opportunities for action latent in the environment and the process of understanding an environment in terms of interaction possibilities is interpreted as the detection of affordances. Gibson himself writes:

> *When the constant properties of constant objects are perceived (the shape, size, color, texture, composition, motion, animation, and position relative to other objects), the observer can go on to detect their affordances. I have coined this word as a substitute for values, a term which carries an old burden of philosophical meaning. I mean simply what things furnish, for good or ill. What they afford the observer, after all, depends on their properties.*
> J. J. Gibson (1966, p. 285)

According to Gibson, affordances arise based on properties of perceived objects in combination with the perceiving agent's capabilities. This ecological view of the relation between agents and environments is called the *animal-environment system*:

> *The affordances of the environment are what it offers the animal, what it provides or furnishes, either for good or ill. The verb to afford is found in the dictionary, but the noun affordance is*

[1] James Jerome Gibson, 1904 - 1979

[2] The term *Ecological Psychology* is sometimes also used in reference to other related schools of psychology, the prefix *Gibsonian* is then used for resolving this ambiguity.

> *not. I have made it up. I mean by it something that refers to both the environment and the animal in a way that no existing term does. It implies the complementarity of the animal and the environment.*
> J. J. Gibson (1986, p. 127)

The term *ecological* in this context means that the foundation for perception is information which is ecologically available to be perceived by capable agents (J. J. Gibson 1966). McGrenere et al. (2000) condense Gibson's ideas in three fundamental properties of affordances:

1. Affordances exist relative to the agent's capabilities.
2. The existence of affordances is independent from the agent's ability to perceive them.
3. Affordances do not change as the needs and goals of the agent change.

Şahin et al. (2007) point out that affordances can be seen from three fundamental perspectives: the *agent perspective*, the *environmental perspective* and the *observer perspective*. While the concepts remain the same, confusion is possible[3] if author and reader do not share the same perspective. Another fundamental and frequently cited idea of the affordance concept is:

> *Perception is economical.*
> J. J. Gibson (1986)

With this statement, Gibson argues that the perception of object affordances is not acquired by relating a possibly huge set of perceived object features to noticed affordances, but rather by relating noticed affordances to small sets of invariantly discriminating features. This finding relates the affordance concept to the ideas of *direct perception*, opposing psychological

[3] And frequent, according to Şahin et al. (2007).

schools which assume indirect perception, e. g. *cognitivism*. The dispute about *direct and indirect perception*[4] can be condensed into the question whether environmental objects and events carry inherent meaning which is directly perceivable by agents without cognitive effort or, in opposition, whether meaning is attributed to environmental objects and events based on acquired agent-internal representations (Jones 2003).

Although Gibson believed that the perception of affordances is acquired over time, he was not interested in the particular question of how affordance perception is learned (Şahin et al. 2007). However, the psychologist Eleanor J. Gibson worked on explaining the developmental aspect of affordance perception. The field of *developmental psychology* is concerned with the development of human beings over the course of their lifetime, primarily within the ages from infancy to adolescence. E. J. Gibson believed that affordances are learned by the acquisition of new motor capabilities, eventually defining perceptual development as a process of learning about affordances (E. J. Gibson 1992; Adolph et al. 2015). Comprehensive surveys of the work of E. J. Gibson and the concept of affordances within developmental psychology are found in Adolph et al. (2015) and Jamone et al. (2016).

In a thorough review of affordance-related literature, Zech et al. (2017) identify three fundamental characteristics of affordances: *hierarchy*, *competitiveness* and *dynamics* which are briefly summarized in the following.

Hierarchy Affordances are an inherently hierarchical concept. This means that complex affordances, which refer to high-level actions, can be composed of less complex affordances, possibly referring to atomic actions.

Competitiveness Affordance detection is a fundamentally competitive process, i. e. perceiving agents deliberately choose among sets of detected affordances based on their individual needs.

[4] Also termed *direct and indirect realism*.

Dynamics The existence of affordances dynamically adapts to environmental changes. This applies e. g. to the *fillability* of a mug which dynamically vanishes once the mug is filled.

These fundamental properties of affordances form an important basis for the successful formalization of the affordance concept. The aspect of hierarchy will play a crucial role in the computational formalization proposed in this thesis (see Chapter 4 and Chapter 5) which allows the hierarchical arrangement of affordances and provides the formal mechanisms for belief propagation in the defined affordance hierarchy. The aspect of competitiveness will be addressed in Chapter 6 where mechanisms for affordance-based autonomous and shared-autonomous control are investigated. Although the aspect of dynamics is undoubtedly important, this thesis will focus on *static affordances*. While certain environmental changes can be addressed by performing a re-perception of the scene, the observation of action effects and the induced changes in affordance existence fall beyond the scope of this thesis. A related but conceptually different idea that is addressed in Chapter 4 is the idea of *affordance validation* which refers to the observation of effects of specific affordance validation actions in order to assess the existence of visually perceived affordance hypotheses.
Gibson's ideas have influenced research in numerous fields, including developmental psychology, neuroscience, industrial design, social sciences and robotics. While affordance-based approaches to autonomous robotics will be the subject of Section 2.2 and Section 2.3, the interested reader is referred to Şahin et al. (2007), Thill et al. (2013), Jamone et al. (2016), and Min et al. (2016) for more complete reviews including affordance-related approaches in other fields.

2.1.1 Attempts to Definition

Though Gibson initially developed the concept of affordances, he missed to provide a precise definition which led to intensive debate among ecological psychologists. Furthermore, Gibson's own view on affordances evolved over time. Horton et al. (2012) provide a brief summary of the scientific discourse about affordances, both within the field of Ecological Psychology and between psychologists and roboticists. Numerous researchers picked up Gibson's ideas for enhancement, definition or formalization. Particularly the precise definition of the term *affordance* caught the attention of many researchers, leading to a set of competing definitions. Early discussions about affordances, including Gibson's own work, often focus on visual perception, particularly on optical flow, which is also reflected in the developed definitions of the affordance concept (Şahin et al. 2007).
While affordances are commonly understood as *emergent properties*, i. e. properties that become apparent in the presence of an agent, discourse particularly exists in the questions if affordances are properties of objects (J. J. Gibson 1966), of the environment (Turvey 1992) or of the animal-environment system (Stoffregen 2003; Chemero 2003; Michaels 2003) and if affordances possess a relational nature (Stoffregen 2003; Chemero 2003; Michaels 2003). In his popular approach, Chemero (2003) defines affordances ϕ as relations:

$$\text{Affords} - \phi(\text{feature}, \text{ability}). \tag{2.1}$$

Chemero hence defines affordances as relations between features of an environment and the capabilities of an agent. This pragmatic approach has gained popularity among roboticists and was for example picked up by Şahin et al. (2007) in the intention of finding a suitable definition of the affordance concept for robotic applications. Thorough reviews of the detailed differences between the individual definitions are found in the comprehensive overviews in Şahin et al. (2007), Dotov et al. (2012), and Zech et al. (2017).

2.1.2 Experimental Evidence

Within the fields of ecological psychology and developmental psychology, numerous researchers attempted to find experimental evidence for the direct perception of affordances in humans and animals. One well-studied aspect is the *body-scaling* of affordances which states that affordances are perceived with respect to the dimensions of the perceiving agent's embodiment. Experiments have been conducted with human subjects for verifying body-scaled perception of the *climbability* of staircase risers with respect to the subject's leg length (Warren 1984), the *passability* of apertures with respect to the subject's eyeheight (Warren et al. 1987) or the *climbability* and *sitability* of surfaces at different heights with respect to the subject's eyeheight (Mark 1987). Costantini et al. (2010), Bub et al. (2010), and Ambrosini et al. (2013) conducted experiments indicating that the spatial relation between object and agent, particularly the object's reachability, plays an important role in the perception of *graspability* affordances. Although not fully understood yet, the *mirror neuron system* is sometimes seen as an indicator for affordance detection in primate brains. One principle argument is that besides *mirror neurons* which fire on action execution and action observation, *canonical neurons* exist which also fire on the observation of objects (Thill et al. 2013). The aspect of direct affordance perception has attracted numerous researches to find neuroscientific evidence for a direct link between perception and action in humans and animals which can in fact be observed for less developed animals. Frogs, for example, have a simple and direct neural detector for objects affording *eatability*, i. e. insects, implemented right behind the eyes (Lettvin et al. 1959). Behavioral studies have further shown that animals like frogs and toads can directly perceive locomotion affordances when approaching prey (Collett 1977; Ingle et al. 1977; Lock et al. 1979). In

sport science, evidence has been found for direct perceptual mechanisms in humans, e. g. for the direct perception of the time-to-contact of approaching objects (Fajen et al. 2008).
While the above experiments focused on different aspect of visual affordance perception, studies from developmental psychology have found evidence for haptic perception of affordances. Experiments have for example been conducted regarding the haptic perception of *traversability* of soft surfaces by crawling and walking infants (E. J. Gibson et al. 1987) or the perception of *traversability* of sloped surfaces by adult participants (Kinsella-Shaw et al. 1992).

2.1.3 Criticism

Gibson's theory of affordances gained large popularity in the field of autonomous robotics. However, it is subject to intense debate within psychology and computer science. In his comprehensive survey, Horton et al. (2012) identifies three central points of controversy in the scientific discourse about affordances which will be briefly addressed in the following.

The Formal Definition of an Affordance Gibson's original definition of the term *affordance* is vague, leaving space for interpretation and debate. While competing and amending definitions exist (see Section 2.1.1), Horton et al. (2012) argue that a uniformly accepted formal definition of an affordance has not yet emerged.

The Compatibility of Psychological and Computational Approaches Horton et al. (2012) state that the two fields interpret the concept of affordances from different directions: Psychologists attempt to *describe* behavior, whereas roboticists try to *implement* behavior. While psychologists and roboticists generally agree that affordances are relations, controversy exists in the question if affordances physically exist as external relations or, in opposition, if affordances are mental constructs of the agent.

The Role of Direct Perception Another point of controversy is the implemented degree of direct perception. While ecological psychologists commonly consider direct perception as a principle foundation, affordance-based approaches in robotics often construct agent-internal models and representations, due to practical reasons. Horton et al. (2012) state that complex behavior that goes beyond the commonly regarded problem of navigation based on optical flow, e. g. tool use, might be impossible to implement solely based on directly perceived affordances.

The addressed points of controversy justify the diversity of affordance-based approaches in robotics as will be reviewed in Section 2.2 and Section 2.3.

2.2 Computational Formalizations of Affordances

The psychological theory of affordances as proposed by Gibson does not provide an inherent computational formalization of the affordance concept. However, since affordance-based approaches were introduced in computer science and robotics, multiple attempts have been taken to develop computational formalizations of Gibson's ideas. In this section, the established formalizations of Steedman (2002a,b), Şahin et al. (2007), Montesano et al. (2008) and Krüger et al. (2011) are briefly introduced and reviewed.

2.2.1 The Formalization of Steedman

In a famous experiment, Köhler (1925) observed that chimpanzees are only able to utilize tools in reaching experiments if the tools are placed within sight of the monkeys. Motivated by this experiment, Steedman (2002a,b) concluded that non-linguistic animals[5] perform *reactive* action planning by forward chaining from the current situation. Humans in contrast, as linguistic animals, have the ability to plan by backward chaining from a defined goal state. Steedman further concluded that affordances are a suitable formalism for representing object-concepts in reactive planning. He proposes to formalize affordances using *Linear Dynamic Event Calculus* (LDEC) descriptions, e. g. :

$$\text{push}(y,x) \rightarrow \left\{ \begin{array}{c} \text{shut}(x) \multimap \text{open}(x) \\ \text{open}(x) \multimap \text{shut}(x) \end{array} \right\}, \tag{2.2}$$

which reads as: *Pushing of a door x by an agent y, yields a shut door to be open and an open door to be shut.* LDEC is capable of expressing sequences of actions or events with preconditions and consequences and allows reasoning about causal relations over events. The set of affordances available for an object, e. g.

$$\text{Affordances}(\text{door}) = \left\{ \begin{array}{c} \text{push} \\ \text{go-through} \end{array} \right\}, \tag{2.3}$$

can be used for action planning. Steedman postulates that universal operations for syntactic and semantic composition exist which apply to affordances as defined above, as well as to natural language expressed in terms of *Combinatorial Categorial Grammars* (CCGs).

Steedman's formalization of affordances draws an interesting similarity between affordance-based action planning and natural language processing. Although Steedman's formalization might be applicable to symbolic planning of whole-body actions in loco-manipulation tasks, it does not inherently

[5] i. e. *non-humans*

link affordances to perception and action execution which is the central topic of this thesis. Furthermore, although Steedman considers learning of affordances as the extension of the affordance-set (Equation 2.3), once novel object-event relations have been discovered, there is no inherent mechanism for representing uncertainty in the acquired relations.

2.2.2 The Formalization of Şahin et al.

In contrast to Steedman's formalization which primarily aims at affordance-driven symbolic planning, Şahin et al. (2007) focus on affordance-based autonomous robot control and navigation. Affordances, in this formalization, are defined as relations between *effects*, *entities* and *behaviors*:

$$\big(effect, (entity, behavior)\big). \tag{2.4}$$

Such a triplet describes the *effect* that is caused by applying *behavior* to *entity*, while *entity* refers to a perceptual representation of a physical entity, e. g. an object. Through constant interaction with the environment and perception of caused effects, autonomous robots can populate a growing database of relation instances, i. e. affordance triplets that have only been observed once. Şahin et al. (2007) define a set of four basic operations for generalizing from individual relation instances to affordances: *entity equivalence*, *behavior equivalence*, *affordance equivalence* and *effect equivalence*. Following the example of bimanual lifting from Şahin et al. (2007), the following representation can be generated from two observed relation instances:

$$\left(lifted, \left(\left\{ \begin{array}{c} blue\text{-}can \\ black\text{-}can \end{array} \right\}, lift\text{-}with\text{-}right\text{-}hand \right) \right). \tag{2.5}$$

By generating entity equivalence classes, the above formulation is condensed into:

$$\big(\textit{lifted}, (<\textit{*-can}>, <\textit{lift-with-right-hand}>)\big). \tag{2.6}$$

Similarly, if further relation instances are observed that demonstrate lifting of cans with the left hand, behavior equivalence classes can be generated in order to obtain a more general representation of the affordance:

$$\big(\textit{lifted}, (<\textit{*-can}>, <\textit{lift-with-*-hand}>)\big). \tag{2.7}$$

Affordance equivalence and effect equivalence work analogously on entity-behavior-tuples and effects, respectively. The generation of equivalence classes can be seen as a mechanism for affordance learning, although Şahin et al. (2007) prefer the term *acquisition* as the employed learning method is not specified in the formalization.

The formalization of Şahin et al. (2007) provides a simple and flexible framework for the representation and acquisition of affordances in the context of autonomous robotics. Reference implementations in Şahin et al. (2007) show that these ideas are feasible. Although the formalization seems entirely symbolic, *entity* and *effect* may refer to sensory percepts. It is important to notice that Şahin et al. (2007) provide a framework for the representation of affordances. Several non-trivial aspects, including feature spaces or learning methods, need to be defined and implemented in real applications. Although uncertainty, e. g. in observations or action execution, is not explicitly represented in the formalization, suitable generalization mechanisms are possible. In contrast to the formalization of whole-body affordances proposed in this thesis which inherently provides basic action parameterization in terms of continuous end-effector poses, such action parameterization is not further considered in the formalization of Şahin et al. (2007).

2.2.3 The Formalization of Montesano et al.

The previously discussed affordance formalizations consider learning about affordances as the process of acquisition and generalization of affordance relations. However, both formalizations provide no inherent solution for dealing with the acquisition of uncertain, redundant or irrelevant affordance relations. Montesano et al. (2008) propose a developmental formalization, maintaining a strong focus on learning. In their formalization, affordances are fundamentally represented as probabilistic relations between objects, actions and effects.

Montesano et al. (2008) propose *Bayesian Networks* (BNs) as a joint framework for learning and querying affordances. BNs are directed acyclic graphs in which nodes represent random variables, while edges correspond to conditional probability distributions. In the formalization of Montesano et al. (2008), the node set X of the BN represents discrete random variables for the executable motor actions A, self-experienced robot features F_r, perceivable object features F_o and perceivable effects E:

$$X = \{A, F_r, F_o, E\}. \tag{2.8}$$

Given a set D of executed actions with observed effects, established methods for model selection are employed for learning the network structure. After the network structure has been fixed, the parameters of the conditional probability distributions corresponding to the network edges can be incrementally updated based on observed data. A learned network can be queried using the *junction tree algorithm* in order to obtain e. g. the probability distribution of effects given a motor action a and a set of observed object features f (Montesano et al. 2008):

$$p(E|A = a, F_o = f). \tag{2.9}$$

The formalization of Montesano et al. (2008) differs from the previously discussed attempts in the inherently probabilistic approach. The results of incrementally acquired experiments can be jointly represented in a BN, eventually allowing affordance-based inference. The affordance formalization proposed in this thesis is inspired by Montesano et al. (2008) in the sense that the probabilistic representation of affordances is considered a key element. However, in contrast to BNs, whole-body affordances in this thesis are represented as Dempster-Shafer belief expressions over the space of end-effector poses which allows the consistent fusion of uncertain affordance-related evidence and provides direct links to action execution parameters. Furthermore, due to the choice of BNs, percepts, action parameters and effects need to be represented in terms of discrete random variables in Montesano et al. (2008). While this is often sufficient, it is difficult to represent the continuous space of end-effector poses in such a formalism.

2.2.4 The PACO-PLUS Formalization

The concept of *Object-Action Complexes* (Krüger et al. 2011), commonly abbreviated as OACs, has been developed within the European research projects *PACO-PLUS*[6] and *Xperience*[7] based on the idea that objects and actions need to be inseparably intertwined in complex cognitive systems. OACs provide a general concept for representing and learning robot behaviors based on sensorimotor experience. The link between symbolic and continuous action descriptions make OACs a powerful formalism, particularly in the context of action and task planning. Krüger et al. (2011) formally define an OAC as a triplet

$$(E,T,M), \tag{2.10}$$

[6] European Union Sixth Framework (IST-FP6-IP-027657) `http://www.paco-plus.org`

[7] European Union Seventh Framework Programme under grant agreement number 270273 `http://www.xperience.org`

consisting of an execution specification E, a prediction function $T : S \rightarrow S$ defined over an attribute space S and a statistical measure of success M over previous executions. The particular implementations of E, T and M depend on the application context.
Originally, affordances have been considered as implicitly modeled within the concept of OACs. For example, an OAC for *grasping* based on visual information decides whether grasping is applicable based on the perceived set of features and therefore implicitly detects *graspability* affordances. This interpretation of affordances is also predominant in Wörgötter et al. (2009), where affordances are considered to be the conditions that allow a state transition of an object O by execution of an action A, denoted as:

$$O \rightarrow^{A} O'. \tag{2.11}$$

In both cases, affordances are implicitly encoded in the OAC definitions, leveraging further formalization and implementation of the actual affordances and the influence of the agent embodiment to the OAC designer.
The affordance formalization proposed in this thesis is largely influenced by the ideas of Wörgötter et al. (2009) and Krüger et al. (2011) and is not intended as a replacement of the concept of OACs, but as a complement:

> *Affordances as formalized in this thesis can be understood as explicit preconditions for the instantiation of OACs.*

The proposed framework for whole-body affordances provides the formal mechanisms for explicitly defining affordances as preconditions for the instantiation of OACs which then provide a direct link to symbolic planning and action execution.

2.3 Affordances in Autonomous Robotics

After introducing the psychological theory of affordances and after further reviewing available computational formalizations of the affordance concept, this section discusses existing approaches to affordance-based autonomous robotics. The concept of affordances has served as a popular source of inspiration within the field of cognitive robotics. Horton et al. (2012) summarizes the early development of affordance-based robotic systems, some of which date back to times before the term *affordance* gained popularity among roboticists. The fundamental idea of these systems, whether they were called affordance-based or not, was to combine the previously mostly separated components of *sensing*, *planning* and *acting* (Brooks 1986) into an ecological approach to autonomous embodied agents. Many of the introduced approaches are inspired by the ideas of *behavior-based robotics* and *developmental robotics*, whose principles will be briefly introduced in Section 2.3.1. The subsequent sections provide a comprehensive overview over affordance-based approaches to autonomous robots, categorized based on the principle definition of the affordance concept in terms of the employed computational model. Discussed definitions include affordances as perceptual invariants (Section 2.3.2), geometric features (Section 2.3.3), probabilistic distributions (Section 2.3.4), probabilistic networks (Section 2.3.5), knowledge bases (Section 2.3.6) and semantic segments (Section 2.3.7). It needs to be noted that the differentiation between the defined categories is not strict and that some approaches fall into multiple categories. In Section 2.3.8, approaches related to the concept of whole-body affordances in loco-manipulation tasks are discussed and Section 2.3.9 particularly reviews approaches seen at the DARPA Robotics Challenge (DRC).

As discussed in Section 2.1.3, affordance-based approaches in robotics are sometimes only loosely related to Gibson's original ideas. This particularly applies to the aspect of direct perception which is central in the psychological definitions of the affordance concept, but often ignored in practical implementations. The survey presented in this chapter further shows that affordance-based approaches in robotics largely vary in their underlying understanding of the affordance concept, as well as in the implemented computational formalizations. In an attempt to organize the plethora of affordance-related approaches in robotics, Zech et al. (2017) develop a taxonomy of available computational models and categorize existing approaches. The survey can be seen as complementary to the following sections as it focuses on more abstract differentiation criteria such as e. g. the taken perspective (see Section 2.1).

2.3.1 Behavior-Based and Developmental Robotics

The concept of affordances, particularly its aspect of direct perception, is fundamentally related to the ideas of *behavior-based robotics* (Brooks 1990; Arkin 1998), where complex (or *complex-appearing*) robotic systems are created based on combinations of simple individual behaviors. A famous example for a behavior-based robotic system is the *Braitenberg Vehicle* (Braitenberg 1986) which is able to autonomously approach light sources (see Figure 2.1).

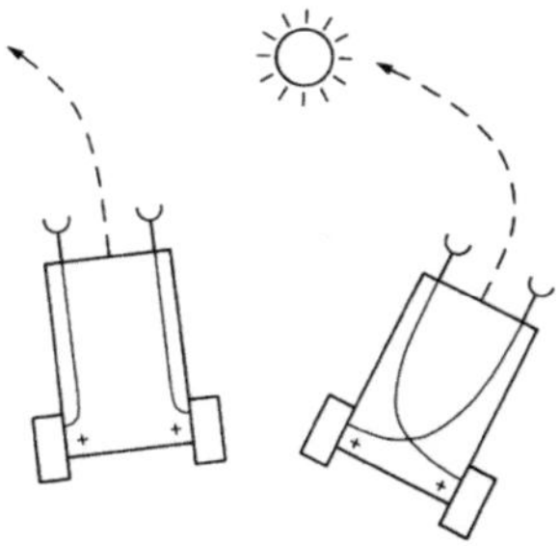

Figure 2.1: A sketch of two Braitenberg Vehicles, one which turns away from light sources (left) and one which approaches light sources (right) (taken from Braitenberg 1986, © 1986 MIT Press).

The field of *developmental robotics* aims at creating robotic systems that pass through phases of developmental learning for developing an evolved understanding of their embodiment, their environment and their capabilities. Such developmental approaches to robotic learning require that the robot is intrinsically motivated to interact with the environment and to directly monitor caused effects. Developmental learning phases can be goal-directed or random, while in the latter case they are commonly termed *motor babbling phases*. While the employed terminology differs, developmental approaches share the aspects of developmental experimenting and monitoring for perceptual invariants.

In *ecological robotics*, researchers attempt to apply concepts from Ecological Psychology to behavior-based or developmental robotic agents, particularly the idea of considering robot and environment as a combined system, the *robot-environment system* (Duchon et al. 1998). As such, ecological robots do not construct internal models, but directly react on effects that their actions cause in the environment:

> *Because the agent is in the environment, the environment need not be in the agent.*
> Duchon et al. (1998, p. 478)

Direct perception of affordances provides efficient mechanisms for triggering behaviors or compositions of behaviors in a behavior-based architecture. This concept has been successfully implemented in the area of autonomous navigation of mobile robots (e. g. Murphy 1999; Şahin et al. 2007).

While the ideas of behavior-based robotics are appealing, it is mostly applied to robots with simple actuation and in unknown, but commonly simple environments. While the methods proposed in this thesis could serve as perceptual basis for a purely behavior-based architecture, one of its interesting features is that it uses the concept of OACs for providing a link from the perception of affordances to the symbolic and sub-symbolic world of deliberate action and task planning. Developmental approaches to affordance learning suffer from the extensive dimensions of the search space and are therefore typically pursued for small amounts of actions with defined parameters and effects, e. g. *pushing* or *pulling*. In the context of whole-body actions, the dimensions of the parameterization space rapidly exceeds the exploratory capabilities of the robot, making auxiliary technologies like off-line training, simulation or heuristics necessary.

2.3.2 Affordances as Perceptual Invariants

Inspired by the concept of direct perception, developmental roboticists often approach the process of affordance learning as learning decision criteria for affordances in a defined space of visual features. This process is often called the detection of *perceptual invariants* during action execution, i. e. the detection of the subset of features that remain constant throughout all successful action executions. The possibility to learn affordances bottom-up only from a set of visual features emphasizes the developmental aspect of these approaches. However, as developmental experiments tend to be time-consuming and expensive, research in this area mostly focuses on simple robots with restricted motor capabilities and associated affordances.

In his early work, MacDorman (2000) implemented an affordance-based approach to mobile robotics in a survival scenario, i. e. seeking contact with advantageous (*tasty*) objects and avoiding contact with disadvantageous (*poisonous*) objects, by learning canonical visual features. Inspired by the exploratory behavior of animals, Stoytchev (2005, 2008) implemented a motor babbling phase for robotic manipulators based on parameterized behaviors, aiming at the autonomous learning of affordances for tool-use. Once an invariant, i. e. a regular pattern in object movement, is detected, the robot attempts to find the shortest behavior sequence that reproduces this invariant and, if successful, adds this sequence and the associated invariants to an *affordance table*. The approach was experimentally validated on a real robotic manipulator using five manually coded behaviors and a set of five tools for manipulating one attractor object. The main drawback of this approach is that the populated affordance table does not generalize to previously not observed settings and tools. To address this issue, Sinapov et al. (2007, 2008) extended the work of Stoytchev (2005, 2008) by replacing the affordance table with a learned predictive model, implemented as a decision tree. Fritz et al. (2006) pursue a similar approach by learning affordance decision trees over a defined set of *affordance cues*, i. e. selected descriptive visual features such as shape or color. The concept is evaluated in simulation using a mobile crane-like robot learning *liftability* affordances. Paletta et al. (2007) embedded the concept of affordance cues into a multi-layer cognitive architecture which allows reasoning about affordance sequences based on *reinforcement learning*. In Stark et al. (2008), visual cues for *graspability* affordances are learned from human demonstration.

Uğur et al. (2007, 2010) proposed a concept for learning *traversability* affordances with mobile robots in cluttered environments, following the affordance formalization of Şahin et al. (2007). The authors employ a *Support Vector Machine* (SVM) for selecting invariant features among a total of 35,100 defined features in a 360×360 pixels range image. After a learning phase the method is successfully employed to detect *traversability* affordances in the defined scenario by utilizing 1% of the defined features. See Figure 2.2 for a visualization of the experimental setup. The initial approach is extended in Çakmak et al. (2007) and Doğar et al. (2007) towards goal-directed autonomous behavior generation based on learned *traversability* affordances. Further extension in Doğar et al. (2008) allows the autonomous learning of novel affordance-related behaviors based on pre-coded primitive behaviors. Related approaches are pursued e. g. in Akgün et al. (2009) for the unsupervised learning of object affordances such as *rollability*, in Dağ et al. (2010) for the categorization of objects based on available affordances and in Katz et al. (2014) for learning *graspability*, *pushability* and *pullability* affordances of objects in cluttered piles. Kostavelis et al. (2012) employ an SVM to learn invariant features for *traversability* in stereo vision disparity maps. In a related scenario, Baleia et al. (2015) learn *traversability* affordances for a mobile robot through haptic exploration with a 3 DOF pan-tilt telescopic antenna.

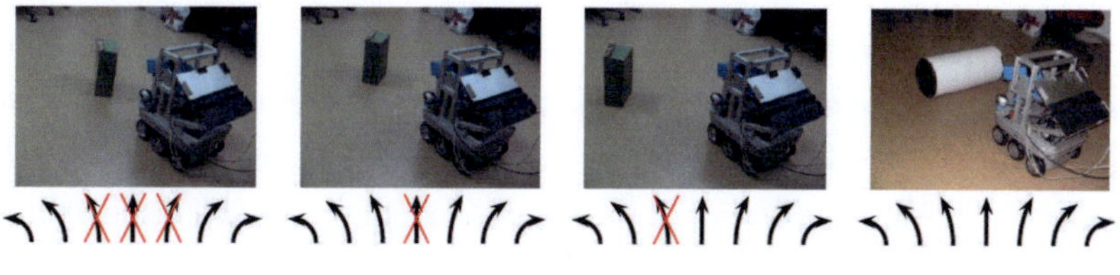

Figure 2.2: Affordance-based navigation with a mobile robot (adapted from Uğur et al. 2007, © 2007 IEEE).

Uğur et al. (2011a,b, 2012) apply the affordance formalization of Şahin et al. (2007) to the developmental learning of manipulation affordances, comparing the implemented learning strategy to the development of infants at the age of seven to ten months. In a developmental phase the robot applies primitive *push* and *lift* behaviors to detected objects of different shapes and categorizes observed effects via *hierarchical clustering*. Subsequently, effect predictors, implemented as SVMs, are trained for each behavior. Learned affordances and their associated effect predictors are then used for action planning. Szedmak et al. (2014) and Uğur et al. (2014) propose to understand affordances learned from perceptual invariants, e. g. *rollability*, as the lowest level of affordance detection on top of which higher-level affordances, e. g. *stackability*, can be learned. This *bootstrapping* process is evaluated by learning paired-object affordances such as *stackability* in a tabletop scenario using a robotic manipulator. The approach is extended in Uğur et al. (2015a,b) towards a holistic framework for developmentally learning and updating relations between perceived objects and symbolic planning entities through clustering of action effects.

The interpretation of affordances as perceptual invariants is popular in developmental robotics. Approaches commonly define a, possibly extensive, visual feature space and attempt to find invariant features during motor babbling phases. Knowledge about the early perceptual development of infants justifies this perspective on affordances (Giagkos et al. 2017). Though the developmental acquisition of affordances is appealing and seems appropriate when considering the human development, the discussed approaches cannot easily be applied to whole-body affordances as examined in this thesis. Basic affordances such as *pushability* or *liftability*, which are commonly investigated in developmental approaches, have immediate and well perceivable visual effects. Furthermore, associated behaviors are simple enough that successful executions are frequently generated by chance during random motor babbling phases. Whole-body affordances on the contrary often refer to complex actions with unapparent effects. Although promising approaches exist that learn complex behaviors and associated affordances based on previously acquired primitive motor behaviors (e. g. Uğur et al. 2015a,b), multi-layered developmental approaches that effectively learn whole-body affordances in loco-manipulation tasks for complex humanoid robots have not been proposed yet.

2.3.3 Affordances as Geometric Features

Another group of affordance-based approaches to autonomous robotics understands local geometric features in perceived object geometries as direct hints for affordances. Some authors even consider geometric features and affordances as equivalent. Although not all approaches in this category can be considered developmental, those that fall into this category are tightly related to the approaches that learn affordances as perceptual invariants. Due to the direct nature of their detection, affordances are usually not explicitly represented and learning of affordances corresponds to learning of decisive geometric features.

By choosing descriptive geometric features, researchers are able to effectively detect *graspability* affordances in different experimental setups. Implemented features include e. g. surface co-planarity and co-colority (Kraft et al. 2008), cylindrical surface patches (ten Pas et al. 2016), SIFT features (Song et al. 2016) and curved surface patches (Kanoulas et al. 2017). Although often not explicitly referring to the concept of affordances, local features of object surfaces are a common approach to data-driven grasp synthesis for familiar and unknown objects (Bohg et al. 2014). While the detection of *graspability* affordances from visual features is a well-studied problem in the field of robotic grasping and manipulation, further approaches exist that attempt to detect *graspability* affordances using other sensor modalities. In Bierbaum et al. (2009), *graspability* affordances for multi-fingered robotic hands are detected by haptically exploring unknown objects for co-planar surface patches (see Figure 2.3).

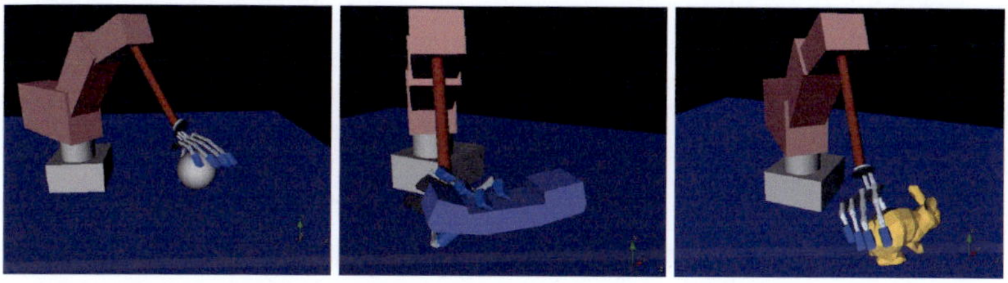

Figure 2.3: Haptic exploration of unknown objects for detecting *graspability* affordances (taken from Bierbaum et al. 2009, © 2009 IEEE).

The above approaches for the detection of *graspability* affordances concentrate on a limited set of selected, highly descriptive features, e. g. surface co-planarity. Other approaches define extensive sets of available geometric features and subsequently attempt to train affordance classificators based on large sets of training examples. Myers et al. (2015) subdivide RGB-D input images into squared patches and extract established geometric features such as surface normals and principle curvatures which are further used for training an SVM to detect tool affordances. In a similar approach from D. Kim et al. (2006), traversability affordances for mobile robots are learned by on-line classificator training based on autonomous exploratory behavior. In

Ridge et al. (2013, 2015), the authors propose *action-grounded features*, i. e. features with dynamic action-related frames of reference which are particularly suited for affordance detection. The proposed features are used for learning *pushability* affordances. Works like Aldoma et al. (2012) and Ruiz et al. (2017) perform the identification of discriminative features off-line using 3D CAD models and use the gained information for detecting affordances in real RGB-D images. Mustafa et al. (2016) train an SVM for the detection of affordances from a kitchen domain, e. g. *pourability* or *stirrability*, based on relations between small patches of detected object surfaces such as distances and angles.

In the motivation of defining geometric features that are as discriminative as possible, Kroemer et al. (2012) introduce a non-parametric representation of object subparts perceived as point clouds and a complementary kernel function that expresses object subpart similarity. The authors perform *kernel logistic regression* in order to obtain a learned model that expresses the probability for an object subpart to bear given affordances. The system is implemented for learning *graspability* and *pourability* affordances from human demonstration using a robotic manipulator equipped with an anthropomorphic hand. This work is extended in Kroemer et al. (2016) towards learning spatial relations between affordance-bearing object parts as preconditions for action execution.

The above works attempt to detect affordances directly from geometric features without constructing intermediate environmental models. On the contrary, numerous researchers approach the problem of affordance detection by explicitly constructing simplified environmental representations in terms of geometric primitives, such as planes, boxes, cylinders or spheres. Note that the transitions between the two types of approaches are smooth which can be seen by the example of Kroemer et al. (2012).

D. I. Kim et al. (2014) construct geometric primitives from RGB-D images for subsequent training of an affordance classifier based on a defined set of geometric features. Considered affordances include *pushability* and *lifta-*

bility, experimentally evaluated using the *PR2* robot. The approach has been extended in D. I. Kim et al. (2015) towards the execution of goal-directed pushing tasks based on *pushability* affordance maps in a warehouse scenario. In Fallon et al. (2015b), planar primitive patches are utilized for the detection of *supportability* affordances for humanoid footstep planning (see Figure 2.4). In a similar approach in Pryor et al. (2016), planar primitives are used for detecting *supportability* and *leanability* affordances for efficient multi-contact motion planning.

Figure 2.4: The detection of *supportability* affordances for bipedal locomotion (taken from Fallon et al. 2015b, © 2015 IEEE).

The idea of detecting affordances directly based on elementary geometric features is closely related to the previously discussed interpretation of affordances as perceptual invariants. However, learning affordance models from geometric feature spaces is also popular in less developmental approaches, in which the considered features can become more sophisticated. A specific branch of approaches, which is particularly related to the methods proposed in this thesis, attempts to construct an intermediate, simplified environmental representation in terms of geometric primitives which is further used for learning affordances. Strictly speaking, these approaches lack the aspect of direct affordance perception, as internal environmental models are created, and do therefore not entirely comply with Gibson (see Section 2.1.3). However, as the approaches introduced in this section show, simplified geometric models allow the detection of more sophisticated affordances, such as *leanability* or *supportability* in the context of humanoid locomotion. They are therefore particularly suited for the detection of whole-body affordances in loco-manipulation tasks. The affordance detection system proposed in this work is based on the so called *H^2T perception pipeline* (see Section 3.1) which pursues a similar approach to environmental representation.

2.3.4 Affordances as Probability Distributions

When considering the visual detection of action possibilities, three principle spaces can be differentiated: the space of available *visual features*, the space of possible *action parameters* and the space of possible *action effects*. Once these three spaces are properly formalized, affordances can be understood and learned as conditional probability distributions. Approaches in this category typically learn such probability distributions for individual affordances. However, they are conceptually related to the affordance formalization of Montesano et al. (2008), in which affordances are represented in joint probabilistic networks. Approaches that demonstrate this joint probabilistic representation of affordances will be discussed in the next section.

Metta et al. (2003) and Fitzpatrick et al. (2003a,b) introduce a neuroscientifically grounded approach to developmental learning of *pushability* affordances in a tabletop scenario by observing immediate action effects. Affordances are represented as probability distributions, termed *maps*, over the possible directions of object movement with respect to the principle object axis. In related approaches, Erdemir et al. (2008) propose a cognitive framework for learning of *reachability* affordances by learning probability distribution models based on *Gaussian mixture models* (GMMs), while Barck-Holst et al. (2009) propose to learn *graspability* affordances by acquiring probability distributions over the spaces of grasp regions, grip forces, object shapes and object sizes. The initial work of Metta et al. (2003) is extended in Tikhanoff et al. (2013) and Mar et al. (2015, 2017) towards the developmental learning of tool categorizations based on detected affordances (see Figure 2.5). Affordances in this case are represented as probability distributions over the space of tool poses and movement directions.

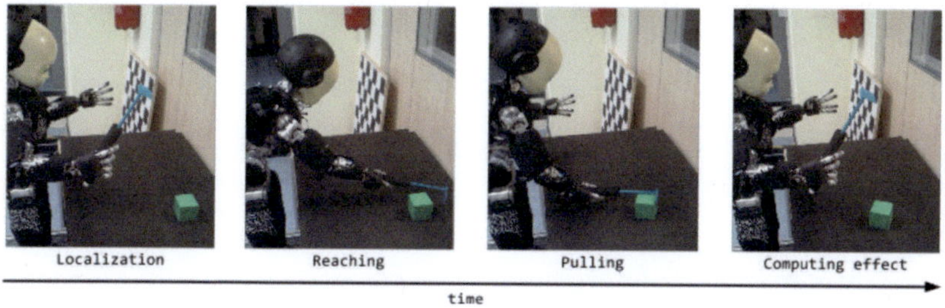

Figure 2.5: Learning of tool affordances in a tabletop scenario using the humanoid robot *iCub* (taken from Mar et al. 2015, © 2015 IEEE).

The representation of affordances as probabilistic densities has been particularly studied in the context of *graspability* affordance detection in which these affordances are commonly understood as object-gripper configurations that result in stable grasping. In the works of de Granville et al. (2006) and Sweeney et al. (2007), *graspability* affordances are represented as probability distributions over the spaces of end-effector positions and orientations. Based on these initial works, Detry et al. (2009, 2010, 2011) propose to represent *graspability* affordances as probabilistic density functions over the space $SE(3)$ of end-effector poses (see Figure 2.6). While density functions are initially constructed from visual cues, the approach is to refine these so called *bootstrap densities* through developmental experiments. Visual cues and successful grasping attempts are collected as particles and further processed into a density function by applying *kernel density estimation* using the kernel function $\boldsymbol{K}$ composed of a normal distribution $\boldsymbol{N}$ for the spatial dimensions and a von Mises-Fisher distribution $\boldsymbol{\Theta}$ for the orientational dimensions:

$$\boldsymbol{K}(x;\mu,\sigma) = \boldsymbol{N}(\lambda;\mu_t,\sigma_t)\cdot\boldsymbol{\Theta}(\theta;\mu_r,\sigma_r). \tag{2.12}$$

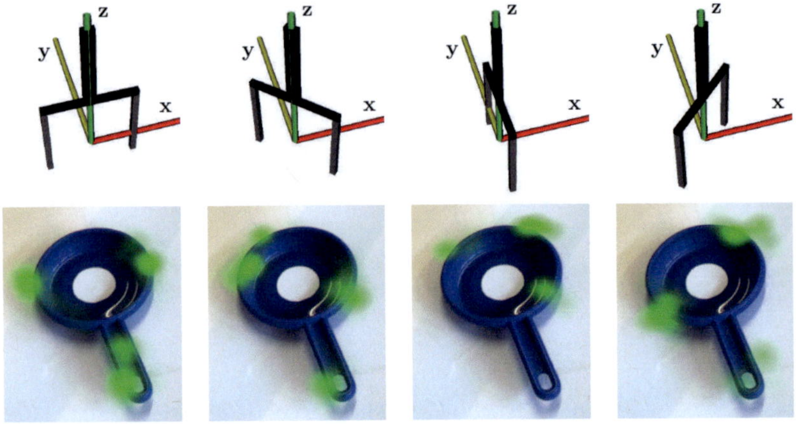

Figure 2.6: Learning of *graspability* affordances as probabilistic densities over the space of end-effector poses. *Top row:* queried end-effector orientations, *bottom row:* visualization of the affordance density function for the corresponding end-effector orientation (taken from Detry et al. 2011, © 2011 R. Detry et al.).

The work is summarized in Piater et al. (2011) as an attempt to emphasize learnable, task-specific representations of visual information over general-purpose task-independent representations.

While the approaches discussed in this category seem different, they share the idea of representing affordances as probabilistic distributions over end-effector or tool poses. Some approaches further include selected action parameters in the definition space of affordance distributions. While end-effector poses are certainly important for the affordances evaluated in the above approaches, e. g. *pushability* or *graspability*, they are also important in the context of whole-body affordances. A central assumption that will be made within this thesis is that whole-body actions can be elementarily explained by fundamental power-grasp affordances, and therefore by end-effector poses, on the lowest level. In fact, affordance densities as introduced by Detry et al. (2010, 2011) are similar to *affordance belief functions* for prismatic grasping which will be defined and discussed in Chapter 4 and Chapter 5.

In contrast to the works discussed in this section, affordance belief functions will be defined over the space of Dempster-Shafer belief expressions, rather than probabilities. This formalism allows the effective combination of affordance-related evidence from multiple sources with different attributed degrees of belief. It furthermore allows the consistent fusion of belief functions for different affordances using elementary logic operations in order to construct higher-level affordance belief functions. A similar representation of affordance-related evidence is found in Sarathy et al. (2016), where *uncertain logic* (Jøsang 2001) is employed for reasoning about symbolic affordances.

2.3.5 Affordances in Probabilistic Networks

The representation of affordances as probabilistic models, as introduced in the previous section, is a popular and established approach. An important and conceptually related subset of affordance-based approaches in autonomous and developmental robotics attempts to learn affordances in probabilistic networks. Such networks realize directed graphical models in which nodes represent random variables and edges represent conditional dependencies between these variables. Affordances in this context are understood as strong dependencies between combinations of objects, actions and effects which are typically represented as network nodes. Popular examples for probabilistic networks are *Bayesian networks* (BNs).

Hart et al. (2005) propose a framework for learning affordances in *relational dependency networks* (RDNs) which express dependencies between *controller attributes*, i. e. action parameters. The learned RDNs express the procedural knowledge for deriving *relational probability trees* (RPTs) for the controller attributes. RPTs are decision tree models which express the values of attributes given the values of their dependency attributes. RPTs are interpreted to learn the affordances of their respective attributes. The framework is evaluated for learning *liftability* affordances with an anthropomorphic bimanual robot in a tabletop scenario. In later works, Hart (2009) and Hart et al. (2011) propose methods for intrinsically motivated learning of control policies for discovering manipulation affordances based on *reinforcement learning* (see Figure 2.7).

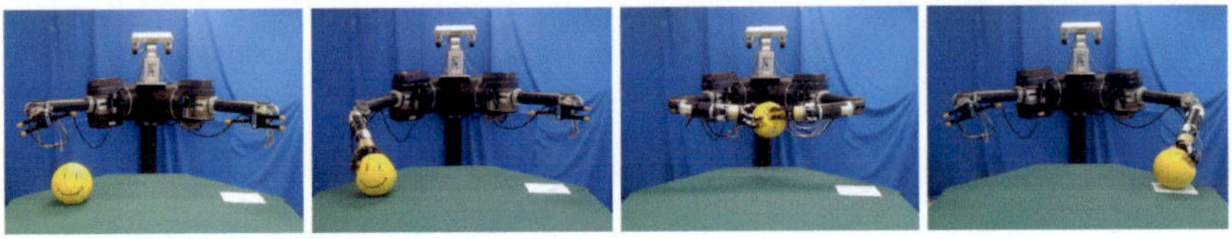

Figure 2.7: Developmental learning of manipulation affordances and associated control policies in a tabletop scenario (taken from Hart et al. 2011, © 2011 IEEE).

The representation of affordances in probabilistic networks has particularly been investigated in the context of learning affordances for tool use. Montesano et al. (2007b, 2008) propose a concept for learning affordances in Bayesian networks, in which object properties, actions and action effects are modeled as discrete random variables, represented by the network nodes. Edges in the BN represent conditional dependencies between nodes. The influential formalization of Montesano et al. (2008) has been covered in the survey of computational formalizations of the affordance concept in Section 2.2.3. The framework for affordance learning is evaluated in an exemplary tabletop scenario, in which affordances for the primitive actions *touch*, *tap* and *grasp* are learned. The same formalism is used in Montesano et al. (2007a) and Lopes et al. (2007) for imitating human action demonstrations based on learned affordances using an anthropomorphic robot and in Montesano et al. (2009) for learning local visual features that indicate *graspability* affordances for an anthropomorphic hand. In Rudolph et al. (2010), affordances are represented in BNs with nodes for actions and features, implicitly modeling action effects as feature changes.

Figure 2.8: Task execution based on a learned relational affordance model using the humanoid robot *iCub* (taken from Moldovan et al. 2017, © 2017 Springer Nature).

The formalization of Montesano et al. (2008) has been extended and improved in different aspects. Osório et al. (2010) state that the structure of the BN proposed in Montesano et al. (2007b, 2008) implicitly assumes complete observability of object properties, as class assignments are discrete. In order to improve the approach with respect to noisy sensor data, Osório et al. (2010) propose an alternative BN structure that implements probabilistic class assignments based on *Gaussian mixture models* (GMMs). Moldovan et al. (2012, 2013) extend the initial approach from Montesano et al. (2008) in order to effectively learn affordances for combinations of physically related objects. Instead of extending the structure of the classical BN by additional object nodes, which quickly becomes infeasible, the authors introduce *relational affordance models* which describe affordances as joint distributions over relations between objects, actions and effects. Relational affordance models are applied in Moldovan et al. (2014) for finding affordance-bearing objects in cluttered kitchen environments by removing as few occluding objects as possible. In Moldovan et al. (2017), a learned relational affordance model is used for symbolic planning of action sequences. The approach is evaluated using the humanoid robot *iCub* (see Figure 2.8).

Gonçalves et al. (2014b,a) use the formalization of Montesano et al. (2008) for learning tool-use affordances by including nodes for *primary objects*, i. e.

the acted objects, and *intermediate objects*, i. e. the tools, in the network. The BN is used to learn *pushability* affordances in simulation using a set of eight objects and tools, and experimentally validated on the real humanoid robot iCub. The framework is further applied in Antunes et al. (2016) for affordance-based probabilistic action planning from human instructions given in natural language. The work of Gonçalves et al. (2014b,a) is extended in Dehban et al. (2016) by using *denoising auto-encoders* in order to circumvent clustering of continuous feature spaces for the use in a BN.

In an approach similar to Montesano et al. (2007b, 2008), Jain et al. (2013) employ BNs for learning affordances of unknown tools based on *functional features*, i. e. tool parts that remain invariant throughout multiple action demonstrations with different tools. Inspired by the formalization of Montesano et al. (2008), the authors of Stramandinoli et al. (2015, 2017) improve the initial implementation of their tool-use affordance learning experiment from Tikhanoff et al. (2013) by employing Bayesian networks. In the experimental setup, the authors learn the affordances of objects and differently shaped tools using the humanoid robot iCub. Price et al. (2016) criticize common approaches for learning affordances in BNs for the dependency of the learned model on a particular robot embodiment. To overcome this issue, the authors propose to use a BN to learn boundaries for affordance feasibility in a wrench-space representation which can be mapped to the capabilities of different robots.

Sun et al. (2010) argue that the direct perception of affordances based on image features is a viable approach for learning individual affordances, but does not scale well as the amount of affordances to learn increases. Based on previous attempts to the direct perception of *traversability* affordances for outdoor navigation in D. Kim et al. (2006), the authors propose the *category-affordance model*, a BN that implements intermediate nodes for visual object categorization, as a general framework for affordance detection. The system is evaluated in two experiments with real robot hardware, learning six affordances, such as *traversability*, *movability* or *supportability*, based on seven defined object categories.

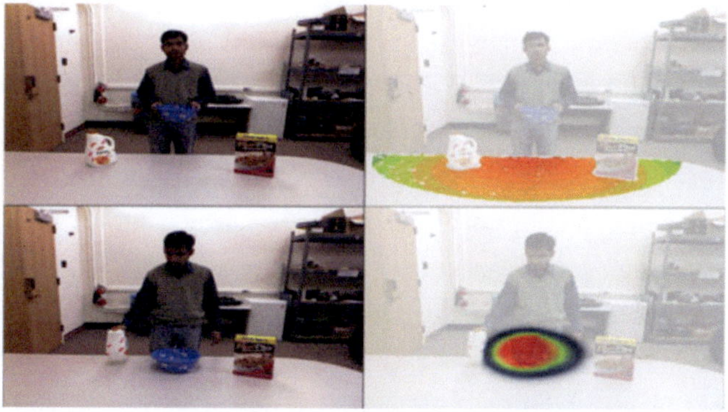

Figure 2.9: Visualization of affordance heatmaps for *placeability* (top) and *purability* (bottom) (taken from Koppula et al. 2016, © 2016 IEEE).

In Kjellström et al. (2011), human demonstrations of human-object interactions are represented in a *Conditional Random Field* (CRF). This representation is used for classifying object-action pairs based on their functional relation. Koppula et al. (2013, 2014, 2016) propose an affordance-based approach to human motion anticipation, in which affordances are understood as object positions with respect to the human body or environmental objects. The authors represent spatio-temporal sequences of human poses and objects in a CRF. Affordances in the approach are represented in *affordance heatmaps*, i. e. distributions of object positions in relation to the human body or the environment. Figure 2.9 displays visualizations of two exemplary affordance heatmaps. In Jiang et al. (2013), affordance heatmaps relative to the human body are employed for improving semantic scene understanding. In an approach similar to Koppula et al. (2016), the authors of Dutta et al. (2016) attempt to predict human motion in a *human-robot interaction* (HRI) scenario by representing affordances as heatmaps generated from demonstrated human activities encoded in probabilistic state machines.

While most approaches to affordance-based autonomous robotics focus on visual detection of affordances, Chu et al. (2016a,b) attempt to learn haptic affordances represented as force/torque profiles in *Hidden Markov Models* (HMMs). Actions are initially demonstrated by means of kinesthetic teaching and experimental repetition of the demonstrated action is performed afterwards in order to learn the characteristic force/torque profile of the affordance. The approach is evaluated using e. g. *openability*, *pushability* or *scoopability* of common container objects from a kitchen environment.

The idea of learning affordances in probabilistic networks can be seen as one of the predominant approaches to the developmental learning of affordances. Probabilistic networks, such as Bayesian networks, provide the possibility to express objects, actions and effects in the same graphical structure and to infer about affordances by marginalizing conditional probability distributions. Bayesian networks are capable of jointly learning multiple affordances in a single network representation. However, the network structure needs to be manually defined or learned using approximative methods. Furthermore, the classical approach of learning affordances in BNs requires large amounts of training samples as the number of involved objects increases (Moldovan et al. 2012). The idea of using probabilistic networks for affordance inference has inspired the hierarchical aspects of the whole-body affordance formalization that will be introduced in Chapter 4. The affordance hierarchy proposed in Chapter 5 can be seen related to a probabilistic network structure based on the concepts of the Dempster-Shafer theory. However, as developmental learning is tedious in the context of sophisticated whole-body actions with humanoid robots, the affordance hierarchy in Chapter 5 is manually defined. While developmental learning of the affordance hierarchy is conceptually possible, it is left for future work in this thesis.

2.3.6 Affordances in Knowledge Bases

The developmental acquisition of affordance-related knowledge as pursued in many of the above approaches can be tedious, particularly when considering complex humanoid robots with large spaces of possible affordances. Several researchers approach this problem by endowing robots with manually or automatically crafted ontological knowledge on objects, actions and affordances. The approaches discussed in this section often draw similarities between object-action relations and natural language. In this understanding, objects and actions correspond to nouns and verbs and sentences expressing object-action relations may convey affordance-related knowledge. This approach makes the utilization of existing linguistic and commonsense knowledge bases such as *WordNet* (Miller 1995) or *ConceptNet* (H. Liu et al. 2004) possible.

In an approach to initiate a knowledge base for affordances, Varadarajan et al. (2012a,b) propose *AfNet*, a database of scalable visual features that define conceptual equivalence classes for objects based on their affordances. The authors define *structural affordances*, i. e. affordances that relate to the object structure, and *material affordances*, i. e. affordances that relate to the object material, that in combination allow the proper classification of over 250 common household objects. In a related approach, Zhu et al. (2014) propose a method to build a knowledge base with object attributes, affordances, human poses and human-object relations as entities and discuss suitable reasoning mechanisms. Relations between entities in the knowledge base represent correlations e. g. between object attributes or between object attributes and affordances. Affordance-related knowledge is often considered part of the human *common sense knowledge* which is rarely explicitly expressed. However, methods for automatic mining of common sense relations from large corpora of natural language text exist, e. g. in Kaiser et al. (2014b), which can be employed for populating affordance knowledge bases.

In the intention of allowing autonomous robots to understand vague task descriptions provided in natural language, Tenorth et al. (2013) propose *KnowRob*, a framework for robotic knowledge processing which incorporates a variety of external sources of information such as human observation, web sites or existing knowledge bases. Although the authors are not explicitly relating their approach to the concept of affordances, affordances are implicitly represented as relations between objects and actions. The framework is embedded into the ambitious *RoboEarth* project (Waibel et al. 2011), a joint effort to provide an open source platform for robotic knowledge exchange. Çelikkanat et al. (2015) propose a concept web for humanoid robots that represents nouns, verbs and adjectives as conceptual entities and *is-a* relations between those. The concept web is implemented as a *Markov Random Field* (MRF), allowing the interactive learning of concepts based on observed co-occurrences and the probabilistic inference in the learned web structure. The creation of affordance-related knowledge bases and ontologies is motivated by the idea of circumventing expensive learning phases by transferring affordance-related knowledge between robots or between humans and robots. Among other information, affordance-related knowledge bases predominantly contain symbolic relations between objects and actions. A central matter of research is the question how symbolic relations can be associated with robotic sensorimotor experience. Some authors approach this *symbol grounding problem* by representing sensorimotor features, e. g. visual object features, in the knowledge base. While the hierarchy of affordance belief functions that will be introduced in Chapter 5 can be seen related to an ontological approach, it does not inherently link continuous affordance belief functions with symbolic entities. However, this link can be implemented by connecting affordance belief functions with OACs as proposed in Chapter 6.

2.3.7 Affordances as Semantic Segments

The detection of affordances from visual information, i. e. RGB or RGB-D images, can be seen as a special case of a *semantic segmentation* problem. Semantic segmentation describes the problem of subdividing input images into semantically meaningful segments which in the context of the discussed approaches refer to affordances. In this sense, affordances are represented as labeled groups of pixels, voxels or points which are assumed to indicate the possibility of an action. Although conceptually different, semantic segments in the context of affordance detection are commonly understood as equivalent to affordances. Semantic segmentation is well studied in the area of computer vision and received great attention with the recent advances in *deep learning*. Many of the discussed approaches employ the *RGB-D part affordance dataset* (Myers et al. 2015) as a baseline for comparison.

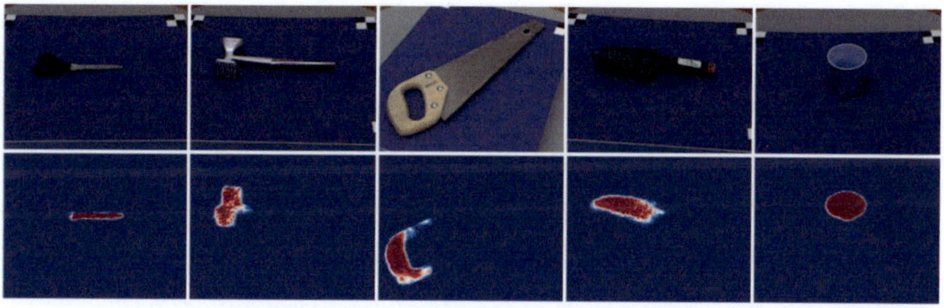

Figure 2.10: Detection of affordances in RGB-D images using an end-to-end deep CNN (taken from Nguyen et al. 2016, © 2016 IEEE).

Multiple groups recently attempted to apply the concepts of semantic segmentation to the problem of affordance detection and achieved remarkable results, particularly with the application of *Convolutional Neural Networks* (CNNs). Deep learning is well suited for the detection of *graspability* affordances as large datasets for robotic grasping exist. Lenz et al. (2015) propose a two-staged approach to detecting *graspability* affordances for robotic grippers in RGB-D images: First, a small deep network is employed for reducing the extensive set of possible grasps to a small set of grasp candidates, while a second deep network then identifies a single optimal grasp from the set of candidates. The network input consist of square image parts including the color, depth and normal information. Nguyen et al. (2016) pursue a similar approach by training an end-to-end deep CNN that detects affordances in RGB-D images. However, in contrast to Lenz et al. (2015), multiple affordances from the context of kitchen and household environments have been learned (see Figure 2.10). The network is evaluated in grasping experiments with the humanoid robot WALK-MAN. In a similar approach, Roy et al. (2016) train a multi-scale deep CNN for detecting *walkability*, *sittability*, *lyability*, *reachability* and *movability* affordances in RGB images on a per-pixel basis by implementing mid-level cues, such as depth maps or surface normals. The work of Nguyen et al. (2016) is extended in Do et al. (2017) towards an end-to-end deep network that jointly detects objects, i. e. object classes and their bounding boxes, together with object affordances in RGB-D images. Training CNNs requires large amounts of annotated training data which is tedious to obtain for affordances. Sawatzky et al. (2017) recently addressed this problem by proposing a weakly supervised CNN for multilabel affordance segmentation in RGB images which can be trained from few annotated keypoints.

In contrast to the above works, Lakani et al. (2017) do not employ methods for semantic segmentation for detecting affordances, but include affordance information during the training phase of a *markov random field* for improved segmentation of objects into semantically meaningful parts. Lüddecke et al. (2016) introduce the concept of *scene affordances* which arise from specific arrangements of environmental objects. The later work of Lüddecke et al. (2017) is motivated by the observation that specific actions are typically afforded by object-parts rather than objects, e. g. only the door handle affords *pinch-graspability*, not the entire door. The authors employ methods for semantic object part segmentation and a manually defined *part affordance table* that maps common object parts to 15 defined affordances in a generic way in order to train an end-to-end CNN. The network is able to successfully detect among 15 common affordances from RGB images, outperforming multiple baselines. In a similar approach, Ye et al. (2017) train an end-to-end CNN for detecting affordances in RGB images based on an ontology of 11 affordances, including different grasp types and the utilization of household appliances and furniture (see Figure 2.11). Besides end-to-end approaches to affordance segmentation, works like Desai et al. (2013) attempt to identify affordances, i. e. *functional regions*, in scenes which are already semantically segmented.

Figure 2.11: Detection of affordances in RGB images using an end-to-end CNN (taken from Ye et al. 2017, © 2017 IEEE).

In McMahon et al. (2017) the performance of different CNN architectures in the detection of *trip hazard affordances* is compared based on a large-scale labeled RGB-D construction site dataset of trip hazards. Porzi et al. (2017) propose a novel general-purpose CNN block *DaConv* suited for RGB-D input which can make use of the depth information to learn scale-aware feature representations. The proposed CNN block shows improvements in different robotic applications, including the detection of affordances.

The interpretation of affordance detection as a semantic segmentation problem is appealing because it allows the application of established methods from computer vision which produce impressive results. Deep CNNs which need to be trained with extensive amounts of training data are particularly popular in the community. While such data exists for particular affordance types, e. g. through the data set of Myers et al. (2015), the transfer of deep architectures to other affordance domains is not trivial. Particularly in the novel context of whole-body affordances in loco-manipulation tasks, labeled training data is rare. Furthermore, segmentation approaches to affordance detection provide no inherent connection between the identified affordance segments and the robot embodiment which is necessary for establishing a link between perception and action execution. Such a link is an important foundation of the affordance formalization proposed in Chapter 4.

2.3.8 Whole-Body Affordances

A central contribution of this thesis is the application of the affordance concept to the detection of possibilities for whole-body actions in loco-manipulation tasks. Such actions are particularly important in the field of humanoid robotics, where loco-manipulation actions are considered essential capabilities. Such actions incorporate the whole robot body for multi-contact stabilization during locomotion, e. g. by *supporting* on or *leaning* against suitable surfaces, and whole-body manipulation, e. g. *pushing* or *pulling* of large objects or *opening* of doors. Figure 1.2 depicts multiple illustrative examples of humans performing whole-body loco-manipulation actions. The problems of motion planning and control of such actions with humanoid robots are challenging, but intensively studied. However, although the previous sections review an extensive body of affordance-based approaches in autonomous robotics, the computational formalization of affordances for whole-body actions is novel. While the terminology of whole-body affordances is developed within the context of this thesis (Kaiser et al. 2014a), few related approaches implement strategies for the detection of corresponding action possibilities which are reviewed within this section.

The work of Fallon et al. (2015b), which has already been mentioned in Section 2.3.3, approaches the detection of whole-body *supportability* affordances for foot placement by detecting horizontal planar primitives in the environment (see Figure 2.4). In accordance with Pryor et al. (2016), detected planes are considered equivalent to the respective affordances and serve as direct hints for end-effector contact planning. In a similar approach in Werner et al. (2016), planar surface patches, which appear large enough to accommodate the robot's feet, are identified in unknown environments for subsequent footstep planning. The authors further propose an integrated pipeline from environmental perception to multi-contact trajectory planning, evaluated at the example of staircase climbing. The example of staircase climbing based on detected planar primitives is also investigated in Oßwald et al. (2011a,b) using the small-scale humanoid robot *Nao* (see Figure 2.13). Lewis et al. (2005) argues that the reliable detection of *supportability* affordances for footstep placement requires surface property estimation besides pure geometric surface features and proposes a method for differing between slippery and solid surfaces.

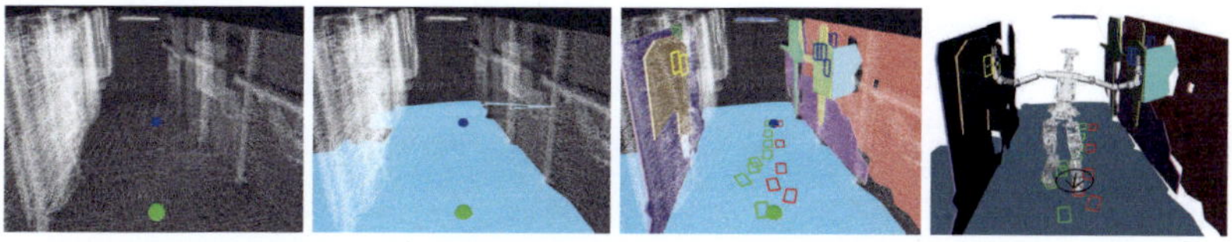

Figure 2.12: The detection of *supportability* and *leanability* affordances for humanoid locomotion planning (taken from Pryor et al. 2016, © 2016 IEEE).

Pryor et al. (2016) address the detection of affordances for humanoid locomotion planning in unknown environments. In an approach similar to the one followed in this thesis, the authors first simplify the perceived environment into planar primitives and subsequently detect *supportability* and *leanability* affordances based on geometric primitive properties. The detected affordances are considered direct hints for end-effector placement during locomotion planning. The key contribution of the work is the combination of iterative affordance detection with the contact sequence planner *ANA** which only needs to consider a local volume of the environment rather than the full scene (see Figure 2.12). While Pryor et al. (2016) share the concept of whole-body affordances with the approach proposed in this thesis, their focus lies in the efficient planning of locomotion trajectories rather than in a novel computational formalization of the affordance concept. The two works can therefore be regarded as complementary.

Figure 2.13: Autonomous staircase climbing based on detected planar primitives (taken from Oßwald et al. 2011a,b, © 2011 IEEE).

While whole-body loco-manipulation actions are well-studied from the perspectives of motion planning and control, the investigation of their perceptual preconditions received little attention. Several groups, whose primary focus lies in locomotion planning, proposed approaches for detecting *supportability* or *leanability* affordances in unknown environments, suiting their particular needs. In this context, the perception of unknown environments with 3D range sensors and the subsequent simplification into geometric primitives appears to be a popular and promising approach. The concept of affordance detection as proposed in this thesis will pursue a similar approach to environmental perception. However, in contrast to the works discussed in this section, discovered geometric primitives are not regarded as direct hints for action planning, equivalent to affordances. Instead, a sophisticated affordance representation based on Dempster-Shafer belief functions is constructed from detected primitives.

2.3.9 The DARPA Robotics Challenge

The detection of whole-body affordances in loco-manipulation tasks was also an essential component of approaches to the DARPA Robotics Challenge.

Figure 2.14: The humanoid robot *Atlas* of the team *WPI-CMU* performing different tasks of the DRC Finals, i. e. utility vehicle egress, walking over rough terrain and staircase climbing (taken from Atkeson et al. 2015, © 2015 IEEE).

The *DARPA Robotics Challenge* (DRC) (Pratt et al. 2013) was a robotics competition held between 2012 and 2015, consisting of three distinct events: The *Virtual Robotics Challenge* (VRC) in June 2013, the *DRC Trials* in December 2013 and the *DRC Finals* in June 2015. Participating teams had to demonstrate complex, semi-autonomous behavior within the context of disaster response. Although not explicitly required, many teams employed a humanoid platform, e. g. the humanoid robot *Atlas* from *Boston Dynamics* (see Figure 2.14). The European team *WALK-MAN*[8] participated with a humanoid robot of the same name (Tsagarakis et al. 2017) and eventually ranking 17th out of 23 participating teams. WALK-MAN is partly used as an evaluation platform throughout this thesis. Table 2.1 summarizes the tasks that had to be solved in the DRC Finals in 2015 together with the total amount of points scored by all teams in the respective tasks. Each successful task execution was awarded one point during the challenge, hence the number of points listed in Table 2.1 equals the number of teams that accomplished

[8] European Union Seventh Framework Programme under grant agreement number 611832 `http://www.walk-man.eu`

the respective task. See Krotkov et al. (2017) for a detailed discussion of the DRC results and insights.

Table 2.1: The tasks of the DRC Finals in the order of a possible challenge attempt (following Krotkov et al. 2017). The column *Pts.* indicates the accumulated amount of points scored by all participating teams.

No.	Name	Description	Pts.
1	*Drive*	Drive a utility vehicle along a lane with obstacles	19
2	*Egress*	Exit the vehicle and locomote to the door	9
3	*Door*	Open the door and locomote through a doorway	17
4	*Valve*	Rotate a 260 mm industrial valve by 360 degrees	16
5	*Wall*	Cut a hole in a wall using a cordless power tool	6
6	*Surprise*	Operate a lever and a magnetic plug	10
7	*Rubble*	Cross one out of two 2.4 m long rubble tracks	9
8	*Stairs*	Climb four steps of 17.8 cm rise	7

The DRC challenges were designed inspired by the idea of robotic disaster response which implies semi-autonomous robot control in unstructured and partly unknown environments. See Figure 2.14 for images showing the humanoid robot *Atlas* performing exemplary tasks of the DRC Finals. As stated above, such conditions require a sophisticated robotic system to implement strategies for autonomous or semi-autonomous affordance detection. However, in a review of the DRC Trials, Murphy (2015) concludes that the degrees of autonomy implemented by the different teams were rather low. This appears appropriate due to the rules of the challenge which were permissive regarding remote human intervention and teleoperation, but strict[9] regarding errors in the task executions, e. g. falls or hardware faults. In such

[9] There were no safety ropes for fall prevention and physical intervention by the teams was punished.

conditions, reliability and safety has priority over autonomy and generality of the approach.

DRC Approaches to Affordance Detection During the DRC Trials in 2013, the tasks and scenarios were accurately defined beforehand. While the task descriptions for the DRC Finals in 2015 were intentionally vague, they were based upon the tasks of the DRC Trials and key elements such as tools were specified.[10] The predominant approach to action possibility perception was therefore to recognize known or familiar objects and structures in the perceived scene and subsequently to utilize known relations between objects and robot skills in order to solve the defined task. For recognizing the involved objects and environmental structures, e. g. the valve in task 4, the teams mostly pursued a semi-autonomous approach, either by using general matching strategies for predefined object models, e. g. the teams *IHMC* (Johnson et al. 2015), *MIT* (Fallon et al. 2015a) and *ViGIR* (Romay et al. 2017), or by using specialized detection methods that identify objects based on task-specific shape features, e. g. the teams *RoboSimian* (Karumanchi et al. 2017), *WPI-CMU* (DeDonato et al. 2017), *SNU* (S. Kim et al. 2017), *NimbRo Rescue* (Schwarz et al. 2017) and *WALK-MAN* (Tsagarakis et al. 2017). Some teams leveraged the perception of objects and environmental structures entirely to the human pilot, e. g. the team *DRC-HUBO* (Zucker et al. 2015). After detecting critical objects, the teams followed predefined task execution strategies incorporating autonomous components like motion planning or stabilization. In critical phases, the pilots of all teams were able to control the robot via basic teleoperation.

Two teams deliberately implemented affordance-based approaches to action possibility detection, allowing a certain degree of flexibility beyond the challenge setup: *ViGIR* (Romay et al. 2017) and *MIT* (Fallon et al. 2015a).

[10] The rule book of the DRC Finals can be obtained from:
`http://archive.darpa.mil/roboticschallenge.`

While both teams based their approaches on the detection of *object templates* in the scene, they employ a different understanding of the term *affordance*. In Romay et al. (2017), an affordance is defined as a motion constraint for the robot end-effector that needs to be satisfied in order to use the detected object in a goal-oriented way. In contrast, Fallon et al. (2015a) define affordances as the detected objects themselves which can be utilized by the robot in a task-oriented way. While the terminology differs, both approaches implement *affordance templates* which link object descriptions, e. g. object models, to descriptions of associated actions, e. g. in terms of grasp poses and motion constraints. While affordance templates are a viable approach within the context of the DRC where objects and scenarios are at least roughly specified, their utility is limited in unknown environments.

The different tasks of the DARPA Robotics Challenge are excellent examples for expected capabilities of humanoid robots in the area of disaster response. The results of the challenge demonstrate that current humanoid robots are able to solve the tasks, while leaving large room for improvement, particularly in the aspects of autonomous perception, multi-contact locomotion and manipulation planning, whole-body stabilization and shared autonomous pilot interaction. The DRC tasks therefore evolved to become popular benchmarks in humanoid robotics research. The affordance system proposed in this thesis provides the foundation for a more general approach to the detection of whole-body affordances in tasks similar to those from the DRC. The DRC also showed that shared autonomous collaboration between a humanoid robot and a human pilot is a viable and appropriate approach to real-world scenarios using state-of-the-art technology. While the formalisms for affordance detection proposed in this thesis is independent of the aspired degree of robot autonomy, the implementation on real humanoid robots is based on shared autonomous robot control (see Chapter 6). This allows the evaluation of the proposed concepts in DRC-inspired scenarios which has partly been done in Chapter 7.

2.4 Autonomous Control in Humanoid Robotics

In the previous sections, the implementation of affordance detection systems was proposed as a key challenge for building autonomous robotic applications. As seen in Section 2.3.9, the state-of-the-art technology in humanoid robotics is able to produce systems that show semi-autonomous behavior while being constantly monitored and controlled by a team of human pilots. This control mode is commonly termed *semi autonomy* or *shared autonomy* and can be localized in between *fully teleoperated* systems, where the pilot controls every individual aspect of the robot, and *fully autonomous* systems which operate without the need of a pilot. As the proposed affordance detection system is evaluated by implementing a pilot interface that allows shared autonomous control of humanoid robots, this section briefly reviews existing autonomous control modes with a particular focus on humanoid robotics.

Table 2.2: Autonomous control modes categorized by the work distribution between the human operator (H) and the (semi-) autonomous robot (R) (adapted from Endsley et al. 1999, © 1999 Taylor & Francis Ltd.).

		Role			
LOA	**Name**	**Mon.**	**Gen.**	**Sel.**	**Imp.**
1	Manual Control	H	H	H	H
2	Action Support	H/R	H	H	H/R
3	Batch Processing	H/R	H	H	R
4	Shared Control	H/R	H/R	H	H/R
5	Decision Support	H/R	H/R	H	R
6	Blended Decision Making	H/R	H/R	H/R	R
7	Rigid System	H/R	R	H	R
8	Automated Decision Making	H/R	H/R	R	R
9	Supervisory Control	H/R	R	R	R
10	Full Automation	R	R	R	R

Endsley et al. (1999) identify three characteristics common to domains which allow the application of autonomous or semi-autonomous systems: Multiple goals and tasks compete for the pilot's attention in situations where tasks are highly demanding and time resources are limited. The application of humanoid robots in disaster response scenarios (see Section 2.3.9) is a viable example for such a domain. Based on an earlier taxonomy from Sheridan et al. (1978), Endsley et al. (1999) develop a taxonomy of autonomous control modes with ten *levels of automation* (LOA). The authors aim at consistently describing autonomous control modes in various different domains, such as air traffic control, air piloting or advanced manufacturing. Control modes are characterized based on four fundamental tasks that have to be performed repetitively (see Endsley et al. 1999):

Monitoring (Mon.): Perception of the system status

Generating (Gen.): Formulation of options or strategies for achieving goals

Selecting (Sel.): Decision on a particular option or strategy

Implementing (Imp.): Carrying out the chosen option

The level of autonomy of a system is defined by the distribution of roles between the human pilot and the robot over the four tasks as shown in Table 2.2.

2.4.1 Autonomy at the DARPA Robotics Challenge

Reports from the DRC, which was held under conditions as realistic as the current state-of-the-art allows, show that operator stress was a non-negligible factor in the teams' successes. Multiple fatal errors happened due to bad interplay between the human pilot and autonomous behaviors of the robot (Atkeson et al. 2015; DRC-Teams 2015). Murphy (2015) reviews the levels of autonomy implemented by the contestants of the DRC Trials and concludes that most teams followed a bottom-up approach to autonomy, starting from pure teleoperation successively enhanced with autonomous behaviors. According to his review, the teams generally implemented tight operator control of autonomous behavior-based on successive execution approval rather than task rehearsal for autonomously planned action sequences. With respect to the LOA taxonomy in Table 2.2, the approaches seen at the DRC Trials can be categorized into the LOAs 2-4: *Action Support*, *Batch Processing* and *Shared Control*. Atkeson et al. (2015), associated with team WPI-CMU, reviews the predominant approaches seen at the DRC and concludes that perception and autonomous behavior are among the key capabilities that need to be improved for producing reliable solutions for the tasks given in the DRC:

> *In the DRC, [the problem of only obtaining mediocre performance by using available standard software components] was solved by over-relying on the human operator and the always-on 9600 baud link. We need to figure out ways to get the perception and autonomy research community interested in helping us make robots that are more aware and autonomous, and going beyond standard libraries.*
> Atkeson et al. (2015, p. 8)

While the DRC was a competition particularly suited to humanoid robotic research platforms, shared autonomous robots are already in application in *urban search and rescue* (USAR) as reviewed in Y. Liu et al. (2013). Although humanoid robots are not a subject of this survey, it shows that shared autonomous and even fully autonomous control modes have been successfully demonstrated in field experiments using single or multiple mobile and aerial robots. Autonomous capabilities include the detection and traversal of rough terrain, e. g. stairs, the creation of 3D maps of the scene via *SLAM*[11] or the identification of victims.

[11] SLAM: *Simultaneous Localization and Mapping*

The affordance detection system developed in this thesis can be seen as a promising step towards more sophisticated humanoid robot systems that do not need to rely on a human operator for performing the roles of *Generating* and *Selecting* (refer to Table 2.2). However, the main contribution of this thesis is not the actual autonomous implementation of *Generating* and *Selecting*, but the perceptive-cognitive foundation as a step towards implementing higher levels of autonomy on humanoid robots.

2.4.2 Pilot Interfaces for Humanoid Robots

As long as humanoid robots applied challenging scenarios are not fully autonomous, there is a need for one or multiple human operators[12] controlling the non-autonomous parts of the robot system via *pilot interfaces*. The design[13] principles of the pilot interface are critical as the interface should at the same time:

1. allow the pilot to control the robot on different LOAs in possibly high detail and precision
2. not overload the pilot with information and possibilities, eventually inducing likelihood for human error in the control process

Pilot interfaces for semi-autonomous humanoid robots, as developed for the DRC, are particularly complex due to the complexity of a humanoid robot and the difficulty of its tasks. In an attempt to balance the work load between the robot and the operator, Birkenkampf et al. (2014) propose a shared autonomous pilot interface for the humanoid robot *Rollin' Justin*. The interface reduces the set of defined actions to those which are afforded by the objects recognized in the current scene. Actions and objects in this work

[12] The terms *operator* and *pilot* are used synonymously throughout this thesis.
[13] *Design* in this case is not to be understood as *visual appearance*.

are defined as PDDL[14] planning operators, while the entire world state is assumed to be known.

As the tasks of the DRC were mostly predefined, the participating teams predominantly implemented task-specific interfaces, in which the operator is presented controls for specific behaviors relevant to the current task (e. g. Tsagarakis et al. 2017). See Figure 2.15 for an exemplary screenshot of the WALK-MAN pilot interface. Furthermore, the operators could observe the robot state and the perceived world state in an integrated 3D visualization of the sensor data which was also used for visualizing essential task parameters (see Figure 2.16). If necessary, operators could switch to more fundamental interfaces for pure teleoperation. The 3D visualization of the robot and its perceived environment provides a viable interface between the human operator and the robot with respect to the perceptual aspects of the challenge. Many teams implemented interactive solutions for conveniently specifying objects of interest within the visualization, e. g. by clicking on points in the visualized point cloud that characterize pose and dimensions of an object (Karumanchi et al. 2017) or by adjusting autonomously detected object templates (Hart et al. 2015; Romay et al. 2015; Fallon et al. 2015a).

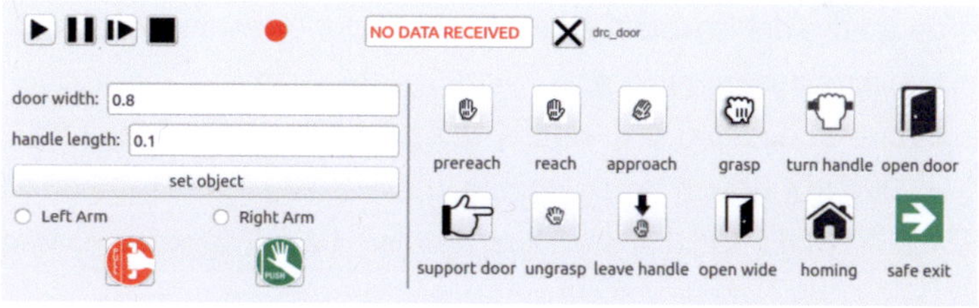

Figure 2.15: Parts of the task-specific pilot interface of the team WALK-MAN for the door-opening task (taken from Tsagarakis et al. 2017, © 2017 Wiley Periodicals, Inc.).

[14] PDDL: *Planning Domain Definition Language*

Experience from the DRC shows that shared autonomous control of humanoid robots in challenging scenarios is possible, but limited to task-specific autonomous behaviors under strict observation and continuous acknowledgment of the human operator. Operator stress and interface complexity has tuned out to be a critical source of error in the intense conditions of the challenge, leading to the conclusion that humanoid robots with more sophisticated autonomous behaviors, particularly in the area of perception, would result in more robust solutions to real-world applications. The affordance detection system developed in this thesis has been evaluated on the humanoid robot platforms ARMAR-III, ARMAR-4 and WALK-MAN based on an exemplary implementation of an affordance-based pilot interface that allows to control humanoid robots on a sophisticated level of autonomy. For the sake of fairness, it has to be mentioned that the pilot interfaces developed for the DRC were pragmatically designed for the purposes of the challenge, leading to impressive results using state-of-the-art humanoid technology. In contrast to these approaches, the prototypical affordance-based pilot interface discussed in this thesis implements more sophisticated control modes, but lacks essential features preventing its direct application under the conditions of the DRC. It can be regarded as a step *towards* more sophisticated pilot interfaces for humanoid robots based on more autonomous perceptive-cognitive capabilities. Furthermore, it is important to mention that neither the pilot interfaces of the DRC, nor the proposed affordance-based pilot interface have been developed with a particular focus on visual appearance, user interface design or ergonomics.

2.5 Summary and Review

This chapter first introduced the theory of affordances in Section 2.1 as a fundamental conceptual basis for the approach taken in this thesis. After reviewing the psychological definitions, discourse and criticism, Section 2.2 summarized four essential attempts to the computational formalization of the affordance concept aiming at application in the area of autonomous robotics. The discussed formalizations approach affordances from different directions and each inspired a broad range of applications in the field of robotics. Section 2.3 provided an overview over affordance-based approaches in autonomous robotics, while discussed works are sorted into six principle categories based on the employed representation of affordances:

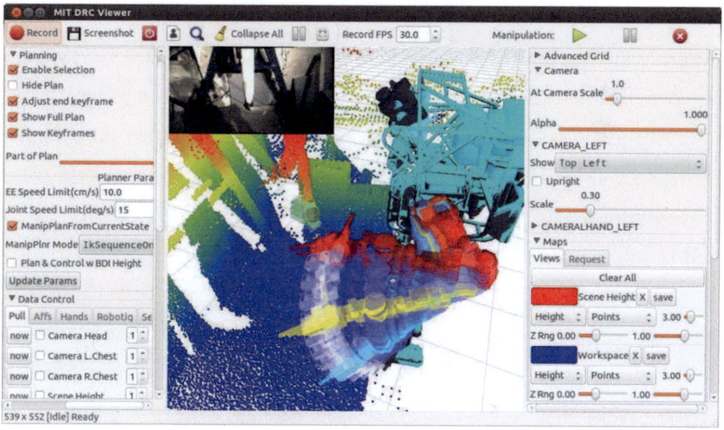

Figure 2.16: The exemplary pilot interface of the team MIT (taken from Fallon et al. 2015a, © 2015 Wiley Periodicals, Inc.).

Perceptual Invariants The first category of affordance-based approaches considers affordances as perceptual invariants in a defined visual feature space. These invariants are commonly learned during developmental phases of motor babbling. Such developmental definitions of the affordance concept allow the implementation of robotic learning phases inspired by human and animal development. However, approaches in this category are typically applied to basic affordances and robots with limited degrees of freedom. Application to the developmental learning of whole-body affordances, although desirable, seems distant.

Geometric Features The second category of affordance-based approaches considers affordances as equivalent to elementary geometric features. Although conceptually related, approaches in this category appear more pragmatic than the developmental learning of perceptual invariants. Some approaches in this category achieve promising results by using handcrafted geometric features rather than learned conditions in a feature space. Individual approaches demonstrate the applicability of this concept to the area of whole-body loco-manipulation, e. g. by detecting *supportability* affordances for footstep planning based on planar primitive patches. The methods introduced in this thesis follow related ideas for geometric primitive extraction. However, the detection of sophisticated affordances and the fusion of affordance-related evidence from multiple sources cannot be properly addressed with an immediate link between perception and action as implemented in approaches from this category.

Probability Distributions The third category of affordance-based approaches introduces probabilistic representations of the affordance concept. Typically, approaches in this category define affordances as probability distributions over the spaces of action parameters and action effects. Approaches particularly related to the one presented in this thesis define affordances as probability distributions over the space of end-effector poses. Probabilistic representations over end-effector pose spaces provide a convenient way for linking affordance detection with action execution, also in the scope of whole-body affordances. However, approaches from this category do not provide solutions for combining affordance-related evidence from different sources or for the hierarchical composition of affordances.

Probabilistic Networks The fourth group of affordance-based approaches extends the ideas of the previous category towards representing affordances in probabilistic networks, such as Bayesian networks. These approaches are particularly popular in the area of developmental learning of affordances, as multiple affordances can be jointly learned in a single network representations. However, appropriate network structures need to be defined or expensively learned and the joint representation and learning of multiple affordances can behave poorly.

Knowledge Bases The fifth group of affordance-based approaches attempts to define and populate knowledge bases or ontologies with relational knowledge. Affordances are predominantly interpreted as relations between objects and actions. While knowledge bases principally allow the transfer of affordance-related knowledge from external sources to a robot or between different robots, the grounding of contained knowledge in the robot's sensorimotor experience is challenging.

Semantic Segments The last category of affordance-based approaches formulates the problem of affordance detection as a particular type of semantic segmentation. Many approaches attempt to apply methods known from computer vision to the problem of affordance detection and achieve remarkable results, particularly with the application of convolutional neural networks. However, approaches in this category typically do not model the link between detected affordances and action parameterization which is essential for the autonomous or shared autonomous control of humanoid robots.

After the broad review of affordance-based approaches given in Section 2.3, approaches particularly related to the conceptual idea of whole-body affordances are reviewed in Section 2.3.8. The survey shows that related approaches are commonly focused on locomotion planning for particular types of whole-body loco-manipulation actions. Section 2.3.9 extends this survey to approaches seen at the DARPA robotics challenge which particularly aimed at demonstrating state-of-the-art skills in humanoid whole-body locomotion and manipulation. However, the participating teams preferred, for good reason, to implement predefined shared autonomous strategies for the tasks of the challenge. The overall analysis shows that a consistent formalization of the affordance concept with respect to whole-body actions in loco-manipulation tasks has not yet been proposed. Finally, Section 2.4 provides insights into the concepts of autonomy and shared autonomy, particularly focusing on the degrees of autonomy employed by the DRC teams. As the concepts proposed in this thesis can be seen as a step towards more autonomous detection and execution of whole-body actions in the context of shared autonomy in loco-manipulation tasks, the review of pilot interfaces given in Section 2.4.2 demonstrates the state-of-the-art in this area.

3 Preliminaries

This thesis aims at the formal conception, implementation and evaluation of an affordance detection and validation system for humanoid robots in whole-body loco-manipulation tasks. Such an affordance system plays a central role in the cognitive architecture of a humanoid robot and is therefore tightly integrated with existing sensorimotor components.
This chapter introduces several important preliminaries which together form the principle foundation of the methods developed within this dissertation. The topics will be briefly introduced and discussed to the degree of detail necessary for a thorough understanding of the later chapters. The foundations introduced in this chapter are the H^2T perception pipeline in Section 3.1, ArmarX together with its concept of statecharts in Section 3.2 and Object-Action Complexes in Section 3.3.

3.1 The H^2T Perception Pipeline

The *H^2T perception pipeline* has been developed in close collaboration with other dissertation projects and serves as a perceptual foundation for the affordance detection system proposed in this thesis. The pipeline is responsible for processing point clouds into sets of geometric primitives which then directly serve as input for the affordance detection system. The pipeline consists of the steps $\boldsymbol{S_1}$, $\boldsymbol{S_2}$ and $\boldsymbol{S_3}$ as outlined in Figure 3.1. The final step $\boldsymbol{S_4}$ constitutes the main contribution of this thesis and will therefore be discussed in extensive detail within the following chapters. Depending on the context, the detection of affordances will be either considered to be an independent addition to the pipeline or its final step $\boldsymbol{S_4}$. Figure 3.2 displays the intermediate results of the individual pipeline steps which will be briefly introduced and discussed in the remainder of this section. This section presents an extended description of the H^{2}T perception pipeline, initially proposed and described in Kaiser et al. (2014a, 2015a).

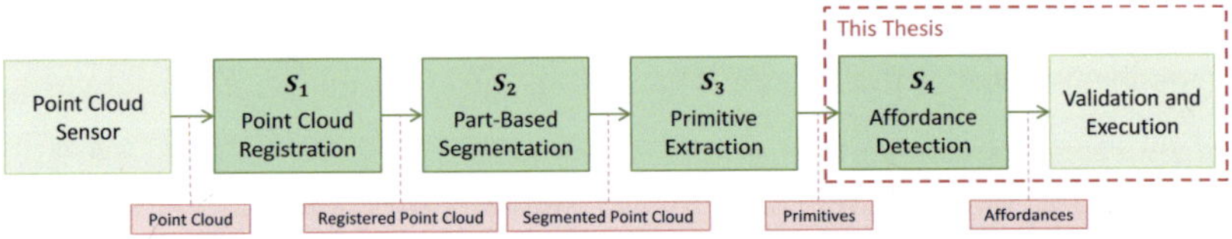

Figure 3.1: The *H^{2}T perception pipeline* (adapted from Kaiser et al. 2018a, © 2018 IEEE). Input point clouds are first registered into a combined representation ($\boldsymbol{S_1}$) and then segmented ($\boldsymbol{S_2}$). The segmented point cloud serves as the basis for extracting geometric primitives ($\boldsymbol{S_3}$) which are subsequently used for affordance detection ($\boldsymbol{S_4}$). The detection of affordances and their later use for the purposes of validation and action execution falls into the scope of this thesis.

Point Cloud Registration The exemplary point cloud shown in Figure 3.3 demonstrates that single point cloud snapshots do often not provide sufficient information about the environment, as important environmental structures can exist outside of the camera's field of view or inside the shadow volume of other structures. Hence, real applications often require a robot to locomote in the scene and to continuously align captured point clouds with previous point clouds in order to obtain a complete image of the environment. This process is called *point cloud registration* and is optionally performed in the earliest stage $\boldsymbol{S_1}$ of the perception pipeline.

The H^{2}T perception pipeline utilizes the state-of-the-art open source SLAM library *RTAB-Map* (Labbé et al. 2014) for this purpose. The real-time capable RTAB-Map registration method is based on the tracking of 2D local image features among consecutive frames. RTAB-Map features loop closure detection and graph pose optimization. While the remaining components of the pipeline can work with arbitrary point clouds, the implementation of the registration step $\boldsymbol{S_1}$ requires RGB-D images. Hence, in the current implementation of the pipeline, the registration step needs to be bypassed if unorganized point clouds are used. Figure 3.4 shows an example for a registered point cloud, resembling a standard scene from the area of whole-body loco-manipulation: a handrail-equipped staircase.

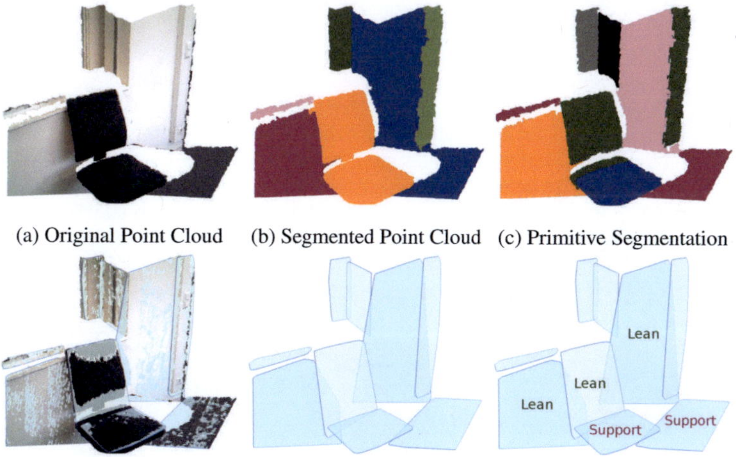

(a) Original Point Cloud (b) Segmented Point Cloud (c) Primitive Segmentation

(d) Geometric Primitives (e) Geometric Primitives (f) Affordances

Figure 3.2: The intermediate steps of the H^{2}T perception pipeline. (a) Multiple individual point clouds are registered and merged into a combined point cloud representation. (b) The point cloud is segmented based on the convexity of surface patches. Each color represents one segment in the visualization. (c-e) Geometric primitives are fitted into the segmented point cloud. (f) Affordances are extracted from the primitives.

The registration step $\boldsymbol{S_1}$ is optional, the perception pipeline can also be configured to work on individual captures or on unregistered sequences of captures. However, some of the experiments on real robotic platforms discussed in Chapter 7 use the registration step for obtaining a larger initial environmental representation.

Figure 3.3: A single exemplary LIDAR point cloud captured in a test environment for loco-manipulation for the humanoid robot WALK-MAN. Although the laser scan produces an extensive depth image of the environment (*left*), shadowed areas are not reflected in the point cloud (*right*). For obtaining a complete point cloud representation of the environment, multiple views from different positions need to be captured and registered.

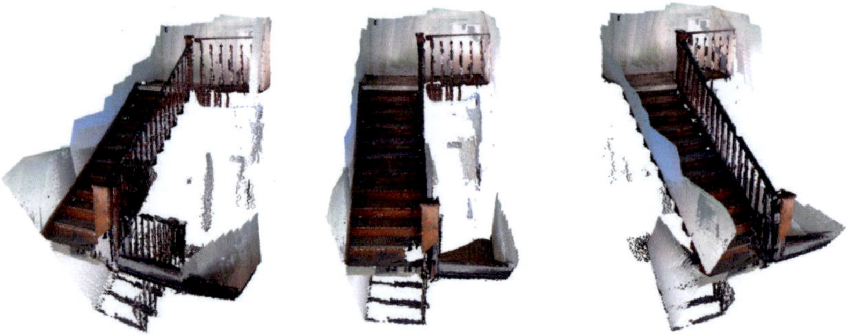

Figure 3.4: Cropped visualization of a registered point cloud resembling a handrail-equipped staircase. The point cloud has been registered using *RTAB-Map* (Labbé et al. 2014) from a set of 64 individual point clouds.

Part-Based Segmentation Once, captured point clouds are registered, the scene is segmented into plausible and distinct regions by employing the segmentation algorithm *LCCP*[1] (Stein et al. 2014). This initial segmentation allows the parallel processing of segmented regions in the subse-

[1] LCCP: *Locally Convex Connected Patches*

quent primitive extraction step. In contrast to conventional segmentation methods that involve model fitting or learning techniques, this approach grows locally connected convex surface regions bounded by concavities. Convexly connected neighbor surface patches are then merged together resulting in a final scene segmentation. While LCCP constitutes the reference segmentation method implemented in the H^2T perception pipeline, other segmentation algorithms, such as region growing, euclidean clustering or deep networks for segmentation can be configured. Figure 3.2b depicts the final part-based segmentation result of the point cloud shown in Figure 3.2a. In the following, the segmentation $\mathcal{S}$ of a registered point cloud $\mathcal{P}$ is formally denoted as a set of disjoint segments s_i:

$$\mathcal{S} = \{s_1, \ldots, s_n\}, \quad s_i \subset \mathcal{P}, \quad s_i \cap s_j = \emptyset \, \forall i \neq j \tag{3.1}$$

Primitive Extraction The third step $\boldsymbol{S_3}$ of the perception pipeline is the extraction of geometric primitives from the segmentation result $\mathcal{S}$ generated by the previous pipeline step $\boldsymbol{S_2}$. Each segment $s_i \in \mathcal{S}$ is iteratively matched against a defined set of geometric models using the *RANSAC*[2] algorithm (Fischler et al. 1981). Currently, three basic primitive types are supported: planes, cylinders and spheres. However, the extension of the pipeline to further geometric shapes is straightforward.

One of the main drawbacks of low-level feature-based segmentation methods is the possible under-segmentation of the scene, i. e. multiple distinct object segments happen to be merged, for instance due to noise in the depth cues. An example for under-segmentation is found in Figure 3.2b, where the segmentation step generates one large segment for the chair. Although the chair constitutes a *semantic entity*, it consists of multiple *geometric primitives*, i. e. the seating and the backrest. In such cases, naive application of model fitting algorithms, such as RANSAC is prone to error. To tackle the

[2] RANSAC: *Random Sample Consensus*

under-segmentation problem, a customized model fitting approach provided in Rusu et al. (2011) is employed as outlined in the following.
For each segment $s \in \mathcal{S}$, the approach computes a set of disjoint geometric primitives $\Psi = \{\psi_1, \ldots, \psi_m\}$, each of which defining either a plane, a cylinder or a sphere. The primitives $\psi_i \in \Psi$ are represented by inlier point clouds $\mathcal{P}_{\psi_i} \subset s$, together with a corresponding set of outliers $\mathcal{O}_s$, i. e. segment points that have not been assigned to any of the primitives ψ_i:

$$\mathcal{O}_s = s \setminus \bigcup_{i=1}^{m} \mathcal{P}_{\psi_i}. \tag{3.2}$$

To partition a segment $s \in \mathcal{S}$ into distinct primitives, RANSAC is iteratively applied. In each iteration, fitting scores δ_{plane}, δ_{cylinder} and δ_{sphere} are computed based on the maximum number of inliers for the three possible models. The model with the highest fitting score is instantiated as a new primitive ψ_{best}. Before adding ψ_{best} to the set of discovered primitives, the underlying point cloud $\mathcal{P}_{\psi_{\text{best}}}$ is further partitioned in a clustering process based on Euclidean distances between points. This step avoids distant clusters of points to be merged into one single primitive. The same procedure is repeated over the remaining outliers $\mathcal{O}$ to generate further primitives, until the number of outliers $|\mathcal{O}|$ is smaller than a threshold τ_{min}. The complete iterative primitive extraction approach is outlined in Algorithm 1.
Figure 3.2e depicts the primitives extracted from the scene segmentation shown in Figure 3.2a. Note that scene parts that are segmented into single segments due to under-segmentation, e. g. the chair, are now successfully partitioned into distinct primitives. The initial step of under-segmentation allows a parallel application of RANSAC for all segments, resulting in an overall faster approach. Figure 3.5 depicts the different steps of the perception pipeline for the staircase point cloud shown in Figure 3.4. Until now the H^2T perception pipeline has been successfully tested with a range of different depth sensing technologies, including the *ASUS Xtion Pro* RGB-D camera,

the *MultiSense S7* stereo camera and the *Hokuyo UTM-30LX-EW* laser scanner (Kaiser et al. 2016b), in a variety of real and simulated environments. This section introduced the pipeline in the version that is used within this thesis. In particular, the employed version of the pipeline does not reason about inter-primitive relations and higher semantic structures. However, extensions to the pipeline have been proposed which address these issues (Grotz et al. 2017).

Algorithm 1 Primitive extraction in the H^{2}T perception pipeline

Require:
$\mathcal{S}$ – Segmentation
$\tau_{\min}$ – Minimum point cloud size
$\tau_{\max}$ – Maximum point cloud size

function PRIMITIVEEXTRACTION($\mathcal{S}$, $\tau_{\min}$, $\tau_{\max}$)
    $\Psi \leftarrow \emptyset$
    for each $s \in \mathcal{S}$ **do**
        $\mathcal{O} \leftarrow s$
        while $|\mathcal{O}| \in (\tau_{\min}, \tau_{\max})$ **do**
            $\psi_{\text{plane}} \leftarrow \text{RANSAC}_{\text{plane}}(\mathcal{O})$
            $\psi_{\text{cylinder}} \leftarrow \text{RANSAC}_{\text{cylinder}}(\mathcal{O})$
            $\psi_{\text{sphere}} \leftarrow \text{RANSAC}_{\text{sphere}}(\mathcal{O})$
            $\psi_{\text{best}} \leftarrow \arg\max_{\psi \in \{\psi_{\text{plane}}, \psi_{\text{cylinder}}, \psi_{\text{sphere}}\}} |\mathcal{P}_\psi|$
            if $\mathcal{P}_{\psi_{\text{best}}} = \emptyset$ **then**
                break
            end if
            $\Psi_{\text{new}} \leftarrow \text{euclideanClustering}(\mathcal{P}_{\psi_{\text{best}}})$
            $\Psi \leftarrow \Psi \cup \Psi_{\text{new}}$
            $\mathcal{O} \leftarrow \mathcal{O} \setminus \mathcal{P}_{\psi_{\text{best}}}$
        end while
    end for
    return Ψ
end function

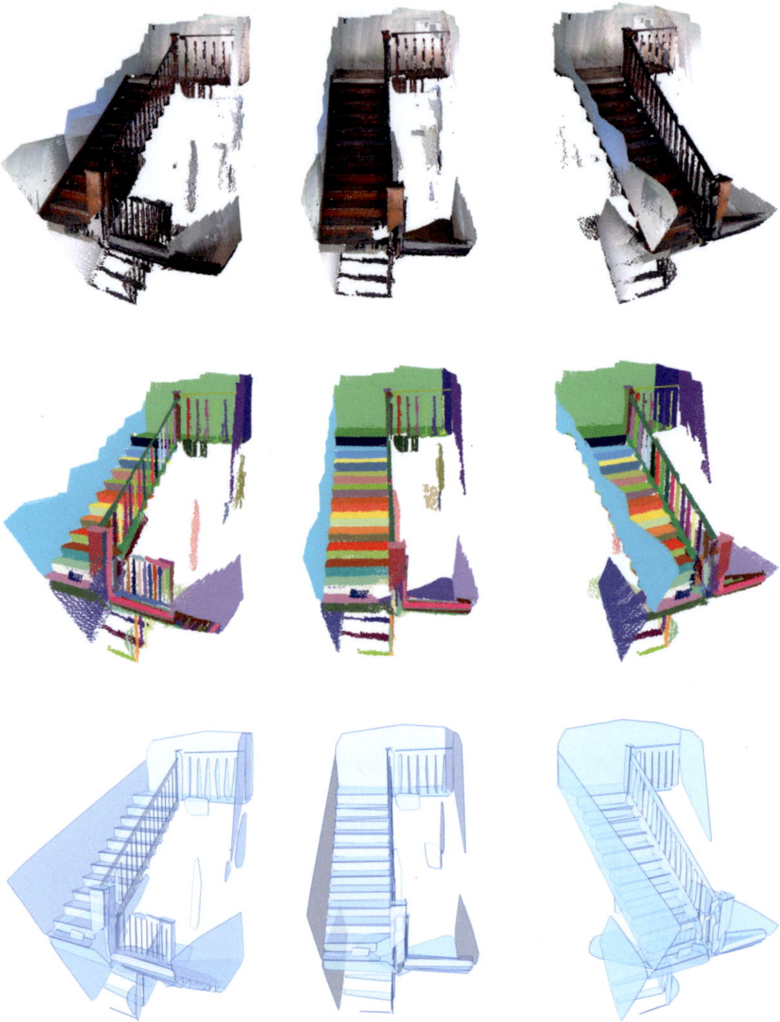

Figure 3.5: Geometric primitives extracted from a manually segmented, registered point cloud of a staircase. The visualizations show the original point clout (*first row*), the manually created segmentation (*second row*) and the resulting set of planar geometric primitives (*third row*).

3.2 The Robot Development Environment ArmarX

The theoretical and conceptual contributions of this thesis can be applied to arbitrary humanoid robots, running with arbitrary software environments. However, the reference implementation, which is used for the evaluation in Chapter 7, is developed within the open source robot development environment *ArmarX*[3]. One of the principle concepts of ArmarX is robot-agnosticism: Few low-level components need to be implemented in addition to a kinematic robot model, in order to port the whole framework to further humanoid robot platforms. These low-level components can either directly interface with the robot hardware, as in the case of ARMAR-4, ARMAR-5 and ARMAR-6, or interface with the native software layer running on the respective robot. This *software bridging approach* has been successfully used for porting ArmarX to the humanoid robots ARMAR-III[4], iCub (Paikan et al. 2015) and WALK-MAN (Kaiser et al. 2016c).

ArmarX realizes a distributed software architecture based on the open source middleware *ZeroC Ice*[5]. An outline of the ArmarX architecture is depicted in Figure 3.6: Besides the middleware layer which is responsible for providing and monitoring communication in the component-based architecture, ArmarX provides a rich set of higher-level components for different aspects of robot programming, including *MemoryX* for data storage, *VisionX* for visual sensor processing, *RobotAPI* for access to the robot hardware and collections of robot independent execution skills. The H^2T perception pipeline introduced in Section 3.1 is part of VisionX.

One benefit of the robot-agnostic architecture is that real robot hardware can be exchanged with a kinematic or dynamic robot simulation without adapting or re-implementing higher-level components. For the purpose of simulation,

[3] ArmarX (Vahrenkamp et al. 2015) is developed at the H^2T as a unified software framework for the ARMAR humanoid robots.

[4] The native software framework of ARMAR-III is *MCA*: `http://www.mca2.org`.

[5] `https://zeroc.com/products/ice`

ArmarX provides convenient means for simulating complex, dynamically changing environments based on the open source physics library *bullet*[6]. The dynamic simulator of ArmarX will be used in the simulated evaluation experiments in Chapter 7.

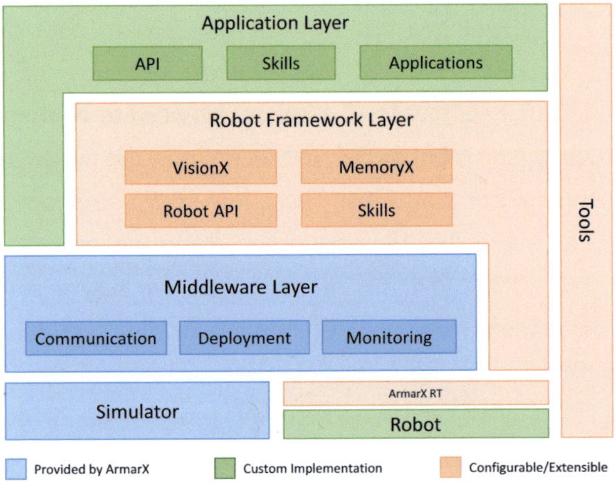

Figure 3.6: Overview over the robot development environment ArmarX (adapted from Vahrenkamp et al. 2015). The H^2T perception pipeline introduced in Section 3.1 is a part of *VisionX*.

Robot Programming in ArmarX: Statecharts One of the core principles of ArmarX is the concept of *hierarchical statecharts* (Wächter et al. 2016) which provides a convenient method for graphical programming of high-level robot skills. Statecharts consist of a hierarchical set of *states* which are connected by event-driven *transitions*. Each state can either be defined as a subordinate statechart or, alternatively, implemented in C++.

Figure 3.7 shows a visualization of the exemplary statechart *MovePlatform* which implements a platform movement for ARMAR-III given a set of target positions. In this example, the initial state *MoveToNext* implements a

[6] `http://bulletphysics.org`

platform movement to a single target position. This state is repeatedly entered on emittance of a *WaypointReached* event. The terminal states *Success* and *Failure* are entered if either all waypoints have been successfully reached or if any type of failure occurred during the execution. ArmarX provides the tools for conveniently editing and starting statecharts, as well as for the inspection of running statecharts. Based on the concept of statecharts, ArmarX provides a rich set of predefined, robot skills on various levels of abstraction.

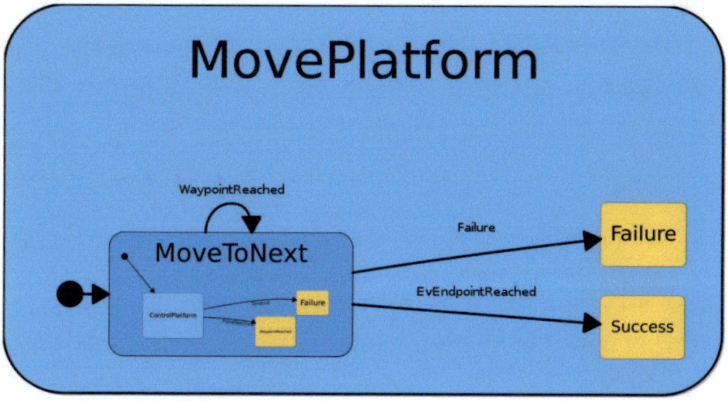

Figure 3.7: An exemplary ArmarX statechart for platform movement: Nested blue boxes represent the state hierarchy and black arrows represent event-driven transitions between states. Yellow boxes identify terminal states which terminate the control flow in the respective statechart.

3.3 Object-Action Complexes

The H^2T perception pipeline provides mechanisms for the pre-processing of depth camera images into a simplified environmental representation that can be used by the affordance detection system developed in this thesis. On the other end, affordances detected in the perceived environment need to be linked to parameterizable action execution specifications available to the robot. This connection will be established via the concept of *Object-Action Complexes* (OACs, Krüger et al. (2011)), eventually enabling the utilization of the proposed affordance system in the context of autonomous and shared autonomous robot control. OACs have been briefly introduced in Section 2.2 as an approach to formalize the affordance concept. OACs provide a general concept for representing and learning robot behaviors based on sensorimotor experience. The link between symbolic and continuous action descriptions make OACs a powerful formalism, particularly with respect to the planning of actions and tasks. The affordance formalization proposed in this thesis is not developed as a replacement of the concept of OACs, but as a complement: *Affordances as formalized in this thesis can be understood as preconditions for the instantiation of OACs.* This relation will be further discussed in Chapter 6. An OAC is formally defined as a triplet

$$(E, T, M), \tag{3.3}$$

consisting of an execution specification E, a prediction function $T : S \to S$ defined over an attribute space S and a statistical measure of success over previous executions M. The particular implementations of E, T and M depend on the application context. Multiple components of an OACs can be learned, e. g. the prediction function, the success measure and the control program, if suitable learning mechanisms are implemented.

3.3.1 An Exemplary OAC for Grasping

While the concept of OACs has been proposed as a conceptual framework for cognitive robotics, the implementation of OACs in practical applications is surprisingly simple. In this section, an exemplary OAC for object-agnostic grasping, an adapted version of the *AgnoGrasp* OAC from Krüger et al. (2011), is introduced. For defining the *AgnoGrasp* OAC, the attribute space S and the three OAC components T, M and E need to be specified as follows:

The Attribute Space S The first step of defining an OAC is the definition of the attribute space S which acts as the definition set and image set of the prediction function T. Hence, the attribute space needs to be chosen expressively enough to encode *preconditions* and *effects* of the intended action. In the case of the *AgnoGrasp* OAC, the attribute space can be defined as:

$$S = \{gripperStatus, \Omega, graspStatus\}, \tag{3.4}$$

while $gripperStatus \in \{full, empty\}$ represents the state of the robotic gripper, i. e. if it is currently grasping an object or not, and $graspStatus \in \{undefined, stable, unstable\}$ represents the condition of the current grasp. The set Ω contains co-planar contours detected in the scene, identifying candidates for graspable objects.

The Prediction Function T The prediction function T maps an initial state S_1 to a predicted state $S_2 = T(S_1)$ which is predicted to be caused by the OAC execution. The prediction function is problem-specific. In the exemplary case of *AgnoGrasp*, the prediction could be implemented by synthesizing and evaluating simulated grasps from the co-planar contours given in Ω.

The Success Measure M The measure of success M can be defined as the ratio of successful executions of the OAC, i. e. the number of successful grasps N, over the last K attempts.

The Execution Specification E The execution specification first ensures a valid initial world state, i. e. an empty gripper and available grasp candidates and then chooses the most promising grasp candidate from Ω using a specified quality rating. After executing a low-level control program, the world state is subsequently updated according to the robot's sensorimotor experience.

3.3.2 The Software Library Spoac

In this thesis, OACs will be used as a framework for action execution and sensorimotor experience with a direct link to symbolic action descriptions which can be used for symbolic action and task planning. The software library *Spoac* (Ovchinnikova et al. 2015) is used for the convenient implementation, storage and execution of OACs. Spoac is tightly integrated with the robot development environment *ArmarX* (see Section 3.2), particularly with its memory subsystem *MemoryX* for the persistent storage of OACs, and the concept of *statecharts* for the definition and execution of the OAC execution specifications. Besides the definition and execution of OACs, Spoac provides interfaces for OAC-based symbolic action and task planning. Figure 3.8 shows an exemplary statechart implementation of an OAC for *prismatic grasping* for ARMAR-III. The OAC implementation first opens the hand, locomotes to a suitable platform pose, moves the end-effector to a suitable approach pose and subsequently approaches the grasp target until a force threshold is exceeded which triggers closing of the hand.

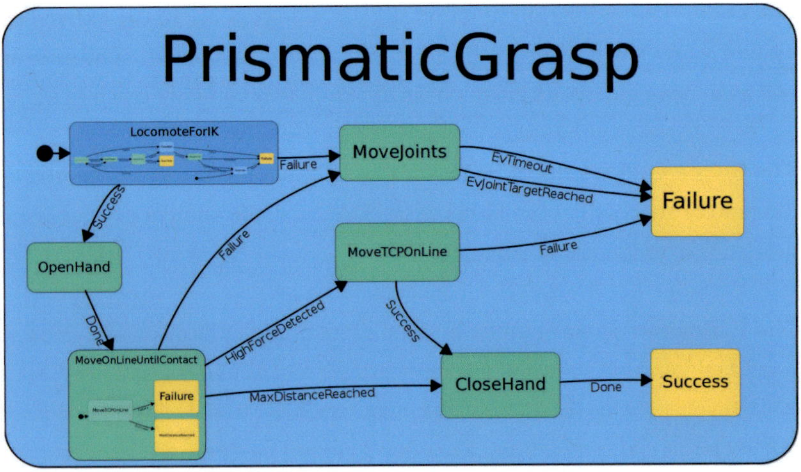

Figure 3.8: An exemplary OAC implementation for prismatic grasping with ARMAR-III: After moving the platform to a suitable position (*LocomoteForIK*), the hand is opened (*OpenHand*) and moved towards the grasp pose until the detection of contact (*MoveOnLineUntilContact*). In the case of a successful approach, the hand is slightly retracted (*MoveTCPOnLine*) and closed (*CloseHand*).

Figure 3.9 demonstrates the hierarchical composition of ArmarX statecharts, in this case for defining a validation OAC for *prismatic grasping* that attempts a prismatic grasp (via the OAC defined in Figure 3.8) and subsequently implements a validation state that assesses the quality of the achieved grasp.

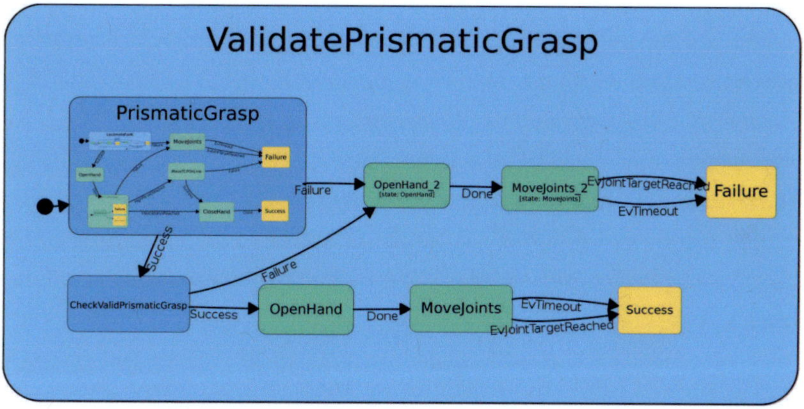

Figure 3.9: An exemplary OAC implementation for prismatic grasp validation with ARMAR-III: After a successful execution of the subordinate statechart for prismatic grasping (*PrismaticGrasp*), the grasp is assessed based on the opening angles of the hand (*CheckValidPrismaticGrasp*). In either case, the hand is opened and retracted before reporting the result.

3.4 Summary and Review

This chapter introduced a number of technical and conceptual prerequisites which are needed for the development and evaluation of the affordance detection and validation system proposed in this thesis. The H^{2}T perception pipeline (Section 3.1) and ArmarX (Section 3.2) are software dependencies of the reference implementation which is used for evaluation and validation in Chapter 7. Both the H^{2}T perception pipeline and ArmarX evolved to become a principle foundation of this thesis, providing robust mechanisms for perception, high-level and low-level robot control and dynamic simulation.

This was particularly useful for the system evaluation in a complex, dynamically simulated environment (Section 7.2.1) and for the validation on the humanoid robot platforms ARMAR-III (Section 7.3.1 and Section 7.3.2) and WALK-MAN (Section 7.3.3). However, despite the choice of the software dependencies for this dissertation project, the affordance system does not principally depend on the H^2T perception pipeline or ArmarX. Alternative implementations which use competing pipelines for primitive extraction, e. g. Pham et al. (2016), or other robot development environments, e. g. ROS[7], are possible.

The concept of Object-Action Complexes discussed in Section 3.3 contributes to both, the theoretical formalism for an affordance-based architecture and to the reference implementation via the software library Spoac. On a conceptual level, OACs provide a viable connection between detected affordances and robot execution skills, as well as between detected affordances and symbolic planning domains.

[7] ROS: *Robot Operating System*

4 Formalizing Whole-Body Affordances

The central theoretic contribution of this thesis is the definition of a computational model for whole-body affordances which allows the hierarchical representation of affordances and the consistent fusion of affordance-related evidence. In the following, these requirements will be briefly reviewed in further detail.

Hierarchical Representation The requirement of a hierarchical representation of affordances becomes self-evident by the observation that large portions of whole-body actions require *power grasping* contact with environmental structures (see Figure 1.2 for examples). Hence, grasping affordances can often be considered prerequisites for higher-level affordances like *pushing* or *pulling* which themselves could serve as prerequisites for even higher levels of affordances, e. g. *bimanual pushing* or *bimanual pulling*. The hierarchical formalization of affordances ensures that evidence of lower-level affordances is appropriately propagated to higher-level affordances.

Consistent Fusion of Evidence The affordance representation should support the *consistent fusion of evidence* about affordances, obtained from arbitrary sensor modalities. The consistent fusion of evidence is important when considering a humanoid robot as an inherently redundant machine, offering a multitude of sensor modalities which can assess the existence of affordances. Furthermore, evidence about affordances could result from human expert knowledge or the robot's own experience. The possible availability of affordance-related evidence from different sources with different attributed reliabilities necessitates a consistent formalism for affordance evidence fusion.

This chapter describes an approach towards a computational model of affordances that satisfies the two requirements above. The formalization is based on the *Dempster-Shafer Theory* (DST) (Dempster 1967; Shafer 1976) and the related *Theory of Subjective Logic* (Jøsang 2001). Parts of the affordance formalization introduced in this chapter have been published in Kaiser et al. (2016a, 2018a).

4.1 Mathematical Notations

Before beginning with a formal definition of the affordance concept as affordance belief functions, this section will provide a brief discussion of mathematical notations that will be used in this and the following chapters. The introduced notations particularly correspond to homogeneous transformations which will be of extensive use within this thesis.

Coordinate Systems Some of the following considerations are made with respect to a coordinate system, e. g. the end-effector coordinate system which will be defined in Figure 4.11. In these cases the symbols $\mathbf{1}_x$, $\mathbf{1}_y$ and $\mathbf{1}_z$ are used for denoting the unit vectors pointing along the positive x-, y- and z-axes, respectively:

$$\mathbf{1}_x = \begin{pmatrix} 1 \\ 0 \\ 0 \end{pmatrix}, \quad \mathbf{1}_y = \begin{pmatrix} 0 \\ 1 \\ 0 \end{pmatrix}, \quad \mathbf{1}_z = \begin{pmatrix} 0 \\ 0 \\ 1 \end{pmatrix}. \tag{4.1}$$

While many of the following considerations are independent of a world coordinate system, it is commonly assumed in this thesis that $\mathbf{1}_z$ points along the global up-direction.

Transformations Many of the formal concepts introduced in the following sections will be based on *end-effector poses* which are represented as transformations in space. The *special Euclidean group* $SE(3)$ is used to denote the space of transformations. A transformation $\boldsymbol{T} \in SE(3)$ is defined as a homogeneous matrix:

$$\boldsymbol{T} = \left(\begin{array}{c|c} \mathfrak{R}(\boldsymbol{T}) & \mathfrak{t}(\boldsymbol{T}) \\ \hline \mathbf{0} & 1 \end{array}\right) \in \mathbb{R}^{4\times 4}. \tag{4.2}$$

The notations $\mathfrak{R}(\boldsymbol{T}) \in \mathbb{R}^{3\times 3}$ and $\mathfrak{t}(\boldsymbol{T}) \in \mathbb{R}^3$ are used when referring to the orientational and translational parts of $\boldsymbol{T}$, respectively.

Boundary The *topological boundary* of a set S is denoted as ∂S. Mathematically, the boundary ∂S is defined as the set of points from the closure $\bar{S} \supseteq S$ which do not belong to the interior $S^{\circ} \subseteq S$:

$$\partial S = \bar{S} \setminus S^{\circ}. \tag{4.3}$$

In the following, the topological boundary operator will be used to specify the boundary set of geometric primitives.

4.2 Affordance Belief Functions

Based on the observation that end-effector contact is crucial for whole-body actions, an affordance $a \in \mathcal{A}$ from the space of known affordances $\mathcal{A}$ is defined to exist with respect to end-effector poses $\boldsymbol{x} \in SE(3)$. The system belief in the existence of a is expressed by an *affordance belief function*

$\Theta_a(\boldsymbol{x})$, mapping end-effector poses $\boldsymbol{x} \in SE(3)$ to belief expressions $d \in \mathcal{D}$ from the *affordance belief space* $\mathcal{D}$:

$$\Theta_a : SE(3) \to \mathcal{D}. \tag{4.4}$$

The affordance belief space $\mathcal{D}$ will be formally defined in Equation 4.9. In order to simplify notations, the index a, denoting the affordance, might be omitted if clear from the context. Equation 4.4 defines affordance belief with respect to single end-effector poses which is suitable for *unimanual affordances* such as *unimanual graspability*. The following sections will consider this unimanual case. However, the extension to multiple end-effectors is possible and will be reviewed in Section 4.6:

$$\Theta_a : \underbrace{SE(3) \times \cdots \times SE(3)}_{N \text{ times}} \to \mathcal{D}. \tag{4.5}$$

For expressing the system belief in the existence of an affordance a with respect to an assumed (and in the following not explicitly mentioned) end-effector pose $\boldsymbol{x} \in SE(3)$, two fundamental hypotheses are defined: a^+ representing the assumption that a exists and a^- representing the assumption that a does not exist. It is the inherent task of the affordance detection and validation system to obtain certainty about which of the two hypotheses is true by combining and evaluating available evidence. The set $\mathcal{X}_a$ of defined hypotheses constitutes the so-called *frame of discernment* or *hypothesis space*:

$$\mathcal{X}_a = \{a^+, a^-\}. \tag{4.6}$$

The set of possible combinations of hypotheses, i. e. the power set $2^{\mathcal{X}_a}$ of $\mathcal{X}_a$ results in:

$$2^{\mathcal{X}_a} = \{\emptyset, \{a^+\}, \{a^-\}, \mathcal{X}_a\}. \tag{4.7}$$

In the interest of simplicity the notations are abbreviated to $a^+ := \{a^+\}$ and $a^- := \{a^-\}$, respectively. Two fundamental properties need to be examined before $\mathcal{X}_a$ can be considered a suitable hypothesis space in the context of the Dempster-Shafer Theory: *completeness* and *mutual exclusiveness*.

Completeness The hypothesis space $\mathcal{X}_a$ must be complete, i. e. it must contain the true hypothesis. As affordances can only either exist or not exist, and as both possibilities are reflected in $\mathcal{X}_a$ as distinct hypotheses a^+ and a^-, $\mathcal{X}_a$ is complete by definition.

Mutual Exclusiveness Elements of the hypothesis space must be mutually exclusive, i. e. only one of the hypotheses can be true. As the complements a^+ and a^- are the only contained hypotheses, $\mathcal{X}_a$ is mutually exclusive.

The above hypothesis space contains two complementary hypotheses and therefore constitutes the simplest non-degenerated case of a hypothesis space. Such hypothesis spaces are called *binary* and are often denoted as $\mathcal{X}_a = \{a, \neg a\}$. The simplicity of $\mathcal{X}_a$ will play an important role for the formalization and for the feasibility of the approach.

4.2.1 Belief, Plausibility and Expected Probability

In the DST, *belief* is formally expressed by attributing probability mass to the set of hypothesis combinations, i. e. to the elements of $2^{\mathcal{X}_a}$. Such a probability mass assignment

$$m : 2^{\mathcal{X}_a} \rightarrow [0,1] \tag{4.8}$$

is called *basic belief assignment* if $m(\emptyset) = 0$ and $\sum_A m(A) = 1$. Probability mass can be intuitively interpreted as follows:

- Probability mass $m(\emptyset)$ is equal to zero by definition;[1]
- Probability mass $m(a^+)$ expresses belief in the existence of a;
- Probability mass $m(a^-)$ expresses belief in the non-existence of a;
- Probability mass $m(\mathcal{X}_a)$ expresses uncertainty about the existence of a.[2]

The affordance belief space $\mathcal{D}$ can now formally be defined as the space of possible basic belief assignments:

$$\mathcal{D} := \left\{ m : 2^{\mathcal{X}_a} \to [0,1] \;\middle|\; m(\emptyset) = 0, \sum_{A \in 2^{\mathcal{X}_a}} m(A) = 1 \right\}. \tag{4.9}$$

In order to simplify the following formalizations, the evaluation of affordance belief functions Θ_a for end-effector poses $\boldsymbol{x} \in SE(3)$ and hypotheses $A \in 2^{\mathcal{X}_a}$ is abbreviated as:

$$\Theta_a(\boldsymbol{x}, A) := \big(\Theta_a(\boldsymbol{x})\big)(A). \tag{4.10}$$

The DST defines two fundamental measures based on a basic belief assignment m: *belief* $\mathrm{bel}(A)$, describing the system's confidence that A contains the true hypothesis, and *plausibility* $\mathrm{pl}(A)$, describing the system's confidence that the true hypothesis does not contradict A[3]:

$$\begin{aligned} \mathrm{bel}(A) &= \sum_{B \subseteq A} m(B) \in [0,1] \\ \mathrm{pl}(A) &= \sum_{B \cap A \neq \emptyset} m(B) \in [0,1]. \end{aligned} \tag{4.11}$$

1 A possible interpretation is *belief in a hypothesis that is known to be false* (Beynon et al. 2000).

2 A possible interpretation is *belief that the true hypothesis is contained in* $\mathcal{X}_a$ which is known to be true.

3 Beynon et al. (2000) describes plausibility as *the extent to which we fail to disbelieve A*.

Belief and plausibility can be expressed for affordance belief functions Θ_a, end-effector poses $\boldsymbol{x} \in SE(3)$ and hypotheses $A \in 2^{\mathcal{X}_a}$ as follows:

$$
\begin{aligned}
\mathrm{bel}_a(\boldsymbol{x},A) &= \sum_{B \subseteq A} \Theta_a(\boldsymbol{x},B) \in [0,1] \\
\mathrm{pl}_a(\boldsymbol{x},A) &= \sum_{B \cap A \neq \emptyset} \Theta_a(\boldsymbol{x},B) \in [0,1].
\end{aligned}
\tag{4.12}
$$

The set-theoretic definitions of belief and plausibility can become computationally hard for large hypothesis spaces. However, exploiting the simplicity of $\mathcal{X}_a$ (Equation 4.6), the equations for belief and plausibility (Equation 4.12) become pleasantly simple:

$$
\begin{aligned}
\mathrm{bel}_a(\boldsymbol{x},A) &= \begin{cases} \Theta_a(\boldsymbol{x},a^+), & \text{if } A = a^+ \\ \Theta_a(\boldsymbol{x},a^-), & \text{if } A = a^- \\ 1, & \text{if } A = \mathcal{X}_a \end{cases} \\
\mathrm{pl}_a(\boldsymbol{x},A) &= \begin{cases} \Theta_a(\boldsymbol{x},a^+) + \Theta_a(\boldsymbol{x},\mathcal{X}_a), & \text{if } A = a^+ \\ \Theta_a(\boldsymbol{x},a^-) + \Theta_a(\boldsymbol{x},\mathcal{X}_a), & \text{if } A = a^- \\ 1, & \text{if } A = \mathcal{X}_a. \end{cases}
\end{aligned}
\tag{4.13}
$$

The DST can be considered an alternative to traditional probability theory with the important distinction that uncertainty can be properly represented. However, a DST belief expression can be interpreted in a probability theoretical way, in which the (classical) probability $p(A)$ of a hypothesis A lies between belief and plausibility:

$$
p(A) \in \big[\mathrm{bel}(A), \mathrm{pl}(A)\big]. \tag{4.14}
$$

Based on this relation, the *expected probability*[4] $E(A)$ (Jøsang 2001) will be used in cases when a belief expression needs to be compacted into a single real number:

$$E(A) = \mathrm{bel}(A) + \frac{1}{2}\big(\mathrm{pl}(A) - \mathrm{bel}(A)\big) = m(A) + \frac{1}{2}m(\mathcal{X}_a). \tag{4.15}$$

The expected probability from Equation 4.15 can be directly applied to affordance belief functions Θ_a for given end-effector poses $\boldsymbol{x} \in SE(3)$:

$$\begin{aligned} E_a(\boldsymbol{x},A) &= \mathrm{bel}_a(\boldsymbol{x},A) + \frac{1}{2}\big(\mathrm{pl}_a(\boldsymbol{x},A) - \mathrm{bel}_a(\boldsymbol{x},A)\big) \\ &= \Theta_a(\boldsymbol{x},A) + \frac{1}{2}\Theta_a(\boldsymbol{x},\mathcal{X}_a). \end{aligned} \tag{4.16}$$

The formalization of affordances as Dempster-Shafer belief functions Θ_a over the space of end-effector poses constitutes the core of the proposed affordance detection and validation system. In the following, the initial requirements of evidence fusion and hierarchy are properly formalized in Section 4.3 and Section 4.4.

4.3 Evidence Fusion

Evidence about affordances can emerge at different points in time, based on different sensory modalities with different attributed degrees of belief. It is the task of the *evidence fusion* formalism to consistently combine such expressions of affordance evidence into a joint system belief. For formalizing the process of evidence fusion, let $\Omega = \{\omega_1, \ldots, \omega_N\}$ be a sequence of *observations*. Each observation $\omega \in \Omega$ is defined as an affordance belief function

$$\omega : SE(3) \to \mathcal{D}. \tag{4.17}$$

[4] The definition of expected probability used here is the special case for binary hypothesis spaces. The general definition can be found in Jøsang (2001).

Hence, observations express affordance-related evidence over the space of end-effector poses. Each value $\boldsymbol{\omega}(\boldsymbol{x}) \in \mathcal{D}$ is a basic belief assignment in the sense of the Dempster-Shafer Theory. Figure 4.1 shows an overview over the concept of evidence fusion.

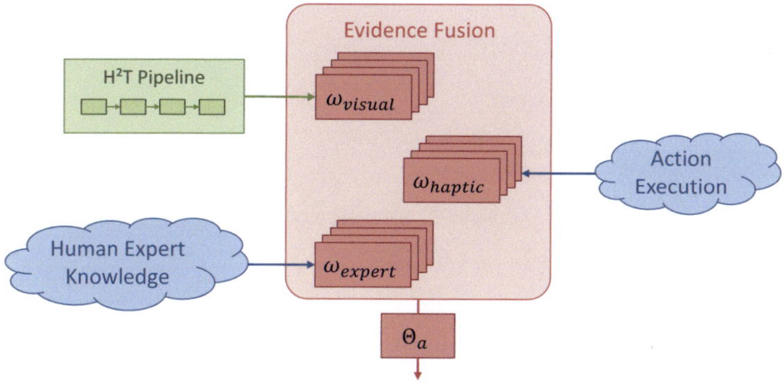

Figure 4.1: The concept of evidence fusion (taken from Kaiser et al. 2018a, ©2018 IEEE): Affordance-related evidence resulting from different sensory modalities under different experimental conditions, is aggregated into a set of observations Ω. Exemplary sources of evidence include visual affordance detection, the execution of exploration and validation actions and human expert knowledge. Evidence fusion describes the process of deriving a joint system belief Θ_a from the available observations under consideration of the certainties attributed to the respective observations.

4.3.1 Dempster's Rule of Combination

The DST defines an associative operator $\oplus$ for combining *compatible* basic belief assignments. Two basic belief assignments are compatible if they are defined over the same hypothesis space. Hence, in the context of affordance belief functions, two observations are compatible if they express evidence related to the same affordance. The combination of compatible observations $\omega_1, \ldots, \omega_N$ is formalized using *Dempster's rule of combination*:

$$\left(\bigoplus_{i=1}^{N}\omega_i\right)(\boldsymbol{x},A)=\begin{cases}0, & \text{if } A=\emptyset\\ \dfrac{1}{1-K(\boldsymbol{x})}\displaystyle\sum_{\left(\bigcap_{j=1}^{N}A_j\right)=A}\prod_{k=1}^{N}\omega_k(\boldsymbol{x},A_k), & \text{otherwise}\end{cases}\tag{4.18}$$

with the *conflict factor* $K(\boldsymbol{x})$:

$$K(\boldsymbol{x})=\sum_{\left(\bigcap_{j=1}^{N}A_j\right)=\emptyset}\prod_{k=1}^{N}\omega_k(\boldsymbol{x},A_k).\tag{4.19}$$

The summation sets $\left(\bigcap_{j=1}^{N}A_j\right)=\mathcal{Z}$ used in Equation 4.18 and Equation 4.19 with $\mathcal{Z}\in\{A,\emptyset\}$ is a shorthand notation for:

$$\left\{(A_1,\ldots,A_N)\in\mathcal{X}_a^N \,\middle|\, \left(\bigcap_{j=1}^{N}A_j\right)=\mathcal{Z}\right\}.\tag{4.20}$$

A simple proof based on the associativity of the combination rule, outlined in Section A.2, shows that incremental evidence fusion is possible:

$$\bigoplus_{i=1}^{N}\omega_i=\omega_1\oplus\cdots\oplus\omega_N.\tag{4.21}$$

Hence, the combination rule can be regarded as a binary operator $\omega_1 \oplus \omega_2$ in the following considerations. Due to the simplicity of the hypothesis space $\mathcal{X}_a$, the combination rule from Equation 4.18 and Equation 4.19 can be simplified into efficiently computable equations:

$$(\omega_1 \oplus \omega_2)(\boldsymbol{x},A) = \frac{1}{1-K(\boldsymbol{x})} \cdot \begin{cases} 0, & \text{if } A = \emptyset \\ \omega_1(\boldsymbol{x},\mathcal{X}_a)\cdot\omega_2(\boldsymbol{x},\mathcal{X}_a), & \text{if } A = \mathcal{X}_a \\ \omega_1(\boldsymbol{x},A)\omega_2(\boldsymbol{x},A) & \\ \quad +\omega_1(\boldsymbol{x},\mathcal{X}_a)\omega_2(\boldsymbol{x},A) & \text{otherwise,} \\ \quad +\omega_1(\boldsymbol{x},A)\omega_2(\boldsymbol{x},\mathcal{X}_a) & \end{cases}$$

with the conflict factor $K(\boldsymbol{x})$:

$$K(\boldsymbol{x}) = \omega_1(\boldsymbol{x},a^+)\cdot\omega_2(\boldsymbol{x},a^-) + \omega_1(\boldsymbol{x},a^-)\cdot\omega_2(\boldsymbol{x},a^+). \tag{4.22}$$

4.3.2 Spatial Generalization of Observations

There are several types of experiments which would produce evidence in terms of observations ω. Depending on the utilized sensors and the experimental setup, two main types of observations, need to be differentiated:

Extensive Observations inherently provide spatially distributed evidence, as the employed sensor and the experimental setup evaluate affordances for whole ranges of possible end-effector poses. Producers of extensive observations include visual affordance detection as affordances in this case are evaluated for all end-effector poses on the boundaries of detected primitives.

Selective Observations provide evidence for specific end-effector poses only. Producers of selective observations include haptic affordance validation as the employed validation experiments are performed for specific end-effector poses.

Selective observations provide affordance-related evidence with respect to individual reference end-effector poses $\boldsymbol{x}_{\text{ref}}$. In order to allow efficient reasoning about affordances in a larger scale, selective observations need to be spatially generalized, producing evidence for a local environment around $\boldsymbol{x}_{\text{ref}}$. The spatial generalization of selective observations is a concept known from the literature of *graspability* affordance learning. In Detry et al. (2011), individual grasping experiments are considered as *particles* which are spatially generalized by means of *kernel density estimation* using Gaussian and von Mises-Fisher distributed kernel functions. In accordance to Detry et al. (2011), spatial generalization in this work is performed by combining two distribution functions

$$\begin{aligned} n(\boldsymbol{x}_{\text{ref}}, \boldsymbol{x}) &\propto \mathcal{N}\left(\mathfrak{t}(\boldsymbol{x}_{\text{ref}}), \sigma_{\text{pos}}^2\right) \\ m(\boldsymbol{x}_{\text{ref}}, \boldsymbol{x}) &\propto \mathcal{M}\left(\mathfrak{R}(\boldsymbol{x}_{\text{ref}}), \sigma_{\text{rot}}^2\right), \end{aligned} \tag{4.23}$$

for the translational component $\mathfrak{t}(\boldsymbol{x}_{\text{ref}})$ and the rotational component $\mathfrak{R}(\boldsymbol{x}_{\text{ref}})$ of $\boldsymbol{x}_{\text{ref}}$, respectively. The distribution function n is proportional to a normal distribution $\mathcal{N}$, modeling the spatial generalization of observations. The distribution function m is proportional to a von Mises-Fisher distribution $\mathcal{M}$, modeling the rotational generalization of observations.[5] Note that both functions m and n are proportional to their respective distribution, but they are no actual probability distributions, as they are normalized to a maximum value of 1. The combined distribution function is defined as:

$$\delta(\boldsymbol{x}_{\text{ref}}, \boldsymbol{x}) = n(\boldsymbol{x}_{\text{ref}}, \boldsymbol{x}) \cdot m(\boldsymbol{x}_{\text{ref}}, \boldsymbol{x}). \tag{4.24}$$

[5] See Appendix A.1 for further details on the choice and the definition of the von Mises-Fisher distribution.

Using the combined distribution function $\delta(\boldsymbol{x}_{\text{ref}}, \boldsymbol{x})$, the spatial generalization of selective observations $\omega(\boldsymbol{x}, A)$ can be modeled as the following belief function:

$$\omega(\boldsymbol{x}, A) = \begin{cases} \delta(\boldsymbol{x}_{\text{ref}}, \boldsymbol{x}) \cdot \omega(\boldsymbol{x}, a^+), & \text{if } A = a^+ \\ \delta(\boldsymbol{x}_{\text{ref}}, \boldsymbol{x}) \cdot \omega(\boldsymbol{x}, a^-), & \text{if } A = a^- \\ 1 - \omega(\boldsymbol{x}, a^+) - \omega(\boldsymbol{x}, a^-), & \text{if } A = \mathcal{X}_a, \end{cases} \tag{4.25}$$

For modeling the general observation certainty $\eta \in [0, 1]$, the definition of $\omega(\boldsymbol{x}, A)$ from Equation 4.25 is extended by adding the observation certainty as a weighting factor to positive and negative belief:

$$\omega_\eta(\boldsymbol{x}, A) = \begin{cases} \eta \cdot \delta(\boldsymbol{x}_{\text{ref}}, \boldsymbol{x}) \cdot \omega(\boldsymbol{x}, a^+), & \text{if } A = a^+ \\ \eta \cdot \delta(\boldsymbol{x}_{\text{ref}}, \boldsymbol{x}) \cdot \omega(\boldsymbol{x}, a^-), & \text{if } A = a^- \\ 1 - \omega_\eta(\boldsymbol{x}, a^+) - \omega_\eta(\boldsymbol{x}, a^-), & \text{if } A = \mathcal{X}_a. \end{cases} \tag{4.26}$$

An observation certainty $\eta < 1$ allows the affordance system to appropriately account for erroneous observations. It further allows to model observations with different attributed degrees of certainty. For example, one could reasonably attribute less certainty to observations from visual affordance detection than to observations from haptic validation experiments.

4.3.3 Examples

Figure 4.2 shows a visualization of the iterative fusion of three selective observations ω_1, ω_2 and ω_3, two in favor and one against the existence of an assumed affordance a on a hypothetic one-dimensional primitive (the x-axis). Belief and plausibility are visualized as green and red lines, respectively, while the interval between belief and plausibility, which contains the existence probability of a in a classical sense, is highlighted in grey. In its initial belief state ω_0, obtained e. g. via visual perception, the system tends towards the existence of the affordance, supposing a certainty of $\eta = 0.6$. Through the iterative fusion of the initial system belief ω_0 with the evidence from ω_1, ω_2 and ω_3, the system belief gradually evolves to a clearer picture of the affordance. In the final joint system belief shown in Figure 4.2d, the affordance is assumed to exist for (roughly) $x \in [0,4]$ and it is assumed to not exist for $x \in [-3,-1]$. Outside of these intervals of relative certainty, there is no sufficient evidence other than the initial system belief ω_0.

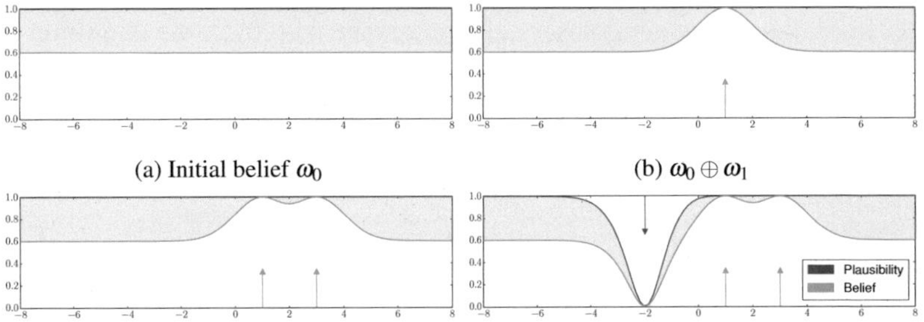

(a) Initial belief ω_0

(b) $\omega_0 \oplus \omega_1$

(c) $\omega_0 \oplus \omega_1 \oplus \omega_2$

(d) $\omega_0 \oplus \omega_1 \oplus \omega_2 \oplus \omega_3$

Figure 4.2: Three observations ω_1, ω_2 and ω_3 applied to an initial belief estimation with a certainty of $\eta = 0.6$. The observations express evidence for different end-effector poses (1, 3 and -2, respectively) which are indicated by red and green arrows. While ω_1 and ω_2 confirm the affordance, ω_3 contradicts it.

In the examples of Figure 4.2, the observations ω_1, ω_2 and ω_3 were attributed absolute certainty, i. e. $\eta = 1$. Figure 4.3 shows the joint belief function $\omega_0 \oplus \omega_1 \oplus \omega_2 \oplus \omega_3$ from Figure 4.2d with varying observation certainties η ranging from observations with fairly low certainty ($\eta = 0.2$) to absolute trust in the observation ($\eta = 1$). It can be seen that observations with smaller attributed certainties have lower impact on the system belief.

The one-dimensional examples shown in Figure 4.2 and Figure 4.3 provide a good intuition of the evidence fusion behavior. However, the type of visualization does not scale with the dimensionality of the end-effector pose space. Affordance belief functions defined over higher dimensional spaces of end-effector poses will be visualized according to the *decision value* $v_a(\boldsymbol{x})$ based on the expected probability defined in Equation 4.15:

$$\begin{aligned} v_a(\boldsymbol{x}) &: SE(3) \rightarrow [0,1], \\ &\boldsymbol{x} \mapsto \frac{1}{2} \cdot \left(E_a(\boldsymbol{x}, a^+) - E_a(\boldsymbol{x}, a^-) + 1\right). \end{aligned} \tag{4.27}$$

The visualization of higher dimensional affordance belief functions is defined in the HSL[6] color space, where the decision value $v_a(\boldsymbol{x})$ determines the hue value, the saturation is fixed to a constant value and the uncertainty $\Theta_a(\boldsymbol{x}, \mathcal{X}_a)$ determines the lightness (see Figure 4.4).

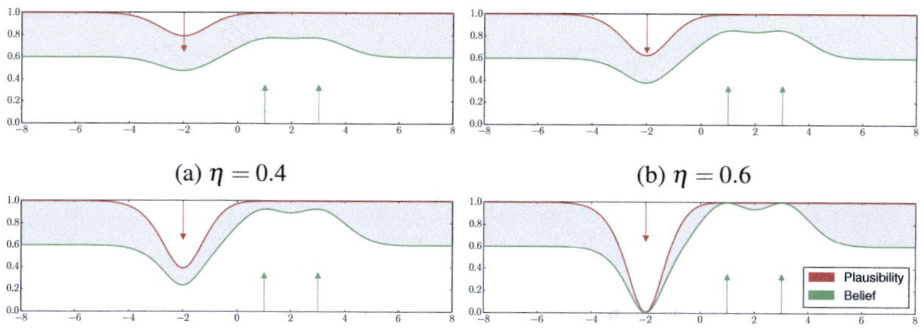

(a) $\eta = 0.4$ (b) $\eta = 0.6$

(c) $\eta = 0.8$ (d) $\eta = 1.0$

Figure 4.3: The influence of different observation certainties η attributed to the joint belief function $\omega_0 \oplus \omega_1 \oplus \omega_2 \oplus \omega_3$.

Figure 4.5 visualizes a two-dimensional affordance belief function constructed from seven consecutive selective observations. Figure 4.6 repeats the same experimental setup based on an initial belief obtained through an extensive observation which could for example result from visual perception. The results show the applicability of the concept to two-dimensional primitive surfaces and that accumulated confirming observations can eventually overrule the initial system belief.

6 HSL: *Hue, Saturation, Lightness*

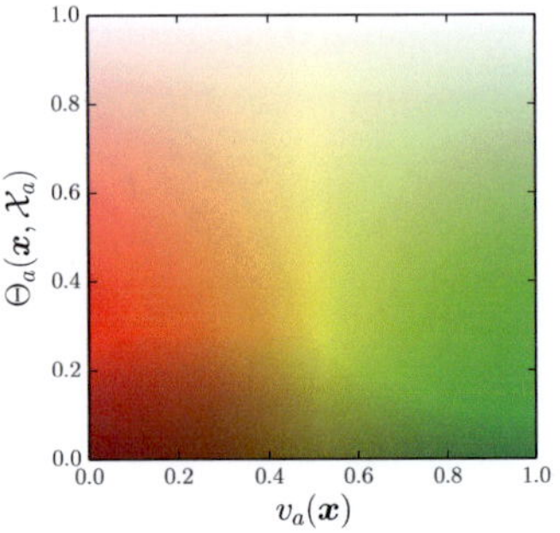

Figure 4.4: Belief functions Θ_a are visualized by projection to the HSL color space (taken from Kaiser et al. 2018a, © 2018 IEEE). The decision value $v_a(\boldsymbol{x})$ is represented by the hue value, ranging from red to green, while red indicates predominant belief in a^- and green indicates predominant belief in a^+. Uncertainty $\Theta_a(\mathcal{X}_a)$ is represented by the lightness value.

4.4 Inference on Affordance Belief Functions

In the previous sections, a formalization was proposed which is able to effectively combine evidence expressed in terms of affordance belief functions $\Theta_a(\boldsymbol{x})$. As Dempster's rule of combination is only defined for belief assignments that share the same hypothesis space, the combination of belief functions Θ_{a_1} and Θ_{a_2} for different affordances a_1 and a_2 is not possible. In order to use affordance belief functions in a hierarchical representation of affordances, a formalism of *inference* needs to be developed which is able to combine belief functions in the sense of logic operations. As a simple example, consider a hierarchical rule for the existence of *supportability* affordances:

> *A supportability affordance exists for a given end-effector pose $\boldsymbol{x}$ if a graspability affordance exists for $\boldsymbol{x}$ and if the underlying primitive is horizontally oriented.*

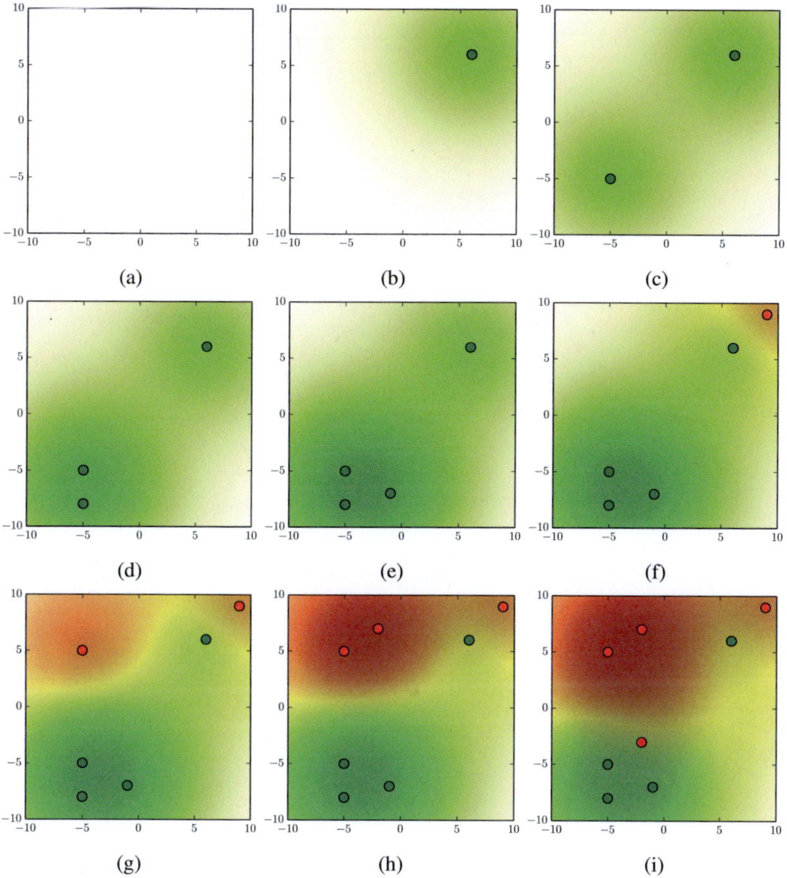

Figure 4.5: Visualization of an affordance belief function composed from eight consecutive observations with attributed certainties $\eta = 0.7$ for a hypothetic 2D primitive surface (taken from Kaiser et al. 2018a, © 2018 IEEE). (a) Without prior information the initial belief represents complete uncertainty. (b-e) Confirming observations emphasize belief in the existence of the investigated affordance, resulting in dark green areas of high belief $\text{bel}(a^+)$. (f-i) Contradicting observations emphasize belief in the absence of the investigated affordance, resulting in dark red color in areas of high belief $\text{bel}(a^-)$.

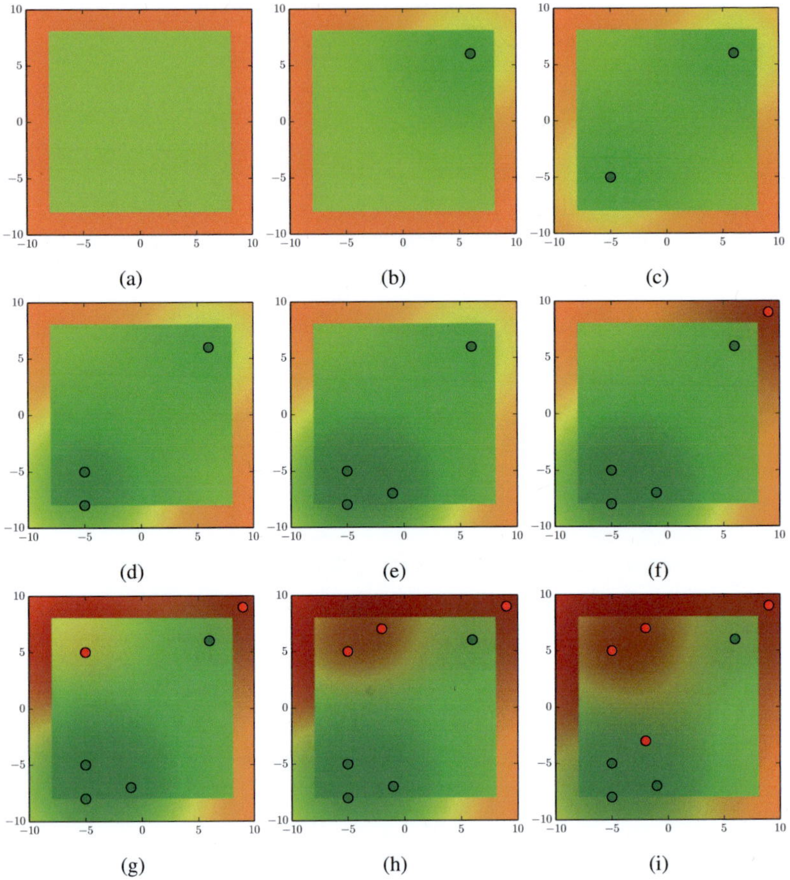

Figure 4.6: Visualization of an affordance belief function composed from eight consecutive observations with attributed certainties $\eta = 0.7$ and prior belief from visual perception with attributed certainty $\eta = 0.6$, for a hypothetic 2D primitive surface. (a) Visual perception produces a prior belief distribution with high belief $\mathrm{bel}(a^+)$ in the primitive interior and high belief $\mathrm{bel}(a^-)$ at the primitive boundaries which, as will be seen later, is characteristic for a *platform graspability* affordance. (b-e) Confirming observations emphasize belief in the existence of the investigated affordance, partially overriding the initial belief assignment. (f-i) Contradicting observations emphasize belief in the absence of the investigated affordance, resulting in dark red color in areas of high belief $\mathrm{bel}(a^-)$.

If the *graspability* affordance and the horizontal primitive orientation are given as belief functions Θ_{Grasp} and $\Theta_{\text{Horizontal}}$, this rule can formally be expressed as:

$$\frac{\Theta_{\text{Grasp}}(\boldsymbol{x}) \wedge \Theta_{\text{Horizontal}}(p)}{\Theta_{\text{Support}}(\boldsymbol{x})}. \tag{4.28}$$

In this case, Θ_{Support} is called the *higher-level affordance* as its existence depends on the *lower-level affordance* Θ_{Grasp}.[7] Other logic operations are possible as well, e. g. in the case of a general *graspability* affordance which exists if one of multiple, more specific *graspability* affordances exists:

$$\frac{\Theta_{\text{Platform-Grasp}}(\boldsymbol{x}) \vee \Theta_{\text{Prismatic-Grasp}}(\boldsymbol{x}) \vee \Theta_{\text{Circular-Grasp}}(\boldsymbol{x})}{\Theta_{\text{Grasp}}(\boldsymbol{x})}. \tag{4.29}$$

It is important to realize that the belief functions Θ_* in the above equations represent belief with respect to different hypothesis spaces, as defined in Equation 4.6. Hence, inference on affordance belief functions cannot be done by means of traditional DST. Dempster's rule of combination is neither theoretically applicable in this case, nor does it practically produce reasonable results. However, the *Theory of Subjective Logic* (Jøsang 2001) provides the theoretical means for applying logic operations to Dempster-Shafer belief values. Let a and b be distinct affordances with respective hypothesis spaces $\mathcal{X}_a$ and $\mathcal{X}_b$ and $\boldsymbol{x} \in SE(3)$ be an end-effector pose. Further, let $A \in 2^{\mathcal{X}_b}$ and $B \in 2^{\mathcal{X}_b}$ be affordance hypotheses. Then the subjective logic operations $A \wedge B$, $A \vee B$ and $\neg A$ are defined as follows:

$$\begin{aligned}
\text{bel}_{a\wedge b}(\boldsymbol{x}, A \wedge B) &= \text{bel}_a(\boldsymbol{x}, A) \cdot \text{bel}_b(\boldsymbol{x}, B) \\
\text{bel}_{a\vee b}(\boldsymbol{x}, A \vee B) &= \text{bel}_a(\boldsymbol{x}, A) + \text{bel}_b(\boldsymbol{x}, B) - \text{bel}_a(\boldsymbol{x}, A) \cdot \text{bel}_b(\boldsymbol{x}, B) \\
\text{bel}_a(\neg A) &= 1 - \text{pl}_a(A).
\end{aligned} \tag{4.30}$$

[7] The existence of *supportability* further depends on the primitive property of *horizontality* which will be formalized in Section 4.5.

Note that with the exception of the negation $\neg A$, resulting belief is expressed over the new hypothesis spaces $\mathcal{X}_{a\wedge b}$ and $\mathcal{X}_{a\vee b}$. For two affordance belief functions Θ_a and Θ_b, defined over the respective hypothesis spaces $\mathcal{X}_a$ and $\mathcal{X}_b$, the subjective logic operations from Equation 4.30 can be written as:

$$\Theta_{a\wedge b}(\boldsymbol{x},A) = \begin{cases} \Theta_a(\boldsymbol{x},a^+)\cdot\Theta_b(\boldsymbol{x},b^+), & \text{if } A = c^+ \\ \Theta_a(\boldsymbol{x},a^-)+\Theta_b(\boldsymbol{x},b^-)-\Theta_a(\boldsymbol{x},a^-)\cdot\Theta_b(\boldsymbol{x},b^-), & \text{if } A = c^- \\ 1-\Theta_{a\wedge b}(\boldsymbol{x},c^+)-\Theta_{a\wedge b}(\boldsymbol{x},c^-), & \text{if } A = \mathcal{X}_c \end{cases}$$

$$\Theta_{a\vee b}(\boldsymbol{x},A) = \begin{cases} \Theta_a(\boldsymbol{x},a^+)+\Theta_b(\boldsymbol{x},b^+)-\Theta_a(\boldsymbol{x},a^+)\cdot\Theta_b(\boldsymbol{x},b^+), & \text{if } A = c^+ \\ \Theta_a(\boldsymbol{x},a^-)\cdot\Theta_b(\boldsymbol{x},b^-), & \text{if } A = c^- \\ 1-\Theta_{a\vee b}(\boldsymbol{x},c^+)-\Theta_{a\vee b}(\boldsymbol{x},c^-), & \text{if } A = \mathcal{X}_c \end{cases}$$

$$\Theta_{\neg a}(\boldsymbol{x},A) = \begin{cases} \Theta_a(\boldsymbol{x},a^-), & \text{if } A = a^+ \\ \Theta_a(\boldsymbol{x},a^+), & \text{if } A = a^- \\ 1-\Theta_{\neg a}(\boldsymbol{x},a^+)-\Theta_{\neg a}(\boldsymbol{x},a^-), & \text{if } A = \mathcal{X}_a. \end{cases}$$

Note that the affordance belief functions $\Theta_{a\wedge b}$ and $\Theta_{a\vee b}(\boldsymbol{x},A)$ are defined over the novel hypothesis spaces $\mathcal{X}_{a\wedge b}$ and $\mathcal{X}_{a\vee b}$, respectively, which are abbreviated as $\mathcal{X}_c$ in the above equations. The initially stated affordance inference rules from (Equation 4.28 and Equation 4.29) can now be written based on subjective logic operations as:

$$\Theta_{\text{Support}}(\boldsymbol{x}) = \Theta_{\text{Grasp}}(\boldsymbol{x}) \wedge \Theta_{\text{Horizontal}}(p) \tag{4.31}$$

and

$$\Theta_{\text{Grasp}}(\boldsymbol{x}) = \Theta_{\text{Platform-Grasp}}(\boldsymbol{x}) \vee \Theta_{\text{Prismatic-Grasp}}(\boldsymbol{x}) \vee \Theta_{\text{Circular-Grasp}}(\boldsymbol{x}).$$

Visualizations of the DS-theoretic logic operators applied to exemplary affordance belief functions Θ_1 and Θ_2 are shown in Figure 4.7, Figure 4.8 and

Figure 4.9. As can be seen, the subjective logic operations applied to affordance belief functions with areas of different belief and uncertainty, produce intuitive results.

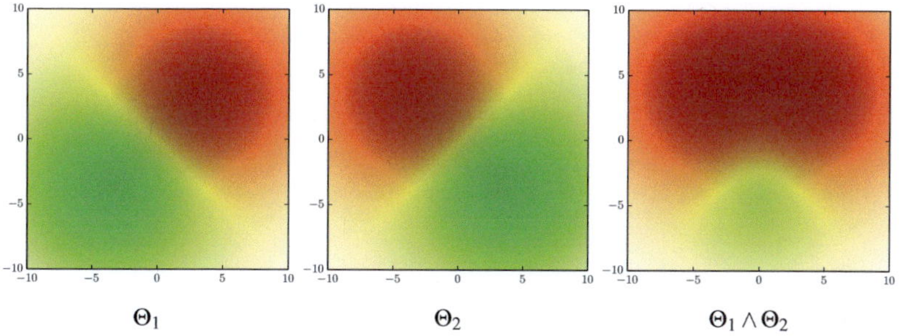

Figure 4.7: The DS-theoretic conjunction (subjective logic AND) applied to two affordance belief functions Θ_1 and Θ_2 (taken from Kaiser et al. 2018a, © 2018 IEEE).

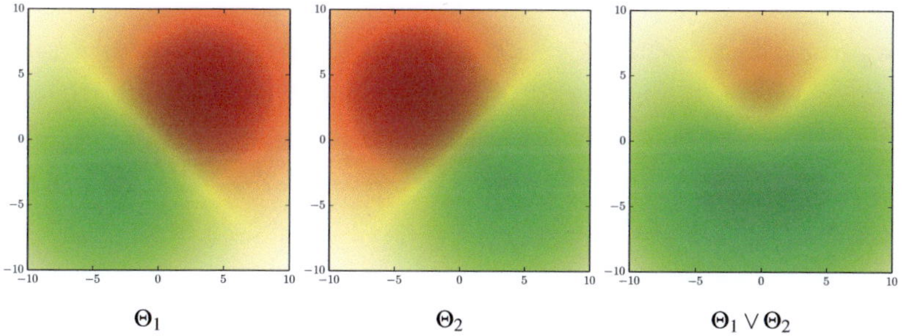

Figure 4.8: The DS-theoretic disjunction (subjective logic OR) applied to two affordance belief functions Θ_1 and Θ_2.

4.5 Sigmoid Decision Functions

The previous sections introduced a formalism that is able to combine experimentally obtained evidence about affordances into a joint system belief (Section 4.3) and to perform logic operations on obtained affordance belief functions (Section 4.4). This section will formalize the process of obtaining belief functions from properties of the environment or properties of the robot's embodiment. These properties are explicitly mentioned in Gibson's work as essential components in affordance perception.

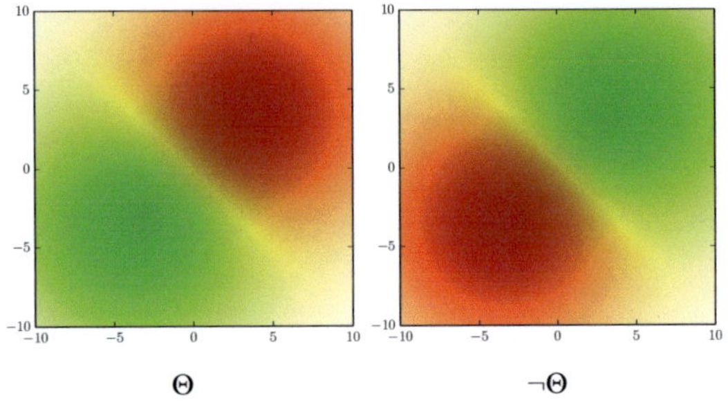

Figure 4.9: The DS-theoretic negation (subjective logic NOT) applied to an affordance belief function Θ.

Properties of environment or embodiment could for example be dimensions of primitives or end-effectors. The consideration of parameters of the robot embodiment in affordance belief functions is necessary as different affordances exist for differently embodied agents, e. g. *graspability* affordances that exists for ARMAR-4 might not necessarily exist for a small-scaled *Nao* robot due to the different end-effector sizes. In this section, properties of environment and embodiment will be incorporated by defining threshold-based belief functions Θ. These belief functions will intuitively express belief that e. g. the primitive length is larger than the robot's hand breadth. The threshold-based belief is modeled through *sigmoid decision functions*:

$$\mathrm{sigm}_{\lambda,\beta}(x) = \frac{1}{1+e^{-\lambda(x-\beta)}} \in (0,1). \tag{4.32}$$

Figure 4.10 visualizes $\mathrm{sigm}_{\lambda,\beta}(x)$ which implements a *greater-than-threshold* decision and two of its variations which implement *lesser-than-threshold* and *in-threshold-interval* decisions. The decision threshold β

defines the point for which $\mathrm{sigm}_{\lambda,\beta}(\beta) = 0.5$, while λ defines the gradient in this point. The combination of two sigmoid decision functions produces a decision interval function with values greater than 0.5 for $x \in [\beta - \varepsilon, \beta + \varepsilon]$:

$$\mathrm{sigm}_{\lambda,\beta-\varepsilon}(x) \cdot \mathrm{sigm}_{-\lambda,\beta+\varepsilon}(x). \tag{4.33}$$

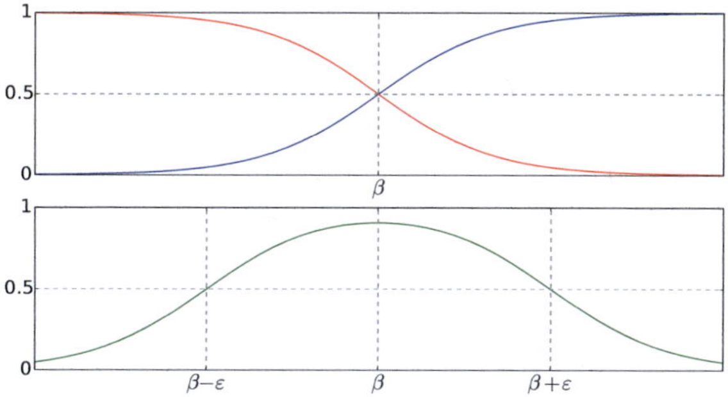

Figure 4.10: The sigmoid functions $\mathrm{sigm}_{\lambda,\beta}(x)$ (*blue*) and $\mathrm{sigm}_{-\lambda,\beta}(x)$ (*red*). The bottom plot displays a sigmoid-based interval function $\mathrm{sigm}_{\lambda,\beta-\varepsilon}(x) \cdot \mathrm{sigm}_{-\lambda,\beta+\varepsilon}(x)$ (*green*) (taken from Kaiser et al. 2016a, © 2016 IEEE).

There are two predominant types of inputs to the sigmoid function: translations $t \in \mathbb{R}$ in *meters* and rotations $r \in [0, 2\pi)$ in *radians*. The parameter λ of the sigmoid function can be fixed to λ_t and λ_r with respect to the input type and will be omitted in the following.[8] Now, three instances of threshold-based decision functions can be defined as:

$$\begin{aligned} \Gamma_{>\beta}(x) &= \mathrm{sigm}_{\lambda,\beta}(x) \\ \Gamma_{<\beta}(x) &= \mathrm{sigm}_{-\lambda,\beta}(x) \\ \Gamma_{\in[\beta,\varepsilon]}(x) &= \mathrm{sigm}_{\lambda,\beta}(x) \cdot \mathrm{sigm}_{-\lambda,\varepsilon}(x). \end{aligned} \tag{4.34}$$

[8] The values have been fixed to $\lambda_t = 1, \lambda_r = 20$ throughout the entire thesis.

In order to utilize the results of threshold operations on environmental and embodiment properties $p \in \mathbb{R}$, the result of the threshold operation has to be converted to a belief function Θ with attributed certainty $\eta \in [0,1]$:

$$\Theta_{p>\beta}(\boldsymbol{x},A) = \begin{cases} \eta \cdot \Gamma_{>\beta}(p), & \text{if } A = p^+ \\ \eta \cdot \Gamma_{<\beta}(p), & \text{if } A = p^- \\ 1 - \Theta_{p>\beta}(\boldsymbol{x},p^+) - \Theta_{p>\beta}(\boldsymbol{x},p^-), & \text{if } A = \mathcal{X}_p, \end{cases} \tag{4.35}$$

and likewise for $\Theta_{p<\beta}(\boldsymbol{x},A)$ and $\Theta_{\in[\beta,\varepsilon]}(\boldsymbol{x},A)$. Note that this definition implicitly assumes an appropriate hypothesis space $\mathcal{X}_p = \{p^+, p^-\}$, whose entries can be interpreted as *parameter p satisfies the threshold condition* (p^+) and *parameter p does not satisfy the threshold condition* (p^-).
The formalization of sigmoid decision functions and their associated belief functions introduced in this section allows the formulation of threshold and interval conditions on environmental and embodiment parameters in terms of a belief function Θ. The resulting belief function can be combined with regular affordance belief functions using the logic operations introduced in Section 4.4 which for example allows the formulation of *supportability* affordances based on *prismatic graspability* and horizontal primitive orientation as suggested in Equation 4.31.

4.6 Extension to Multiple End-Effectors

The formalization introduced and discussed in this chapter defines affordance belief functions over the space of end-effector poses:

$$\Theta_a : SE(3) \to \mathcal{D}. \tag{4.36}$$

While the case of unimanual affordances has been used for illustration in this chapter, the formalism is not limited to this case. Arbitrary numbers of end-effectors can be considered by extending the definition space of affordance belief functions to the Cartesian product of individual end-effector pose spaces:

$$\Theta_a : \underbrace{SE(3) \times \cdots \times SE(3)}_{N \text{ times}} \to \mathcal{D}. \tag{4.37}$$

As the definition space of affordance belief functions was never explicitly used, the formalization introduced in this chapter is also valid for the case of multiple end-effectors. The only difference is that wherever single end-effector poses $\boldsymbol{x} \in SE(3)$ are used, the case of multiple end-effectors requires tuples of $(\boldsymbol{x}_1, \ldots, \boldsymbol{x}_N) \in SE(3) \times \cdots \times SE(3)$ of end-effector poses. The extension of the proposed formalism to arbitrary numbers of end-effectors is possible, but will likely cause computational problems even for small values of N. Hence, the case of $N > 2$ lies beyond the scope of this thesis. However, special attention will be paid to the case of $N = 2$ which defines *bimanual* or *bipedal* affordances, referring to an important set of actions in the area of whole-body loco-manipulation.

4.7 Discrete Affordance Belief Functions

Affordance belief functions Θ_a are continuously defined over the space of end-effector poses. While the continuous nature of the approach is appealing, real-world applications require appropriate discretization. The naive approach of defining fixed discretization step sizes δ_{spatial} and $\delta_{\text{orientational}}$ for the spatial and orientational components of $SE(3)$ is infeasible even for unimanual affordances as Table 4.1 suggests.[9] Hence, this section discusses approaches to reduce the size of the end-effector pose space before discretization in order to ensure feasibility for unimanual and bimanual affordance belief functions.

[9] Memory consumption per sampling is estimated as two 32 bit floating point values for storing belief and plausibility.

Table 4.1: Naive sampling of a 1 m^3 cube in $SE(3)$.

δ_{spatial}	$\delta_{\text{orientational}}$	**Sampling Size**	**Memory**
10 cm	$\frac{\pi}{2}$ rad	32,000	250 KiB
1 cm	$\frac{\pi}{2}$ rad	32,000,000	244 MiB
1 cm	$\frac{\pi}{4}$ rad	256,000,000	1.9 GiB
1 cm	$\frac{\pi}{8}$ rad	2,048,000,000	15.3 GiB
1 mm	$\frac{\pi}{8}$ rad	2,048,000,000,000	15.3 TiB

Sampling of End-Effector Positions The first important observation that implies a large reduction of the sampling sizes is that affordances in Section 4.2 are defined based on end-effector contact. The implication is that affordance belief functions, by definition, do only attribute nonzero belief $\text{bel}_a(a^+)$ to end-effector poses $\boldsymbol{x} \in SE(3)$ which lie at the boundaries of geometric primitives. Let $\Pi = \{p_1, \ldots, p_K\}$ be the set of detected geometric primitives and let $\partial\Pi \subset SE(3)$ be the space of end-effector poses in contact with the primitive boundaries:

$$\partial\Pi = \{\boldsymbol{x} \in SE(3) \mid \exists p \in \Pi : \boldsymbol{x} \in \partial p\}, \tag{4.38}$$

then it holds that:

$$\text{bel}_a(\boldsymbol{x}, a^+) = 0 \;\; \forall \boldsymbol{x} \in SE(3) \setminus \partial\Pi, \;\; \forall a \in \mathcal{A}. \tag{4.39}$$

Hence, the fundamental approach to discretization is the discretization of the primitive boundaries $\partial\Pi$.

Sampling of End-Effector Orientations The definition space $\partial\Pi \subset SE(3)$ can further be reduced by exploiting a second observation: As all affordances are hierarchically defined based on fundamental power grasp affordances, which will be formally discussed in Chapter 5,

affordance belief functions can only take nonzero values for end-effector poses for which these fundamental grasping affordances are feasible.
As can be seen in Figure 4.11, the end-effector coordinate systems are defined with respect to a *grasp direction* which equals to the z-axis of the end-effector coordinate frame. Hence, end-effector poses $\boldsymbol{x}$ for which the local z-axis does not point towards the primitive are not considered feasible for fundamental grasping and can therefore be discarded.

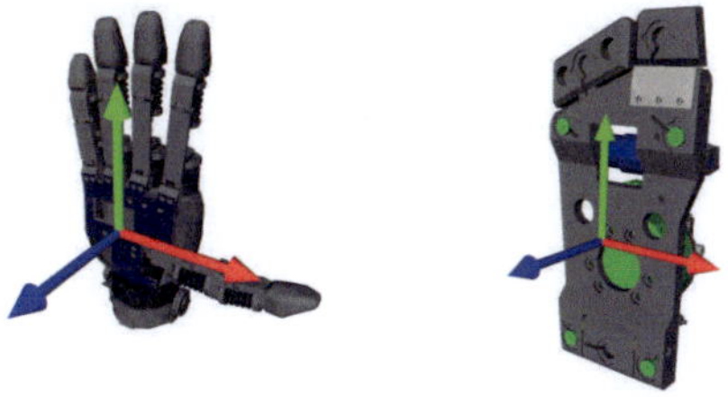

(a) (b)

Figure 4.11: Examples for the *local end-effector coordinate system* of (a) the right hand of ARMAR-4 and (b) the right foot of ARMAR-4 (taken from Kaiser et al. 2016a, © 2016 IEEE). The z-axis (blue) points into grasp direction and the y-axis (green) points into the direction of the longest end-effector extent. This definition of the local end-effector coordinate system will be assumed for all end-effectors of all employed robots throughout this thesis.

Implementation As discussed in the previous sections, the sampling of primitive boundaries is equivalent to an efficient version of sampling the definition space of affordance belief functions. A sampling Σ_p in this context is represented as a single matrix containing feasible end-effector poses alongside the boundaries of a primitive p:

$$\Sigma_p = [\boldsymbol{x}_{p,1} | \dots | \boldsymbol{x}_{p,N}] \in \mathbb{R}^{4 \times 4N} \tag{4.40}$$

Affordance belief functions are implemented with respect to a reference primitive sampling according to the following procedure. First, an affordance belief function Θ_a is separated into multiple disjoint affordance belief functions $\Theta_{a,p_1},\dots,\Theta_{a,p_K}$ which only attribute nonzero belief to end-effector poses $\boldsymbol{x} \in \partial p_i$ on the boundary of a primitive $p_i \in \Pi$. Each belief function $\Theta_{a,p}$ refers to the sampling Σ_p generated for $p \in \Pi$ and evaluates to a matrix containing the DS belief expressions to the corresponding end-effector poses from Σ_p:

$$\Theta_{a,p_j} = [\boldsymbol{d}_1|\dots|\boldsymbol{d}_N] \in \mathbb{R}^{2\times N}, \tag{4.41}$$

while each DS belief expression $\boldsymbol{d}_j \in \mathbb{R}^2$ is composed as:

$$\boldsymbol{d}_j = \begin{bmatrix} \Theta_a(\Sigma_p[j], a^+) \\ \Theta_a(\Sigma_p[j], a^-) \end{bmatrix}. \tag{4.42}$$

Examples The difference in the sampling sizes obtained with the reduced definitions space compared to the naive approach (Table 4.1) obviously depends on the primitive density in the scene. Table 4.2 lists the reduced sampling sizes of exemplary scenes introduced throughout this thesis. The listed scenes are categorized into three sections:

A This section contains single-view point clouds captured using an *ASUS Xtion Pro* structured light sensor as employed on the humanoid robot ARMAR-III.

B This section contains single-view point clouds captured using an *Hokuyo UTM-30LX-EW* laser scanner embedded into the *Carnegie Robotics MultiSense-SL* robot head[10], as employed on the humanoid robot WALK-MAN.

[10] `http://carnegierobotics.com/multisense-sl`

C This section contains large-scale point clouds constructed by registering multiple individual views into a single point cloud representation. The individual point clouds are obtained via an *ASUS Xtion Pro* sensor (*Large Staircase*) or via a simulated point cloud sensor based on a CAD environment model (*Kitchen* and *Kitchen Counter*). In contrast to the categories **A** and **B**, point clouds in this section are used with manual segmentation within this thesis.

The sampling sizes and memory consumptions given in Table 4.2 show that the reduced definition space makes efficient samplings of affordance belief functions feasible, even for large-scale, registered environments like the staircase (Figure 3.4) and the kitchen (Figure 7.9). Performance measurements of the primitive extraction and affordance detection steps are presented in Section 7.4 for the scenes from Table 4.2.

Table 4.2: Sampling sizes for exemplary scenes (δ_{spatial} =2.5 cm, $\delta_{\text{orientational}} = \frac{\pi}{8}$ rad).

	Scene	Reference	Num. Points	Prim. Area	Sampling Sz.
	Chair	Figure 3.2	144,832	2.47 m^2	277,952
A	Sm. Staircase	Figure 5.6	119,615	2.95 m^2	173,536
	Ladder	-	61,100	1.15 m^2	79,584
	Bar	Figure 7.26	412,044	1.26 m^2	78,112
B	Board	Figure 7.28	418,171	1.47 m^2	89,008
	Valve	Figure 7.29	392,267	1.35 m^2	85,936
	Lg. Staircase	Figure 3.4	759,400	58.45 m^2	3,281,200
C	Kitchen	Figure 7.9	1,599,320	37.00 m^2	2,111,540
	Kitchen Ctr.	Figure 7.9	205,101	11.78 m^2	672,752

4.8 Summary and Review

This chapter introduced a formalism for the hierarchical representation of whole-body affordances which allows the consistent fusion of affordance-related evidence at different levels. The formalism is based on affordance belief functions which map end-effector poses to Dempster-Shafer belief expressions. Evidence is expressed as affordance belief functions, independently of its source and certainty, and is combined using Dempster's rule of combination. The Theory of Subjective Logic is employed for applying logic operations on affordance belief functions in order to allow the hierarchical composition of higher-level affordances based on more simple, lower-level affordances. The integration of environmental properties or properties of the robot's embodiment is possible by creating sigmoid belief functions which can be consistently used together with affordance belief functions. The chapter concluded with a review of techniques for reducing the definition space of affordance belief functions with the aim of generating computationally feasible samplings of belief functions.

The representation of affordances through affordance belief functions provides the formal foundation for the hierarchical definition of whole-body affordances introduced in Chapter 5, as well as for the practical implementation of an affordance detection system based on visual sensor information and for the consistent fusion of observation obtained through validation actions. The approach to discretization discussed in Section 4.7 is crucial for the efficient implementation in realistic, large-scale environments, as will be described in Chapter 7.

5 A Hierarchy of Whole-Body Affordances

The previous chapter introduced and discussed a formalism for the representation and combination of affordance-related evidence based on affordance belief functions Θ. In this chapter, the formalization will be used for defining a hierarchy of whole-body affordances. The underlying assumption that *affordances are hierarchical* is justified by the observation that many whole-body affordances, e. g. *holdability* of a handrail, require the existence of lower-level affordances, e. g. *prismatic graspability* of the handrail. The definition of affordances developed in this chapter enables the effective propagation of evidence from lower to higher levels in the hierarchy. In the context of the example above, if the robot gains evidence about *prismatic graspability*, this evidence will automatically also be considered for the system's belief in *holdability* affordances.

The affordance definitions will be hierarchical in the sense that higher-level affordance belief functions can be composed of lower-level affordance belief functions using the logic operations defined in Section 4.4. Intra-affordance evidence, i. e. evidence defined over a common hypothesis space and therefore concerning a single affordance, is combined using Dempster's rule of combination as introduced in Section 4.3. Environmental properties, e. g. primitive orientation or extent, and properties of the robot embodiment, e. g. end-effector dimensions, can be considered in the composition of affordance belief functions based on the concept of sigmoid decision functions (Section 4.5). After the introduction of preliminary concepts in Section 5.1, *fundamental power grasp affordances* will be defined in Section 5.2 as the

root of the affordance hierarchy. These lowest-level affordances are only composed of environmental and embodiment properties. Section 5.3 and Section 5.4 introduce the entire affordance hierarchy for unimanual and bimanual affordances.
Parts of the whole-body affordance hierarchy and of the underlying formalisms have been published in Kaiser et al. (2016a, 2018a).

5.1 Preliminaries

For the formalization of the process of visual affordance detection, let Π denote the set of detected environmental primitives:

$$\Pi = \{p_1, \dots, p_K\}. \tag{5.1}$$

In this section, multiple fundamental functions are introduced that express basic geometric properties of primitives $p \in \Pi$, possibly with respect to an end-effector pose $\boldsymbol{x} \in SE(3)$. Some of the defined property functions refer to the *local end-effector coordinate system* as defined in Figure 4.11.

Shape Functions Formally, a set of shape functions is defined in order to determine the degree to which a primitive $p \in \Pi$ belongs to an associated shape class. Possible shape functions, matching the current capabilities of the H^2T perception pipeline, are:

$$\begin{aligned} &\text{planar}(p) \in [0,1] \\ &\text{circular}(p) \in [0,1] \\ &\text{spherical}(p) \in [0,1] \\ &\text{cylindrical}(p) \in [0,1] \end{aligned} \tag{5.2}$$

The shape functions are not mutually exclusive per definition, for example a planar and circular primitive[1] is possible. The perception pipeline as well as the following considerations are agnostic with respect to the types of primitives, meaning that the extension of the system to further shape classes is possible and straightforward. However, the evaluation shows that the reliable extraction of primitives from real sensor data is prone to noise and error. It turns out that planes are the most reliable and usable primitive type. The H^2T perception pipeline is therefore configured to prefer planar segmentations if possible.

Dimension Functions For assessing the primitive extent, the *dimension functions* $\text{width}(p)$, $\text{height}(p)$ and $\text{depth}(p)$ are defined which determine width, height and depth of the primitive's object-aligned bounding box. While the names *width, height* and *depth* imply a defined order based on the primitive's local coordinate system, this order is not further considered in the affordance definitions.

Grasp Volume Extent Functions In order to assess the graspability of geometric primitives p, the notion of *grasp volumes* is introduced which represent the sub-volume $\mathcal{V}_g(\boldsymbol{x}, p) \subseteq p$ that is enclosed by the grasping hand. In the case of a non-prehensile grasp, e. g. a platform grasp, the grasp volume is defined as the sub-volume of p that is in supporting contact with the end-effector. See Figure 5.1 for visualizations of grasp volumes in different power grasping examples. The grasp volume $\mathcal{V}_g(\boldsymbol{x}, p)$ is not formally defined at this point as it cannot directly be used for the purpose of *graspability* affordance definition, particularly due to its dependency on the concrete hand shape. However, *grasp volume extent functions* will be defined in the following

[1] One example for such a primitive is an industrial valve which will play an important role in the experiments shown in Chapter 7.

which characterize the *biggest possible grasp cuboid* based on the primitive geometry and the robot embodiment, i. e. its end-effector dimensions.
The interesting aspect of the grasp volume is its extent orthogonally to the grasp direction, i. e. in x- and y-direction of the local grasp coordinate system (see Figure 4.11), as these properties characterize the applicable grasp types. Hence, the *grasp volume extent functions* $v_x(\boldsymbol{x}, p, \beta_F)$ and $v_y(\boldsymbol{x}, p, \beta_F)$ are introduced which determine the extent of the biggest possible grasp volume in x- or y-direction of the local grasp coordinate system based on the end-effector pose $\boldsymbol{x} \in SE(3)$ and the primitive p. The grasp volume extent is computed with respect to the body-scaled forehand length β_F which describes the maximum depth to which the end-effector can wrap around the primitive in grasp direction. The forehand length will be formally introduced in Section 5.2 (see Figure 5.5) together with further body-scaled parameters of the robot end-effector. The grasp volume extent functions can be defined in an absolute version, in which the grasp volume can be arbitrarily shifted in the hand, and in a symmetric version, in which the end-effector pose needs to be centered in the grasp volume. This differentiation leads to four grasp volume extent functions which are defined in Table 5.1. See Figure 5.2 for exemplary visualizations of absolute and symmetric grasp volumes.

Table 5.1: Grasp volume extent functions

Function	**Description**
$v_x^a(\boldsymbol{x}, p, \beta_F)$	Length of the biggest absolute grasp volume in x-direction
$v_x^s(\boldsymbol{x}, p, \beta_F)$	Length of the biggest symmetric grasp volume in x-direction
$v_y^a(\boldsymbol{x}, p, \beta_F)$	Length of the biggest absolute grasp volume in y-direction
$v_y^s(\boldsymbol{x}, p, \beta_F)$	Length of the biggest symmetric grasp volume in y-direction

Orientation Function The orientation function $\mathrm{up}(p)$ describes the orientation of a primitive $p \in \Pi$ with respect to the global up-vector $\boldsymbol{u}$. While this vector can be arbitrarily defined, $\boldsymbol{u} := \mathbf{1}_z$ is used throughout the entire thesis. The primitive orientation function evaluates the angle between the primitive normal $\boldsymbol{n}(p)$ and $\boldsymbol{u}$:

$$\mathrm{up}(p) = \arccos\left(\frac{\boldsymbol{n}(p) \cdot \boldsymbol{u}}{\|\boldsymbol{n}(p)\| \cdot \|\boldsymbol{u}\|}\right) \in [0, \pi] \tag{5.3}$$

For the definition of bimanual affordances, three further property functions are defined which compute geometric relations between two end-effector poses $\boldsymbol{x}_1 \in SE(3)$ and $\boldsymbol{x}_2 \in SE(3)$: The *end-effector distance function*, the *end-effector angle function* and the *bimanual orientation function*.

Figure 5.1: Visualization of grasp volumes (*yellow*) for exemplary grasps on planar and cylindrical primitives (*green*).

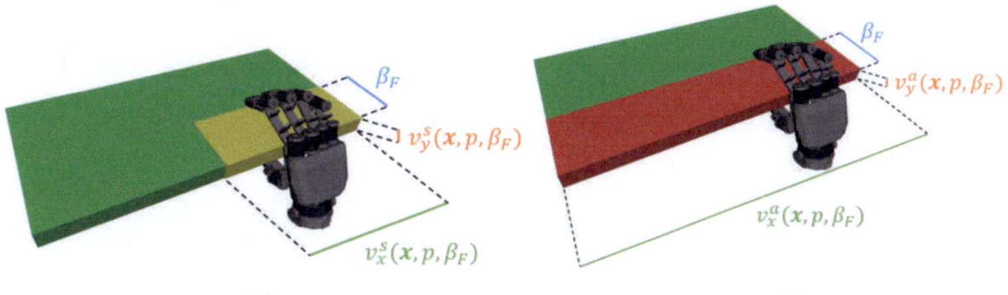

(a) (b)

Figure 5.2: Visualization of a symmetric grasp volume *(a)* and an absolute grasp volume *(b)* with respective maximum extent for an exemplary primitive (*green*).

End-Effector Distance Function The distance between two end-effector poses is relevant as too large or too small distances make bimanual operation infeasible. The end-effector distance function $d(\boldsymbol{x}_1, \boldsymbol{x}_2)$ is defined as:

$$d(\boldsymbol{x}_1, \boldsymbol{x}_2) = \|\mathfrak{t}(\boldsymbol{x}_1) - \mathfrak{t}(\boldsymbol{x}_2)\| \in \mathbb{R}^+ \tag{5.4}$$

End-Effector Angle Function The angle $\alpha(\boldsymbol{x}_1, \boldsymbol{x}_2)$ between two end-effector poses characterizes the difference in grasp orientation and is defined as the angle between the y-axes of the local end-effector coordinate systems (see Figure 4.11):

$$\alpha(\boldsymbol{x}_1, \boldsymbol{x}_2) = \arccos\Big(\big(\mathfrak{R}(\boldsymbol{x}_1) \cdot \mathbf{1}_y\big) \cdot \big(\mathfrak{R}(\boldsymbol{x}_2) \cdot \mathbf{1}_y\big) \Big). \tag{5.5}$$

This definition of the angular difference between end-effector poses applies to aligned and opposed bimanual end-effector configurations.

Bimanual Orientation Function The bimanual orientation $\mathrm{up}(\boldsymbol{x}_1, \boldsymbol{x}_2)$ characterizes the orientation of the bimanual end-effector configuration with respect to the global up-vector $\boldsymbol{u}$:

$$\mathrm{up}(\boldsymbol{x}_1, \boldsymbol{x}_2) = \arccos\left(\frac{\big(\mathfrak{t}(\boldsymbol{x}_1) - \mathfrak{t}(\boldsymbol{x}_2)\big) \cdot \boldsymbol{u}}{\|\mathfrak{t}(\boldsymbol{x}_1) - \mathfrak{t}(\boldsymbol{x}_2)\|} \right) \tag{5.6}$$

In the following, the introduced geometric functions will be used for defining fundamental power grasp affordances which serve as the lowest-level affordances in the hierarchy.

5.2 Fundamental Power Grasp Affordances

This section formally defines the root of the proposed whole-body affordance hierarchy. As the hierarchy is intended to reflect the hierarchical composition of affordance belief functions, root affordances need to be lowest-level affordances which are only used for composing higher-level affordances, not vice versa. Whole-body actions are fundamentally understood as multi-contact actions in this thesis, i. e. actions that establish environmental contact with one or multiple end-effectors. While environmental contact with body parts other than end-effectors is possible, consider e. g. *sitting*, such actions are not further considered. In this sense, the natural root affordances of the whole-body affordance hierarchy are end-effector contact affordances, i. e. *graspability* affordances. Note that *graspability* is defined in its most general sense here.

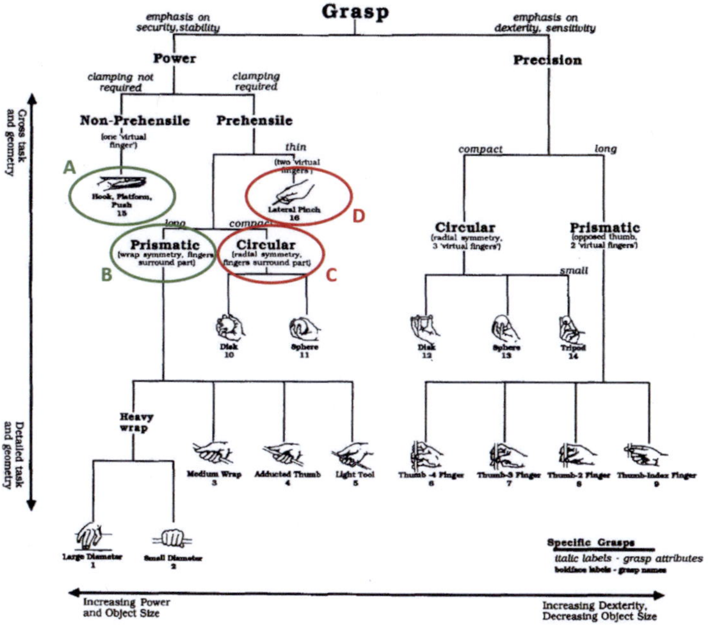

Figure 5.3: The taxonomy of human grasp types from Cutkosky (1989) with highlighting of the four basic types of power grasps: *platform grasps* (A), *prismatic grasps* (B), *circular grasps* (C) and *lateral pinch grasps* (D). Green color indicates grasp types that are represented in the affordance hierarchy while grasp types in red are not further considered (adapted from Cutkosky 1989, © 1989 IEEE).

The well-known taxonomy of Cutkosky (1989), depicted in Figure 5.3, distinguishes between *precision grasps* and *power grasps*. While precision grasps are used for dexterous manipulation actions, power grasps are employed when larger forces need to be exerted. As whole-body actions, particularly within loco-manipulation tasks, most exclusively employ power grasping (see Figure 1.2 for examples), precision grasps are not further considered in this work. Within Cutkosky's taxonomy of power grasps depicted in Figure 5.3, four principle grasp types, labeled A to D, are distinguished which will briefly be reviewed in the following.

Platform Grasps (A) refer to planar contact between a suitable end-effector, such as the palm of a hand or the sole of a foot, and a planar environmental primitive. Platform grasps are commonly observed in whole-body actions, e. g. in *leaning*, *supporting* or *bimanual grasping*, and *platform graspability* will therefore be considered as the first root affordance in the proposed hierarchy.

Prismatic Grasps (B) refer to a class of grasp types for prismatic objects, e. g. cylinders. While Cutkosky (1989) distinguishes between five different types of prismatic grasps, these differentiations appear too meticulous to be performed on an affordance level. Grasp surveys such as Bullock et al. (2013) and Vergara et al. (2014) show that prismatic grasps are the predominant power grasp types used by humans during tasks of daily living. Hence, *prismatic graspability* will be considered as the second root affordance in the hierarchy.

Circular Grasps (C) refer to a class of grasp types for circular or spherical objects. According to Bullock et al. (2013) and Vergara et al. (2014) circular grasps belong to the most frequently used power grasp types. However, the execution of circular grasps relies on the ability of finger spreading which is not implemented in the robotic hands considered throughout this thesis.

Hence, *circular graspability*, although principally possible, is not further considered in the proposed whole-body affordance hierarchy.

Lateral Pinch Grasps (D) refer to a specific power grasp type for small objects. The object is clamped between the thumb and the side of the index finger. Similar to *circular graspability*, *lateral pinch graspability* is not further considered in this work, as the employed robotic hands are not capable of reproducing this grasp type.

In the following, the two fundamental power grasp affordances are formally defined based on the concept of belief functions introduced in Chapter 4. The existence of fundamental affordances solely depends on properties of environmental primitives and robot embodiment, as no lower-level affordances exist. Most important for grasping are end-effector dimensions which are shown in Figure 5.5. Table A.1 lists possible values for these parameters for the embodiments of an average human and the humanoid robots ARMAR-III, ARMAR-4 and WALK-MAN.

(a) Prismatic grasp (b) Platform grasp

Figure 5.4: The two fundamental grasp types considered to form the root of the affordance hierarchy (taken from Kaiser et al. 2016a, © 2016 IEEE).

Platform Graspability Affordance The first fundamental grasp affordance is *platform graspability*, as shown in Figure 5.4b. In platform grasping, the hand is opened to full extent and put in contact with large, planar surfaces which is particularly useful for whole-body actions such as *supporting*, *pushing* or *bimanual grasping*. Narratively, platform graspability affordances can be defined as follows:

> *A platform graspability affordance exists for a given end-effector pose $\boldsymbol{x}$ and a primitive p if the primitive is large enough to accommodate the dimensions of the end-effector.*

This intuitive definition can be formally expressed as an affordance belief function based on the body-scaled parameters for the hand length β_L and hand breadth β_B (see Figure 5.5) and based on the dimensions of p in the end-effector pose frame $\boldsymbol{x}$ (see Table 5.1):

$$\Theta_{\text{G-Platform}}(p,\boldsymbol{x}) = \Theta_{v_x^s(\boldsymbol{x},p,\beta_F)>\beta_B}(\boldsymbol{x}) \wedge \Theta_{v_y^s(\boldsymbol{x},p,\beta_F)>\beta_L}(\boldsymbol{x}) \qquad (5.7)$$

The axes x and y refer to the local end-effector coordinate systems as shown in Figure 4.11.

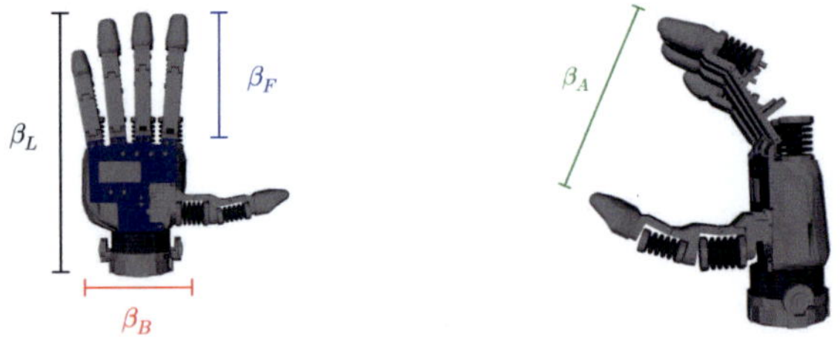

Figure 5.5: The body-scaled parameters β_L (*black*), β_B (*red*), β_F (*blue*) and β_A (*green*) as foundation for perceiving grasp affordances (adapted from Kaiser et al. 2016a, © 2016 IEEE). The parameters refer to *hand length*, *hand breadth*, *forehand length* and *hand aperture*, respectively, as defined in Garrett (1971).

Prismatic Graspability Affordance The second fundamental grasp affordance is *prismatic graspability*, as shown in Figure 5.4a. In prismatic grasping, fingers and thumb are opposedly wrapped around objects that fit into the hand aperture. This grasp type is particularly useful for whole-body actions, such as *holding*, *pulling* or *bimanual grasping*. Narratively, prismatic graspability affordances can be defined as follows:

> *A prismatic graspability affordance exists for a given end-effector pose $\boldsymbol{x}$ and a primitive p if the primitive width is larger than the hand breadth β_B and the primitive height is smaller than the hand aperture β_A.*

This intuitive definition can be formally expressed as an affordance belief function based on the body-scaled parameters for the hand breadth β_B and hand aperture β_A (see Figure 5.5) and the dimensions of p in the end-effector pose frame $\boldsymbol{x}$ (see Table 5.1):

$$\Theta_{\text{G-Prismatic}}(p, \boldsymbol{x}) = \Theta_{v_x^s(\boldsymbol{x},p,\beta_F)>\beta_B}(\boldsymbol{x}) \wedge \Theta_{v_y^a(\boldsymbol{x},p,\beta_F)<\beta_A}(\boldsymbol{x}) \tag{5.8}$$

Figure 5.6 shows visualizations of affordance belief functions for *platform graspability* and *prismatic graspability* for the example of a handrail-equipped staircase. The belief functions have been generated using the formalisms from Equation 5.7 and Equation 5.8. The example shows that the resulting belief functions take high values for end-effector poses for which the respective grasp type would be well applicable, e. g. in the inner areas of planar surfaces for platform grasping and at the boundaries of planar and cylindrical primitives for prismatic grasping.

5.3 Unimanual Affordance Hierarchy

This section defines the hierarchy of unimanual whole-body affordances which will subsequently be extended to bimanual affordances in Section 5.4.

[2] See Figure 4.4 for an explanation of the color mapping.

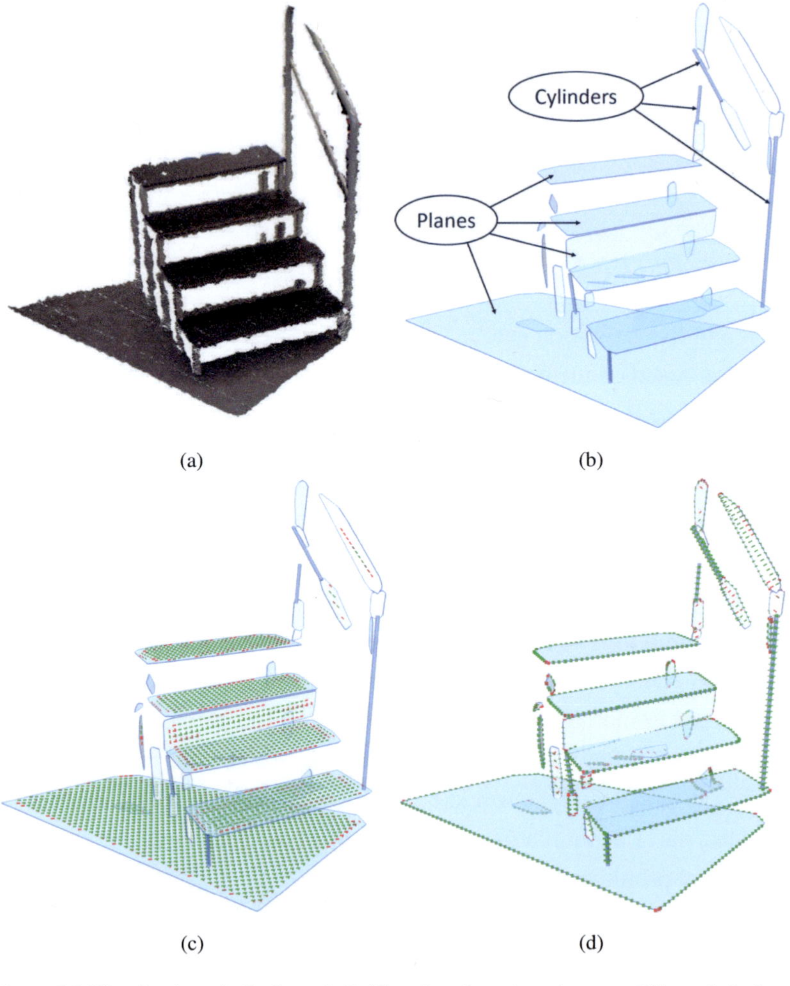

Figure 5.6: Visualization of affordance belief functions for *prismatic graspability* and *platform graspability* to an exemplary staircase scenario[2](taken from Kaiser et al. 2016a, © 2016 IEEE). The figures show (a) the original point cloud, (b) the geometric primitives obtained via the H^2T perception pipeline, (c) the affordance belief function $\Theta_{\text{G-Platform}}$ and (d) the affordance belief function $\Theta_{\text{G-Prismatic}}$.

The hierarchy of whole-body affordances is sorted in layers based on the distance to the fundamental power grasp affordances defined in Section 5.2 which form the root of the affordance hierarchy. Belief functions from a layer $\boldsymbol{L}_k$ can be composed of lower-level belief functions from layers $\boldsymbol{L}_0, \ldots, \boldsymbol{L}_{k-1}$. Depending on the types of contained belief functions, layers will be denoted as $\boldsymbol{A}_i$, containing affordance belief functions (see Section 4.2), or as $\boldsymbol{P}_i$, containing property decision functions (see Section 4.5).

The Property Layer $\boldsymbol{P}_0$ Table 5.2 defines the belief functions for fundamental environmental properties of a primitive p, assorted into layer $\boldsymbol{P}_0$. This layer contains the belief functions $\Theta_{\text{Vertical}}(p)$ and $\Theta_{\text{Horizontal}}(p)$ for expressing the primitive orientation[3] and $\Theta_{\text{Round}}(p)$ for expressing the degree of circularity of p. The belief functions $\Theta_{\text{Movable}}(p)$ and $\Theta_{\text{Fixed}}(p)$ have a more complex definition based on the dimensions of the primitive's object-aligned bounding box. Refer to Section 5.1 for details on the employed property functions.

Table 5.2: The whole-body affordance hierarchy (layer $\boldsymbol{P}_0$)

Layer	Symbol	Composition of Belief Function
	$\Theta_{\text{Vertical}}(p)$	$\Theta_{\text{up}(p)\approx_\varepsilon 0}(p)$
	$\Theta_{\text{Horizontal}}(p)$	$\Theta_{\text{up}(p)\approx_\varepsilon \pi}(p)$
$\boldsymbol{P}_0$	$\Theta_{\text{Round}}(p)$	$\Theta_{\text{circular}(p)\approx_\varepsilon 1}(p)$
	$\Theta_{\text{Movable}}(p)$	$\Theta_{\text{width}(p)<\lambda_1}(p) \wedge \Theta_{\text{height}(p)<\lambda_1}(p) \wedge \Theta_{\text{depth}(p)<\lambda_1}(p)$
	$\Theta_{\text{Fixed}}(p)$	$\Theta_{\text{width}(p)>\lambda_1}(p) \vee \Theta_{\text{height}(p)>\lambda_1}(p) \vee \Theta_{\text{depth}(p)>\lambda_1}(p)$

The Affordance Layers $\boldsymbol{A}_0$ and $\boldsymbol{A}_1$ Table 5.3 defines the lowest layer $\boldsymbol{A}_0$ of affordance belief functions, containing the fundamental grasp affordances $\Theta_{\text{G-Prismatic}}$ and $\Theta_{\text{G-Platform}}$. It further defines the layer $\boldsymbol{A}_1$ which contains

[3] The notation $\text{up}(p) \approx_\varepsilon x$ is a short writing for $\text{up}(p) \in [x-\varepsilon, x+\varepsilon]$.

only one affordance belief function, Θ_{Grasp}. The general *graspability* affordance defined in layer $\boldsymbol{A}_1$ can be used when no particular grasp type is required. It is defined based on the fundamental grasp affordances from layer $\boldsymbol{A}_0$.

The Affordance Layer $\boldsymbol{A}_2$ The grasp affordances $\Theta_{\text{G-Platform}}$, $\Theta_{\text{G-Prismatic}}$ and Θ_{Grasp} from layers $\boldsymbol{A}_0$ and $\boldsymbol{A}_1$ can now be combined with environmental properties from layer $\boldsymbol{P}_0$ to form higher-level affordance belief functions for unimanual whole-body actions, such as *supporting*, *leaning*, *holding*, *lifting*, *pushing*, *pulling* and *turning*. Table 5.4 defines the belief functions assorted to layer $\boldsymbol{A}_1$. Figure 5.7 displays the exemplary composition of a *leanability* affordance based on the lower-level affordance belief function $\Theta_{\text{G-Platform}}$ for *platform graspability* and the property belief functions Θ_{Vertical} and Θ_{Fixed} which characterize a vertical and large primitive.

Table 5.3: The whole-body affordance hierarchy (layers $\boldsymbol{A}_0$ and $\boldsymbol{A}_1$)

Layer	Symbol	Composition of Affordance Belief Function
$\boldsymbol{A}_0$	$\Theta_{\text{G-Platform}}(p, \boldsymbol{x})$	$\Theta_{v_x^s(\boldsymbol{x},p,\beta_F)>\beta_B}(\boldsymbol{x}) \wedge \Theta_{v_y^s(\boldsymbol{x},p,\beta_F)>\beta_L}(\boldsymbol{x})$
	$\Theta_{\text{G-Prismatic}}(p, \boldsymbol{x})$	$\Theta_{v_x^s(\boldsymbol{x},p,\beta_F)>\beta_B}(\boldsymbol{x}) \wedge \Theta_{v_y^a(\boldsymbol{x},p,\beta_F)<\beta_A}(\boldsymbol{x})$
$\boldsymbol{A}_1$	$\Theta_{\text{Grasp}}(p, \boldsymbol{x})$	$\Theta_{\text{G-Platform}}(p, \boldsymbol{x}) \vee \Theta_{\text{G-Prismatic}}(p, \boldsymbol{x})$

Table 5.4: The whole-body affordance hierarchy (layer $\boldsymbol{A}_2$)

Layer	Symbol	Composition of Affordance Belief Function
	$\Theta_{\text{Support}}(p, \boldsymbol{x})$	$\Theta_{\text{G-Platform}}(p, \boldsymbol{x}) \wedge \Theta_{\text{Fixed}}(p) \wedge \Theta_{\text{Horizontal}}(p)$
	$\Theta_{\text{Lean}}(p, \boldsymbol{x})$	$\Theta_{\text{G-Platform}}(p, \boldsymbol{x}) \wedge \Theta_{\text{Fixed}}(p) \wedge \Theta_{\text{Vertical}}(p)$
	$\Theta_{\text{Hold}}(p, \boldsymbol{x})$	$\Theta_{\text{G-Prismatic}}(p, \boldsymbol{x}) \wedge \Theta_{\text{Fixed}}(p)$
$\boldsymbol{A}_2$	$\Theta_{\text{Lift}}(p, \boldsymbol{x})$	$\Theta_{\text{G-Prismatic}}(p, \boldsymbol{x}) \wedge \Theta_{\text{Movable}}(p)$
	$\Theta_{\text{Push}}(p, \boldsymbol{x})$	$\Theta_{\text{Grasp}}(p, \boldsymbol{x}) \wedge \Theta_{\text{Movable}}(p)$
	$\Theta_{\text{Pull}}(p, \boldsymbol{x})$	$\Theta_{\text{G-Prismatic}}(p, \boldsymbol{x}) \wedge \Theta_{\text{Movable}}(p)$
	$\Theta_{\text{Turn}}(\boldsymbol{x})$	$\Theta_{\text{G-Prismatic}}(p, \boldsymbol{x}) \wedge \Theta_{\text{Movable}}(p) \wedge \Theta_{\text{Round}}(p)$

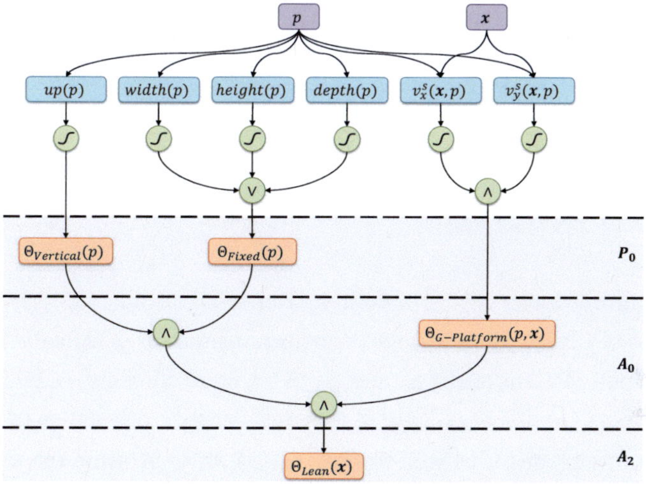

Figure 5.7: The hierarchical composition of the affordance belief function Θ_{Lean} based on the lower-level affordance belief function $\Theta_{\text{G-Platform}}$ and the property belief functions Θ_{Vertical} and Θ_{Fixed}.

The layers $\boldsymbol{A}_0$, $\boldsymbol{A}_1$ and $\boldsymbol{A}_2$ define basic unimanual whole-body affordances and specify their composition rules within the affordance hierarchy. While the specified set of affordances is rich enough for performing a variety of different tasks in real environments, as will be demonstrated in Chapter 7, the hierarchy is not considered complete. In the following section, bimanual affordances will be introduced into the hierarchy as an extension of the previously defined layers.

5.4 Bimanual Affordance Hierarchy

The hierarchy of unimanual whole-body affordances introduced in Section 5.3 contains the layers $\boldsymbol{P}_0$ and $\boldsymbol{A}_0$ to $\boldsymbol{A}_2$. In this section, the results of Section 4.6 are used for extending the hierarchy with layers $\boldsymbol{P}_1$ and $\boldsymbol{A}_3$ to $\boldsymbol{A}_6$ for bimanual whole-body affordances. As discussed in Section 4.6, the definition space of bimanual affordance belief functions is $SE(3) \times SE(3)$, i. e. the Cartesian product of end-effector poses. Hence, bimanual affordance belief functions can be composed of end-effector specific unimanual affordance belief functions, e. g. a *bimanual platform graspability* affordance for the end-effector pose pair $(\boldsymbol{x}_1, \boldsymbol{x}_2)$ is defined based on *unimanual platform graspability* affordances for the individual end-effector poses $\boldsymbol{x}_1$ and $\boldsymbol{x}_2$.

The Property Layer $\boldsymbol{P}_1$ For defining bimanual affordances, a new property layer $\boldsymbol{P}_1$ is introduced which contains properties of the relation between the two end-effector poses $\boldsymbol{x}_1$ and $\boldsymbol{x}_2$: This layer contains the belief functions $\Theta_{\text{Vertical}}(p)$ and $\Theta_{\text{Horizontal}}(p)$ for expressing the orientation of the end-effector arrangement, as well as $\Theta_{\text{Feasible}}(p)$ for expressing the degree of feasibility of the distance between the end-effector poses. The belief functions $\Theta_{\text{Aligned}}(p)$ and $\Theta_{\text{Opposed}}(p)$ specify if the end-effector arrangement is aligned or opposed. Refer to Table 5.5 for details on the employed property functions.

Table 5.5: The whole-body affordance hierarchy (layer $\boldsymbol{P}_1$)

Layer	Symbol	Composition of Belief Function
	$\Theta_{\text{Vertical}}(\boldsymbol{x}_1, \boldsymbol{x}_2)$	$\Theta_{\text{up}(\boldsymbol{x}_1, \boldsymbol{x}_2) \approx_\varepsilon 0}(\boldsymbol{x}_1, \boldsymbol{x}_2)$
	$\Theta_{\text{Horizontal}}(\boldsymbol{x}_1, \boldsymbol{x}_2)$	$\Theta_{\text{up}(\boldsymbol{x}_1, \boldsymbol{x}_2) \approx_\varepsilon \pi}(\boldsymbol{x}_1, \boldsymbol{x}_2)$
$\boldsymbol{P}_1$	$\Theta_{\text{Feasible}}(\boldsymbol{x}_1, \boldsymbol{x}_2)$	$\Theta_{d(\boldsymbol{x}_1, \boldsymbol{x}_2) > \beta_L}(\boldsymbol{x}_1, \boldsymbol{x}_2) \wedge \Theta_{d(\boldsymbol{x}_1, \boldsymbol{x}_2) < \beta_{\text{Sh}}}(\boldsymbol{x}_1, \boldsymbol{x}_2)$
	$\Theta_{\text{Aligned}}(\boldsymbol{x}_1, \boldsymbol{x}_2)$	$\Theta_{\alpha(\boldsymbol{x}_1, \boldsymbol{x}_2) \approx_\varepsilon 0}(\boldsymbol{x}_1, \boldsymbol{x}_2)$
	$\Theta_{\text{Opposed}}(\boldsymbol{x}_1, \boldsymbol{x}_2)$	$\Theta_{\alpha(\boldsymbol{x}_1, \boldsymbol{x}_2) \approx_\varepsilon \pi}(\boldsymbol{x}_1, \boldsymbol{x}_2)$

The Affordance Layers A_3, A_4 and A_5 In the same way as with the definition of the fundamental *unimanual graspability* affordances in layer $\boldsymbol{A}_0$, the fundamental *bimanual graspability* affordances $\Theta_{\text{Bi-G-Platform}}$ and $\Theta_{\text{Bi-G-Prismatic}}$ can now be defined based on their unimanual counterparts. Bimanual grasping is considered possible if the respective unimanual grasp affordances exist for the individual end-effector poses and if the distance between the end-effector poses is considered feasible. The general *bimanual graspability* affordance defined in layer $\boldsymbol{A}_4$ is defined based on the fundamental bimanual grasp affordances and is used when no particular grasp type is required. Now, further bimanual grasp affordances can be differentiated by considering the relative orientation of the end-effectors. Based on these affordances, bimanual grasping can be categorized into *aligned* and *opposed* end-effector configurations. Refer to Table 5.6 for details on the employed property functions.

Table 5.6: The whole-body affordance hierarchy (layers $\boldsymbol{A}_3$, $\boldsymbol{A}_4$ and $\boldsymbol{A}_5$)

Layer	Symbol	Composition of Belief Function
$\boldsymbol{A}_3$	$\Theta_{\text{Bi-G-Platform}}(p, \boldsymbol{x}_1, \boldsymbol{x}_2)$	$\Theta_{\text{G-Platform}}(p, \boldsymbol{x}_1) \wedge \Theta_{\text{G-Platform}}(p, \boldsymbol{x}_2) \wedge \Theta_{\text{Feasible}}(\boldsymbol{x}_1, \boldsymbol{x}_2)$
	$\Theta_{\text{Bi-G-Prismatic}}(p, \boldsymbol{x}_1, \boldsymbol{x}_2)$	$\Theta_{\text{G-Prismatic}}(p, \boldsymbol{x}_1) \wedge \Theta_{\text{G-Prismatic}}(p, \boldsymbol{x}_2) \wedge \Theta_{\text{Feasible}}(\boldsymbol{x}_1, \boldsymbol{x}_2)$
$\boldsymbol{A}_4$	$\Theta_{\text{Bi-Grasp}}(p, \boldsymbol{x}_1, \boldsymbol{x}_2)$	$\Theta_{\text{Bi-G-Platform}}(p, \boldsymbol{x}_1, \boldsymbol{x}_2) \vee \Theta_{\text{Bi-G-Prismatic}}(p, \boldsymbol{x}_1, \boldsymbol{x}_2)$
$\boldsymbol{A}_5$	$\Theta_{\text{Bi-G-Aligned}}(p, \boldsymbol{x}_1, \boldsymbol{x}_2)$	$\Theta_{\text{Bi-Grasp}}(p, \boldsymbol{x}_1, \boldsymbol{x}_2) \wedge \Theta_{\text{Aligned}}(\boldsymbol{x}_1, \boldsymbol{x}_2)$
	$\Theta_{\text{Bi-G-Opposed}}(p, \boldsymbol{x}_1, \boldsymbol{x}_2)$	$\Theta_{\text{Bi-Grasp}}(p, \boldsymbol{x}_1, \boldsymbol{x}_2) \wedge \Theta_{\text{Opposed}}(\boldsymbol{x}_1, \boldsymbol{x}_2)$
	$\Theta_{\text{Bi-G-Aligned-Platform}}(p, \boldsymbol{x}_1, \boldsymbol{x}_2)$	$\Theta_{\text{Bi-G-Platform}}(p, \boldsymbol{x}_1, \boldsymbol{x}_2) \wedge \Theta_{\text{Aligned}}(\boldsymbol{x}_1, \boldsymbol{x}_2)$
	$\Theta_{\text{Bi-G-Aligned-Prismatic}}(p, \boldsymbol{x}_1, \boldsymbol{x}_2)$	$\Theta_{\text{Bi-G-Prismatic}}(p, \boldsymbol{x}_1, \boldsymbol{x}_2) \wedge \Theta_{\text{Aligned}}(\boldsymbol{x}_1, \boldsymbol{x}_2)$
	$\Theta_{\text{Bi-G-Opposed-Platform}}(p, \boldsymbol{x}_1, \boldsymbol{x}_2)$	$\Theta_{\text{Bi-G-Platform}}(p, \boldsymbol{x}_1, \boldsymbol{x}_2) \wedge \Theta_{\text{Opposed}}(\boldsymbol{x}_1, \boldsymbol{x}_2)$
	$\Theta_{\text{Bi-G-Opposed-Prismatic}}(p, \boldsymbol{x}_1, \boldsymbol{x}_2)$	$\Theta_{\text{Bi-G-Prismatic}}(p, \boldsymbol{x}_1, \boldsymbol{x}_2) \wedge \Theta_{\text{Opposed}}(\boldsymbol{x}_1, \boldsymbol{x}_2)$

The Affordance Layer $\boldsymbol{A}_6$ As for the unimanual affordance layer $\boldsymbol{A}_2$, higher-level affordances can now be defined based on the lower-level bimanual grasp affordances. See Figure 5.8 for the exemplary composition of the belief function $\Theta_{\text{Bi-Support}}$ for *bimanual supportability*. Refer to Table 5.7 for details on the employed property functions.

5.5 Summary and Review

Based on the hypothesis that platform grasping and prismatic grasping are essential foundations for whole-body actions, this chapter introduced and formally defined a hierarchy of whole-body affordances. The root of this affordance hierarchy consists of two fundamental power grasp affordances. The hierarchical arrangement of affordances allows the composition of affordance belief functions from lower-level affordance belief functions. In this concept, affordances for supporting, leaning, holding, lifting, pushing, pulling and turning are defined which represent essential skills from the area of whole-body loco-manipulation. Furthermore, by extending the definition space of the underlying affordance belief functions, Section 5.4 extended the given hierarchy to include bimanual affordances. The full set of defined affordances together with their composition rules can be found in Table A.2. One benefit of the hierarchical formalization of affordances presented in this chapter is that the set of affordances can easily be extended on all layers and gained evidence will be appropriately propagated to newly defined affordances as well. Although the affordance hierarchy as defined in this chapter is intended to capture significant portions of the space of whole-body actions that are relevant in humanoid robotic applications, the hierarchy cannot be considered complete.

Table 5.7: The whole-body affordance hierarchy (layer $\boldsymbol{A}_6$)

Layer	Symbol	Composition of Belief Function
	$\Theta_{\text{Bi-Support}}(p, \boldsymbol{x}_1, \boldsymbol{x}_2)$	$\Theta_{\text{Bi-G-Platform}}(p, \boldsymbol{x}_1, \boldsymbol{x}_2) \wedge \Theta_{\text{Fixed}}(p) \wedge \Theta_{\text{Horizontal}}(p)$
	$\Theta_{\text{Bi-Lean}}(p, \boldsymbol{x}_1, \boldsymbol{x}_2)$	$\Theta_{\text{Bi-G-Platform}}(p, \boldsymbol{x}_1, \boldsymbol{x}_2) \wedge \Theta_{\text{Fixed}}(p) \wedge \Theta_{\text{Vertical}}(p)$
	$\Theta_{\text{Bi-Hold}}(p, \boldsymbol{x}_1, \boldsymbol{x}_2)$	$\Theta_{\text{Bi-G-Prismatic}}(p, \boldsymbol{x}_1, \boldsymbol{x}_2) \wedge \Theta_{\text{Hold}}(p, \boldsymbol{x}_1) \wedge \Theta_{\text{Hold}}(p, \boldsymbol{x}_2)$
$\boldsymbol{A}_6$	$\Theta_{\text{Bi-Lift}}(p, \boldsymbol{x}_1, \boldsymbol{x}_2)$	$\Theta_{\text{Bi-G-Prismatic}}(p, \boldsymbol{x}_1, \boldsymbol{x}_2) \wedge \Theta_{\text{Lift}}(p, \boldsymbol{x}_1) \wedge \Theta_{\text{Lift}}(p, \boldsymbol{x}_2)$
	$\Theta_{\text{Bi-Push}}(p, \boldsymbol{x}_1, \boldsymbol{x}_2)$	$\Theta_{\text{Bi-G-Aligned}}(p, \boldsymbol{x}_1, \boldsymbol{x}_2) \wedge \Theta_{\text{Push}}(\boldsymbol{x}_1) \wedge \Theta_{\text{Push}}(\boldsymbol{x}_2)$
	$\Theta_{\text{Bi-Pull}}(p, \boldsymbol{x}_1, \boldsymbol{x}_2)$	$\Theta_{\text{Bi-G-Aligned-Prismatic}}(p, \boldsymbol{x}_1, \boldsymbol{x}_2) \wedge \Theta_{\text{Pull}}(\boldsymbol{x}_1) \wedge \Theta_{\text{Pull}}(\boldsymbol{x}_2)$
	$\Theta_{\text{Bi-Turn}}(p, \boldsymbol{x}_1, \boldsymbol{x}_2)$	$\Theta_{\text{Bi-G-Opposed-Prismatic}}(p, \boldsymbol{x}_1, \boldsymbol{x}_2) \wedge \Theta_{\text{Round}}(p)$

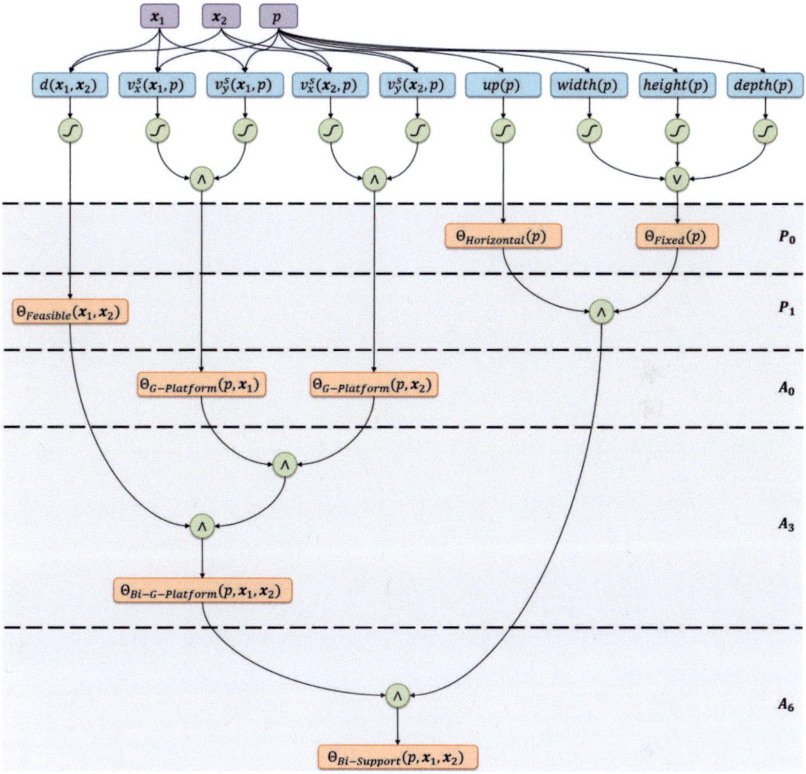

Figure 5.8: The hierarchical composition of the affordance belief function $\Theta_{\text{Bi-Support}}$ for *bimanual supportability*, based on lower-level affordance belief functions.

6 Affordance-Based Autonomy

This chapter provides the conceptual and practical foundations for applying the affordance detection system, as introduced and discussed in the previous chapters, to the control of real humanoid robots. Section 2.4 introduced different levels of autonomy that can be used for robotic control. In particular *full autonomy* as the ultimate goal and *shared autonomy* as a practical solution to high-level control for state-of-the-art humanoid robots are introduced. The formalization of affordances in terms of affordance belief functions and OACs provides the necessary means for convenient integration into autonomous and shared-autonomous control schemes which will be discussed in Section 6.1 and Section 6.2, respectively. The concept of affordance-based shared autonomy is accompanied by the implementation of a pilot interface which allows the practical application of the proposed affordance detection system on real humanoid robots. This pilot interface will be used in Chapter 7 for the evaluation of the affordance detection system in real applications.

6.1 A Concept for Affordance-Based Autonomy

Fully autonomous humanoid robots need to implement sophisticated mechanisms not only in the perception of action possibilities, but also in higher-level components, such as action or task planning. In order to realize a complete cognitive architecture based on the proposed system for affordance detection, perceived affordances need to provide links to both, action execution descriptions and symbolic planning entities.

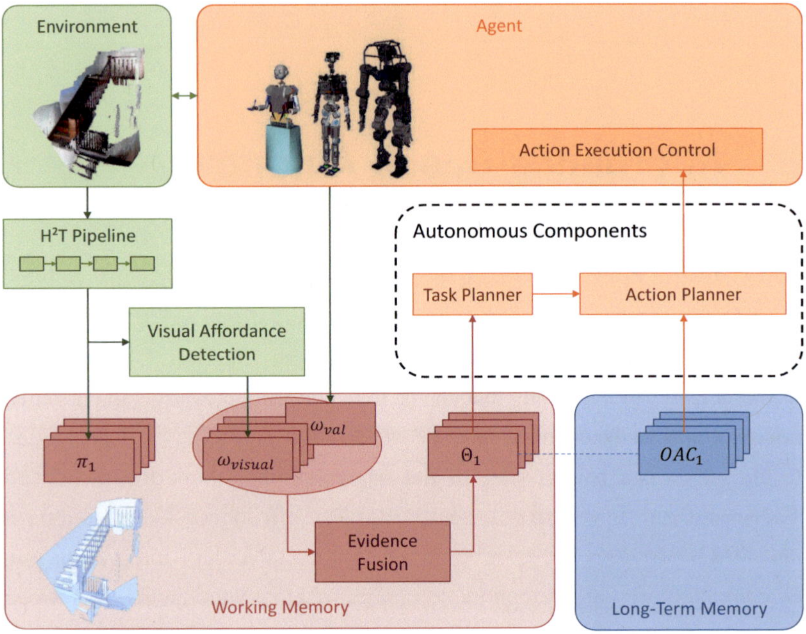

Figure 6.1: Affordance belief functions embedded in a conceptual framework that integrates affordance detection with symbolic planning. The fusion of evidence from multiple observations ω form affordance belief functions Θ (*red*) which directly contribute to the instantiation and parametrization of OACs (*blue*). Execution of selected OACs enrich Θ with additional validation observations ω_{val} (*green*).

The *Xperience* project[1] provides a sophisticated cognitive architecture based on the formalism of Object-Action Complexes (OACs) (Krüger et al. 2011). OACs have been introduced in Section 2.2 and Section 3.3 as representations of object-action dependencies which comprehensively combine action execution strategies (*control programs*) and symbolic representations of *preconditions* and *action effects*. OACs integrate well into the general symbolic planning architecture *Spoac* (Ovchinnikova et al. 2015) which is integrated in

[1] European Union Seventh Framework Programme under grant agreement number 270273 http://www.xperience.org

the robot software environment ArmarX (Vahrenkamp et al. 2015) developed at the H^2T. In the context of Spoac, OACs are directly linked with action execution strategies formulated as ArmarX statecharts (Wächter et al. 2016). Figure 6.1 outlines the integration of the affordance detection system into a higher-level cognitive architecture based on the formalism of OACs. In the following, the individual components of the cognitive architecture for affordance-based autonomy are explained in further detail.

Visual Affordance Detection In the first step, the environment is perceived using depth sensing technology[2], resulting in point cloud representations. The H^2T perception pipeline then processes the point clouds as explained in Section 3.1, resulting in sets of geometric primitives $\pi_1, \ldots, \pi_K$ which are stored in the robot's working memory. In the final pipeline stage, visualized as a separate component in Figure 6.1, the detected geometric primitives are used as a basis for the visual detection of affordances by evaluating the affordance hierarchy introduced in Chapter 5. The process of visual affordance detection produces affordance belief functions which are stored as observations ω_{visual} in the robot's working memory.

Evidence Fusion Affordance belief functions from different observations, possibly also from different experimental conditions using different sensors, are collected in the robot's working memory. These affordance belief functions in combination assemble the robot's belief in the respective affordance. The evidence fusion component is responsible for consistently combining available evidence into joint affordance belief functions, expressing the overall belief in the existence of respective affordances. These joint belief functions are denoted as $\Theta_{\text{Affordance}}$ and stored in the robot's working memory for further use by affordance-based system components.

[2] This could be e. g. RGB-D cameras, stereo cameras or LIDAR laser scanners.

OACs The long-term memory contains the OACs that are available to the robot. While OACs provide a generic and flexible concept for coupling objects and actions, this section refers to OACs as implemented in the software library *Spoac* introduced in Section 3.3. Linking affordances with OACs is an important element in the affordance-based architecture as OACs provide a link between action execution skills implemented as ArmarX statecharts and symbolic descriptions of preconditions and effects of implemented actions with respect to an appropriate planning domain. OACs further provide information about their parameterization, particularly with respect to the amount of end-effectors involved in the action execution.

Autonomous Task and Action Planning A cognitive architecture for autonomous robots requires two essential components which realize high-level cognitive behavior based on given task descriptions: A *task planner* that produces sequences of intermediate goals from an abstract task specification and an *action planner* that produces action sequences based on their symbolic preconditions and effects. As suggested in the architecture, the combination of affordance belief functions and OACs provides valuable information that can be used for realizing these components. However, autonomous task and action planning is an unsolved field of fundamental research in robotics, and hence this thesis does not further elaborate on the concrete implementation of these components. Instead, Section 6.2 proposes to leverage these tasks to a human pilot.

Action Execution Once action sequences have been planned by high-level autonomous planning components, the corresponding sequences of OACs are passed to the action execution control component which controls and supervises their execution. Depending on the control programs of executed OACs, affordance-related evidence can be collected during action execution. This is particularly true for *affordance validation actions*, whose sole purpose is the collection of affordance-related evidence. This evidence is represented as observations ω_{val} and is stored in the working memory, alongside other available observations.

6.2 A Concept for Affordance-Based Shared Autonomy

The concept for affordance-based autonomy proposed in Figure 6.1 is feasible in the way that collected affordances inform higher-level autonomous components. However, the state-of-the-art in the field of autonomous task and action planning does not provide true autonomy in these components, even when informed by autonomously detected affordances. Hence, the application of the affordance detection system proposed in this thesis is focused on *shared autonomous control modes* which allow high-level autonomous capabilities to be leveraged to a human pilot.

Figure 6.2 visualizes the role of the *affordance-based pilot interface* within the autonomous cognitive architecture from Figure 6.1: Detected affordances and intermediate perceptual representations are presented to a human pilot, including the original point clouds, extracted geometric primitives, the detected affordances and their associated OACs. Based on this information, the human pilot can conveniently control the robot on an abstract level by selecting among the affordances and OACs proposed by the robot. In this system, the pilot essentially replaces the autonomous components of task and action planning displayed in Figure 6.1. The concept of affordance-based shared autonomy and the affordance-based pilot interface have been published in Kaiser et al. (2016c).

Based on the concepts of affordance-based autonomy and shared autonomy discussed in the previous sections, an affordance-based pilot interface has been developed within the context of this thesis. This pilot interface allows a human pilot to interact with the affordance detection system. The pilot interface itself is agnostic to the employed robot and to the circumstances of its application, e. g. if it is connected to a simulated robot in a simulated environment or to a real humanoid robot in a full-scale demonstration environment. In the following, the pilot interface will be discussed based on the simulated humanoid robot ARMAR-III in a simulated kitchen environment (see Figure 6.3), while the application on real humanoid robots will be discussed in Chapter 7.

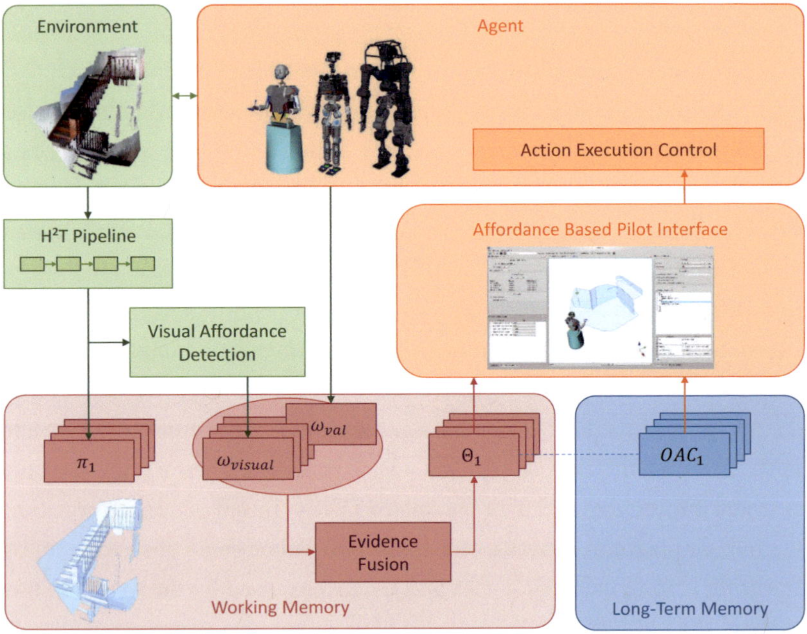

Figure 6.2: An affordance-based pilot interface embedded in the affordance-based cognitive architecture from Figure 6.1: The abstract and conceptually challenging functions of task and action planning are leveraged to a human pilot.

The simulation environment used in this section and throughout the evaluation in Chapter 7 is *SimulationX*, the default dynamics simulation environment of ArmarX (Vahrenkamp et al. 2015). Besides simulating multibody dynamics, the ArmarX simulation environment features simulated depth camera images which allows the direct application of the H^2T perception pipeline in simulated scenarios. ArmarX implements a transparent interface between higher-level components and low-level components that connect to the simulation environment or to actual robotic hardware (see Figure 3.6). Hence, the implementation of the pilot interface in ArmarX allows its convenient application to simulated and real scenarios.

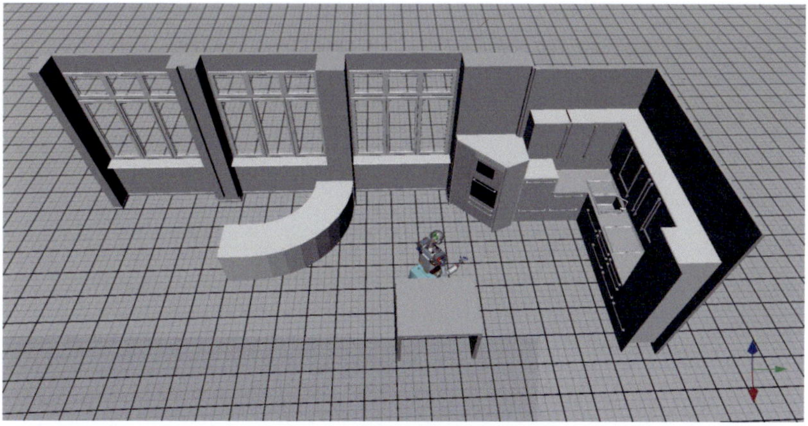

Figure 6.3: The humanoid robot ARMAR-III in a simulated kitchen environment.

Figure 6.4 shows a screenshot of the affordance-based pilot interface, while its individual components are tagged with labels from **A** to **E**. These components will be discussed in further detail below.

Pipeline Control (A) The top left area of the pilot interface allows the pilot to configure and control the H^2T perception pipeline and to introspect the current pipeline status (see Figure 6.5). The pilot selects the sensor device to use, the desired cropping strategy and a predefined set of segmentation parameters. The widget further allows the pilot to start the perception pipeline, either in a continuous or in a one-shot mode. The current pipeline status is visualized at the bottom of the widget, indicating the capture timestamp of the point cloud that just passed the respective pipeline step.

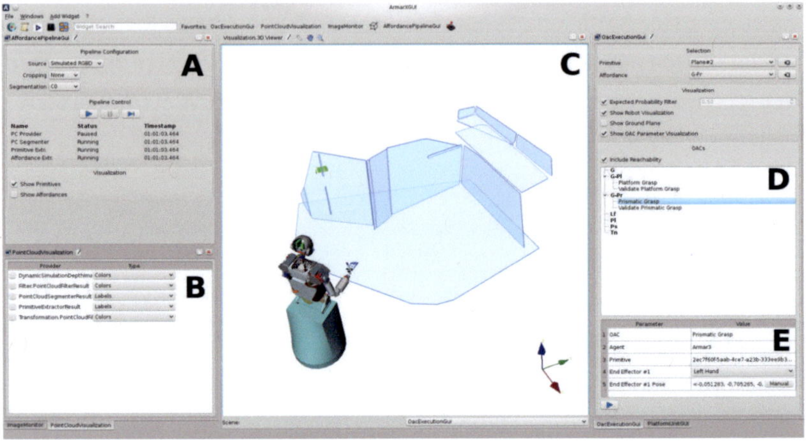

Figure 6.4: The affordance-based pilot interface for shared autonomous control of a humanoid robot in unknown scenarios. In this example, the pilot interface is connected to the simulated humanoid robot ARMAR-III in a kitchen environment (see Figure 6.3). The configured 3D visualization (**C**) shows geometric primitives extracted from the current robot view based on the simulated situation shows in Figure 6.3.

Point Cloud Visualization Setup and Camera Images (B) By default, the bottom left area of the pilot interface shows a configured camera image of the robot (see Figure 6.6a). This is necessary for providing the pilot with as much information as possible for orientation in the unknown environment. However, the camera images are not further used for the affordance detection system. In a second tab, the widget allows the configuration of the point cloud visualization setup (see Figure 6.6b). This is essential for the pilot as the processed point clouds that result from the intermediate steps of the perception pipeline carry valuable information which can in some cases support the pilot's understanding of the scene.

In the point cloud visualization setup widget, the pilot can enable, disable and configure the visualization of the point clouds generated in all pipeline steps. This includes the original captured point cloud, the globally transformed captured point cloud, the filtered (i. e. down-sampled) captured point cloud, the segmented point cloud and the final point cloud with geometric primitive labels. Some of these point clouds are labeled which is appropriately displayed by the visualization component.

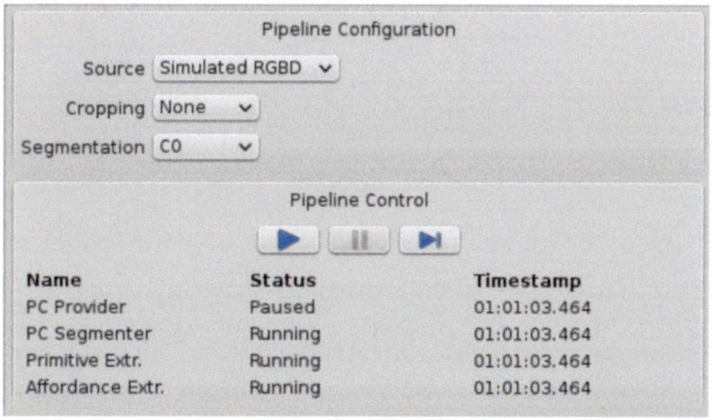

Figure 6.5: Pipeline control and status overview component of the pilot interface (Widget **A** in Figure 6.4).

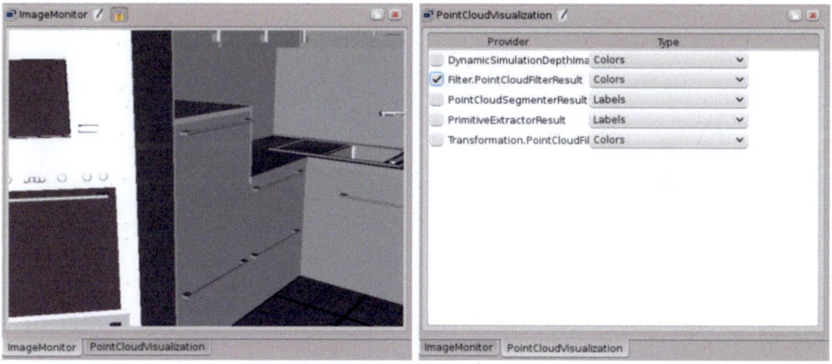

(a) (b)

Figure 6.6: Point cloud visualization setup and camera images (Widget **B** in Figure 6.4): (a) Simulated camera images in the exemplary kitchen environment (see Figure 6.3) and (b) widget for point cloud visualization setup.

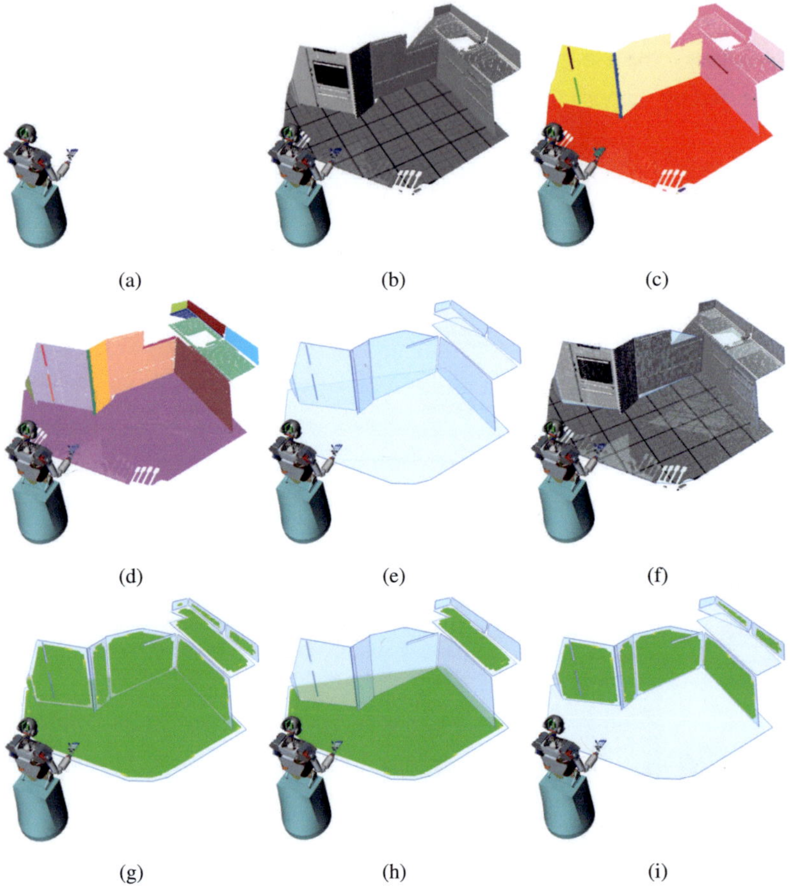

Figure 6.7: Different visualization configurations in the pilot interface (Widget **C** in Figure 6.4): (a) no visualization, (b) the captured point cloud, (c) the segmented point cloud, (d) extracted primitives as labeled point cloud, (e) extracted primitives as 3D shapes, (f) combined visualization of the captured point cloud and extracted primitives, (g) affordance belief function $\Theta_{\text{G-Platform}}$ for *platform graspability*, (h) affordance belief function Θ_{Support} for *supportability* and (i) affordance belief function Θ_{Lean} for *leanability*.

3D Visualization of the Robot Perception (C) The main component of the pilot interface is the 3D visualization of the robot perception. This includes the robot itself in its current configuration and everything the robot sensed and learned about its environment using the affordance detection and validation system. By using the widgets for point cloud visualization setup (**B**) and affordance selection (**D**), the pilot is able to efficiently tailor a custom visualization that conveniently displays the information needed to interpret the current robot environment. Figure 6.7 displays different visualization setups that can be configured in the pilot interface. The camera can be freely adjusted by the pilot in all visualization setups.

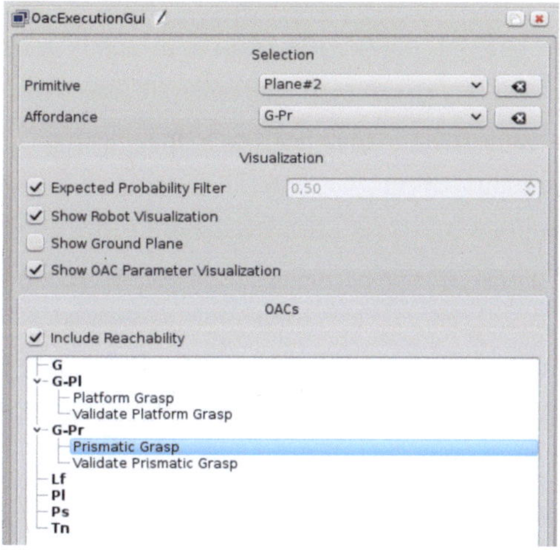

Figure 6.8: List of detected affordances and corresponding OACs (Widget **D** in Figure 6.4). In the depicted state, the OAC *Prismatic Grasp* is selected based on a detected *prismatic graspability* affordance (*G-Pr*) for a planar primitive (*Plane #2*). After selection, automatically proposed end-effector poses are visualized in the 3D scene allowing the pilot to review and adjust the OAC parameterization.

Affordances and OACs (D) The top right component of the pilot interface displays the detected affordances (see Figure 6.8). The pilot is able to select among the presented affordances in order to obtain a visualization of the corresponding affordance belief function. Furthermore, the pilot can interactively select a primitive in the 3D visualization and obtain a list of affordances that exist for the selected primitive. Depending on the detected affordances, the pilot interface automatically proposes related action execution strategies, i. e. OACs, from the robot's long-term memory. The pilot can select one of the proposed OACs and is then presented a visualization of its automatically determined parameterization, particularly the end-effector poses.

OAC Parameter Configuration and Execution (E) In the bottom-right corner of the pilot interface, the pilot is presented an automatically determined parameterization for the selected OAC (see Figure 6.9). Each OAC requires an individual set of input parameters that the pilot has to specify while the most elementary type of parameter is an end-effector pose. Predefined end-effector poses constrain the considered whole-body action in order to support subsequent automatic action planning. High-level task-related parameters cannot be determined based on affordance belief functions and have to be provided by the pilot. The evaluation of affordance belief functions generated by the affordance detection system produces a list of end-effector poses with assigned belief values. Further feasibility checks, such as reachability tests, are performed by the pilot interface in order to provide the pilot with a restricted set of good suggestions for end-effector poses.

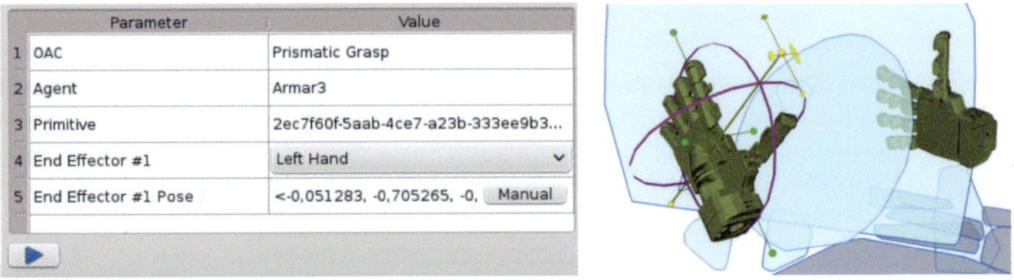

Figure 6.9: Widget for the display and configuration of OAC parameters (*left*, Widget **E** in Figure 6.4) and the adjustment of automatically proposed end-effector poses in the 3D visualization (*right*) (taken from Kaiser et al. 2016c, © 2016 IEEE).

The pilot selects an OAC and receives a visualization of the automatically proposed OAC parameterization which consists of either a single end-effector pose or two end-effector poses in case of a bimanual OAC. The pilot can manually adjust the end-effector poses in the 3D environment if the proposed parameterization is not sufficient (see Figure 6.9). The final step of the pilot workflow is the execution of the selected OAC. The pilot receives feedback on the progress of the OAC execution in terms of a simple status report (*in progress*, *success* or *failed*) and in terms of the robot's self perception during action execution.

6.3 Summary and Review

This chapter introduced and discussed concepts for affordance-based autonomy and affordance-based shared autonomy based on the coupling of the affordance detection system defined in Chapter 4 and Chapter 5 with the concept of OACs for action execution. OACs provide the necessary means for linking execution skills with symbolic planning domains needed for autonomous task and action planning.

The concept of affordance-based shared autonomy, which leverages the challenging tasks of task and action planning to a human pilot, is complemented by the implementation of an affordance-based pilot interface within the robot development environment ArmarX. The pilot interface allows the shared autonomous control of a humanoid robot based on detected geometric primitives and derived affordances. It can be applied to the control of a simulated robot as well as to the control of a real humanoid robot by using the layers of abstraction provided by ArmarX. In Chapter 7, the pilot interface will be a central component enabling affordance-related experiments on the real humanoid robots ARMAR-III and WALK-MAN.

7 Evaluation

The methods developed in this thesis are evaluated in several synthetic, simulated and real experiments which are presented and discussed in this chapter. Parts of the evaluation experiments and results have been published in Kaiser et al. (2015a,b, 2016a,c, 2018a,b). While the synthetic experiments introduced in Section 7.1 aim at the evaluation of the fundamental mechanisms of evidence fusion, the simulated and real experiments introduced in Section 7.2 and Section 7.3 aim at the evaluation of the affordance detection and validation system as a whole. In the following, the three classes of experiments are briefly introduced.

Synthetic Experiments The first set of experiments, which is presented and discussed in in Section 7.1, aims at the evaluation of affordance belief functions and the associated mechanisms for affordance-related evidence fusion as the fundamental building block of the affordance detection and validation system. The synthetic experiments are performed in artificial setups, in which joint affordance belief functions generated from the fusion of multiple observations are compared against randomly generated ground-truth affordances. The central question is if affordance belief functions composed of several iterative observations provide adequate means for accurately resembling available action possibilities.

Simulated Experiments After evaluating the formalism of affordance belief functions, two simulated experiments are presented and discussed in Section 7.2. The first experiment in Section 7.2.1 evaluates the affordance detection and validation system as a whole in a dynamic simulation environment. In the simulated experiment, the humanoid robot ARMAR-III is exposed to a kitchen environment, for which initial affordance belief is generated based on simulated visual perception. Subsequently the robot performs affordance validation experiments in order to validate the initial hypotheses, iteratively refining the belief about *prismatic graspability* affordances. In the second experiment in Section 7.2.2, the integration of the affordance detection system with an existing approach for whole-body pose sequence planning from Mandery et al. (2016) is briefly discussed and evaluated in order to demonstrate the feasibility of affordance-based multi-contact locomotion pose sequence planning for the humanoid robot ARMAR-4. The established link between affordance belief functions and whole-body pose sequence planning is an important prerequisite for affordance-based locomotion planning.

Real Experiments Section 7.3 discusses the results of multiple affordance detection and validation experiments on real humanoid robots in different scenarios. The validation of novel approaches on real hardware is important in robotics as it demonstrates the conceptual and computational feasibility of the approaches and their ability to handle inaccurate and noisy sensor data. Furthermore, the experimental validation of the proposed concepts on different robots is essential in order to demonstrate their generality and robot-agnosticism. The experiments have been conducted on the real humanoid robots ARMAR-III and WALK-MAN.

Performance Measurements Finally, after the different evaluation experiments are discussed, Section 7.4 presents the results of performance measurements of the different steps of the H^2T perception pipeline and the affordance detection system in several exemplary scenes.

7.1 Synthetic Experiments

This section presents the evaluation of the fundamental building block of the affordance detection and validation system: *affordance belief functions* and the associated principles of *evidence fusion* as introduced in Chapter 4. The evaluation experiments presented in this section are performed in synthetic setups based on randomized ground-truth affordances which are generated as described in Section 7.1.1. After introducing the evaluation methodology in Section 7.1.2, generated ground-truth affordances are employed in Section 7.1.3 for assessing the quality of affordance belief functions resulting from iterative evidence fusion of equidistant observations. In Section 7.1.4, a more realistic strategy is employed and evaluated, in which observation locations are determined based on a combined measure of uncertainty and conflict. In the interest of visualization, the spaces of end-effector positions and orientations are evaluated separately, both in 2D. Parts of this section are extended versions of the experimental evaluation published in Kaiser et al. (2018a).

7.1.1 Ground-Truth Affordances

Ground-truth affordances g determine the locations for which an hypothesized affordance exists. This information is used for generating observations and it is the implicit task of the evidence fusion mechanism to appropriately approximate the ground-truth affordance through iterative fusion of observations. While ground-truth affordances g and affordance belief functions Θ share the same definition space of end-effector poses, the image set of ground-truth affordances is binary, indicating the true existence of the hypothesized affordance or its absence. For positions, ground-truth affordances g_{pos} are defined over a planar, square primitive with side lengths of $[-1,1]$:

$$g_{\text{pos}} : [-1,1] \times [-1,1] \rightarrow \{0,1\}. \tag{7.1}$$

In the case of orientations, ground-truth affordances g_{rot} are defined over the 2D spherical coordinates[1] $\theta \in [0, \pi]$ and $\phi \in [0, 2\pi]$:

$$g_{\text{rot}} : [0, \pi] \times [0, 2\pi) \to \{0, 1\}. \tag{7.2}$$

Ground-truth affordances are generated as intersections of randomly sampled half-spaces[2] as outlined in Algorithm 2. The definition of ground-truth affordances as intersections of randomly generated half-spaces leads to convex affordance polygons in the ground-truth data. In order to avoid degenerated ground-truth affordances with very small areas of affordance existence or non-existence, generated ground-truth affordances are rejected if one of the two classes covers less than 20% of the definition space. In the following evaluation experiments, the positional and orientational definition spaces of affordance belief functions and ground-truth affordances are discretized into 200×200 grids and 100×200 grids, respectively. The maximum number of half-spaces to intersect was set to four. See Figure 7.1 for visualizations of multiple randomly generated ground-truth affordances for the space of end-effector positions.

7.1.2 Methodology

The synthetic evaluation experiments target the formalism of evidence fusion in affordance belief functions based on the principles of the Dempster-Shafer theory. The evidence fusion formalism as introduced in Section 4.3 provides

[1] Spherical coordinates represent points in the three-dimensional space by a triplet (r, θ, ϕ), containing the *radial distance* r from a given origin, the *polar angle* θ and the *azimuth angle* ϕ. In order to obtain unique coordinates, the angular components are constrained to $\theta \in [0, \pi]$ and $\phi \in [0, 2\pi)$, while other conventions exist. For representing 2D orientations from $SO(2)$, the value r is omitted in the above considerations, i. e. $r = 0$.

[2] A hyperplane splits an affine space into two *half-spaces*. In the case of the two-dimensional Euclidean space $\mathbb{R}^2$, a line $\boldsymbol{n} \cdot \boldsymbol{x} = c$ with normal $\boldsymbol{n} \in \mathbb{R}^2$ and distance $c \in \mathbb{R}$ to the origin splits the space into the half-spaces $H_1 = \{\boldsymbol{x} \in \mathbb{R}^2 \mid \boldsymbol{n} \cdot \boldsymbol{x} \leq c\}$ and $H_2 = \{\boldsymbol{x} \in \mathbb{R}^2 \mid \boldsymbol{n} \cdot \boldsymbol{x} > c\}$.

the means for consistent fusion of affordance-related observations. The primary question which is investigated in this evaluation experiment is:

> *Does the proposed formalism allow the consistent combination of affordance-related evidence into joint affordance belief functions which approximate randomly generated ground-truth affordances?*

In the evaluation experiments, K observations $\omega_1, \ldots, \omega_K$ are selected from a randomly generated ground-truth affordance g. Two strategies for observation location selection are employed in the evaluation experiments: observation location selection based on an equidistant grid (Section 7.1.3) and observation location selection based on a combined measure of uncertainty and conflict (Section 7.1.4). In either of the cases, the formalism for evidence fusion based on spatially generalized observations (see Section 4.3) is employed for deriving a joint affordance belief function $b = \omega_1 \oplus \cdots \oplus \omega_K$.

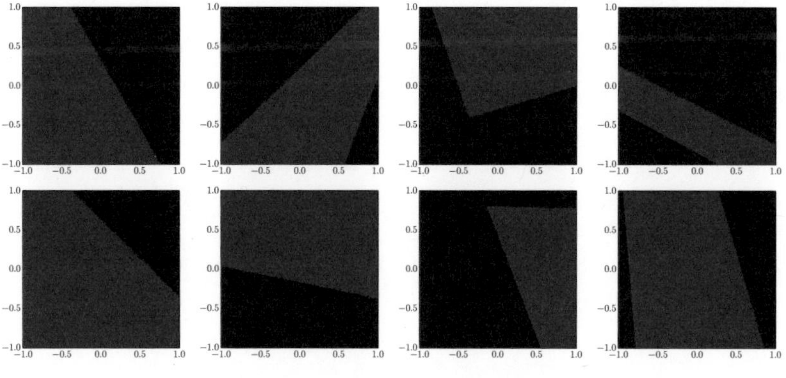

Figure 7.1: Examples for randomized ground-truth affordances for 2D end-effector positions on a planar square primitive. Green areas indicate the existence of the affordance, while red areas indicate the absence of the affordance.

For comparing Dempster-Shafer-valued joint belief functions b (i. e. $b(\boldsymbol{x}) \in \mathcal{D}$) with binary ground-truth affordances g (i. e. $g(\boldsymbol{x}) \in \{0,1\}$), the belief functions are binarized by applying a threshold of $\frac{1}{2}$ to the *expected probability* E_a (see Equation 4.15).

Algorithm 2 Randomized Ground-Truth Affordance Generation

Require:
$D \subset \mathbb{R}^2$ – Discretized definition space
maxHalfSpaces – Maximum number of half-spaces

function GENERATEGROUNDTRUTHAFFORDANCE(D, *maxHalfSpaces*)
  while True **do**
    $g \leftarrow$ Empty map
    for $\boldsymbol{x} \in D$ **do**
      $g_{\boldsymbol{x}} \leftarrow 1$
    end for
    $N \leftarrow$ uniformChoice($\{1, \ldots, maxHalfSpaces\}$)
    for $i \in 1, \ldots, N$ **do**
      $\boldsymbol{r} \leftarrow$ uniformChoice(D)
      $s \leftarrow$ uniformChoice($\{0, 1\}$)
      $\boldsymbol{n} \leftarrow \frac{1}{\|\boldsymbol{r}\|}\boldsymbol{r}$
      $c \leftarrow \|\boldsymbol{r}\|$
      for $\boldsymbol{x} \in D$ **do**
        $$g_{\boldsymbol{x}} \leftarrow g_{\boldsymbol{x}} \wedge \begin{cases} s, & \text{if } \boldsymbol{n} \cdot \boldsymbol{x} \leq c. \\ 1 - s, & \text{otherwise.} \end{cases}$$
      end for
    end for
    $\alpha^+ \leftarrow \frac{|\{\boldsymbol{x} \in D \mid g_{\boldsymbol{x}} = 1\}|}{|D|}$
    $\alpha^- \leftarrow \frac{|\{\boldsymbol{x} \in D \mid g_{\boldsymbol{x}} = 0\}|}{|D|}$
    if $\alpha^+ \geq 0.2$ **and** $\alpha^- \geq 0.2$ **then**
      return g
    end if
  end while
end function

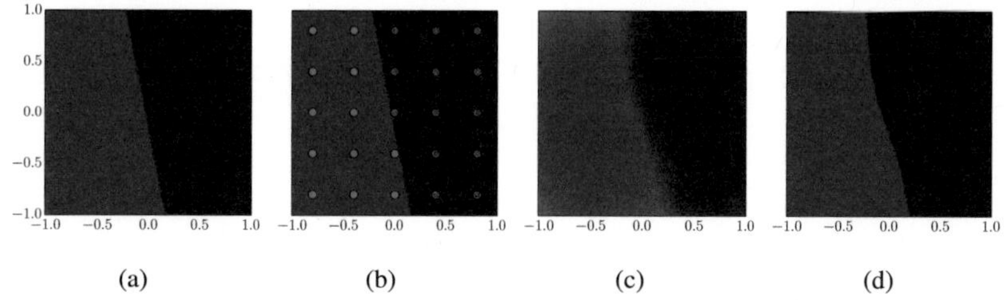

Figure 7.2: A joint affordance belief function generated from a set of 25 observations: *(a)* ground-truth affordance, *(b)* observations, *(c)* joint affordance belief function and *(d)* binarized joint affordance belief function. The joint affordance belief function receives an F_1 score of 0.98. See Figure 4.4 for further details on the visualization method.

The conversion to a binary decision function is necessary in order to comply with the formal definitions in Chapter 4.

$$[b]_a(\boldsymbol{x}) = \begin{cases} a^+, \text{ if } E_a\big(b(\boldsymbol{x}, a^+)\big) \geq \frac{1}{2} \\ a^-, \text{ otherwise.} \end{cases} \tag{7.3}$$

The index a in the above equation refers to the affordance which is represented by the ground-truth affordance g. In the interest of simplicity, $[b]_a$ and $[g]_a$ are abbreviated as b and g, implicitly referring to binarized belief function related to the hypothesized affordance a given in the evaluation scenario. To quantify the degree of similarity between b and g, the evaluation experiments employ the *macro-averaged F_1-measure* (Sokolova et al. 2009):

$$F_1(b,g) = \frac{\text{Precision}(b,g) \cdot \text{Recall}(b,g)}{\text{Precision}(b,g) + \text{Recall}(b,g)}, \tag{7.4}$$

with

$$\text{Precision}(b,g) = \frac{1}{2}\left(\frac{\text{TP}_{b,g,a^+}}{\text{TP}_{b,g,a^+} + \text{FP}_{b,g,a^+}} + \frac{\text{TP}_{b,g,a^-}}{\text{TP}_{b,g,a^-} + \text{FP}_{b,g,a^-}}\right), \tag{7.5}$$

and

$$\mathrm{Recall}(b,g) = \frac{1}{2}\left(\frac{\mathrm{TP}_{b,g,a^+}}{\mathrm{TP}_{b,g,a^+} + \mathrm{FN}_{b,g,a^+}} + \frac{\mathrm{TP}_{b,g,a^-}}{\mathrm{TP}_{b,g,a^-} + \mathrm{FN}_{b,g,a^-}}\right), \quad (7.6)$$

where $\mathrm{TP}_{b,g,a^\pm}$, $\mathrm{FP}_{b,g,a^\pm}$ and $\mathrm{FN}_{b,g,a^\pm}$ refer to the amount of *true positives*, *false positives* and *false negatives* in the discretized belief functions with respect to the existence statement $a^\pm$.

7.1.3 Evidence Fusion with Equidistant Observations

In this evaluation experiment, observations are sampled on an equidistant grid in the definition space $[-1,1] \times [-1,1]$ of affordance belief functions (see Equation 7.1). Figure 7.2 shows an example for a set of 25 observations generated from a ground-truth affordance over the space of 2D end-effector positions and the resulting joint affordance belief function. The results in Figure 7.3 show the averaged F_1-score (Equation 7.4) together with the averaged conflict $\Theta_a(\boldsymbol{x},a^+) \cdot \Theta_a(\boldsymbol{x},a^-)$ and the averaged uncertainty $\Theta_a(\boldsymbol{x},\mathcal{X}_a)$ over the numbers of generated observations. Section 4.3.2 introduces the concept of spatial generalization of selective observations by means of a Gaussian distribution in the positional space and a von Mises-Fisher distribution in the orientational space. As the standard deviation σ of the employed distribution has an influence on the evidence fusion, Figure 7.3 contains multiple plots for different values of σ. The results suggest that the formalism for evidence fusion in affordance belief functions based on selective observations as proposed in Section 4.3.2 can produce joint affordance belief functions that accurately represent the hypothesized ground-truth affordance. For small standard deviations $\sigma \in \{0.05, 0.1\}$, observations have little spatial influence and hence, the overall degree of conflict is low while a high degree of uncertainty remains. Larger standard deviations show better performance in spatial generalization of observations by reducing the degree of uncertainty while at the same time moderately increasing conflict. Too large standard deviations ($\sigma = 0.8$) show poor approximation behavior with F_1-scores lower than 0.8.

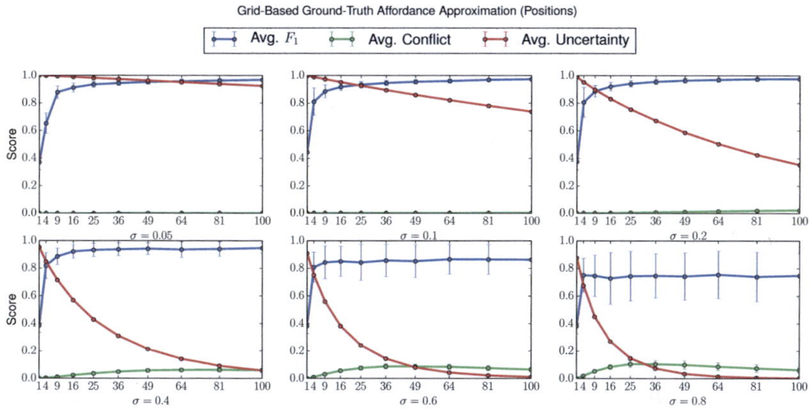

Figure 7.3: Average F_1-scores of joint affordance belief functions resulting from the fusion of 1, 4, 16, 25, 36, 49, 64, 81 and 100 grid-aligned observations (x-axes) in a 2D position space for different standard deviations σ which model the spatial extension of observations. Each result has been averaged over 400 randomly generated ground-truth affordances (see Algorithm 2).

The results suggest that the choice of σ modeling the spatial extension of observations is a trade-off between ground-truth approximation and spatial generalization. Obviously, the choice of the parameter σ depends on the intended density of validation experiments. Further experiments have shown that changes in the observation certainty η (see Section 4.3.2) do not have a significant impact on the approximation behavior.

7.1.4 Uncertainty and Conflict for Observation Location Selection

The evaluation experiment discussed in the previous section demonstrates that the mechanisms of evidence fusion proposed in Section 4.3 provide the means for accurately approximating ground-truth affordances based on the fusion of observations. However, in the experiment, the observation locations are sampled on a uniform grid in the 2D end-effector position space which is not suitable for practical affordance validation experiments. In real applications, the next observation location needs to be determined based on the existing belief state, i. e. validation experiments should be performed for end-effector poses for which the belief state exhibits either a high degree uncertainty or a high degree of conflict. In this section, a measure $C_a(\boldsymbol{x})$ is proposed and employed for observation location selection which solely considers uncertainty and conflict:

$$C_a(\boldsymbol{x}) = \underbrace{\Theta_a(\boldsymbol{x}, \mathcal{X}_a)}_{\text{Uncertainty}} + \underbrace{\Theta_a(\boldsymbol{x}, a^+) \cdot \Theta_a(\boldsymbol{x}, a^-)}_{\text{Conflict}}. \tag{7.7}$$

The algorithm for sampling observation locations evaluates this measure for all end-effector poses $\boldsymbol{x}$ and randomly selects a pose $\boldsymbol{x}_{\text{obs}}$ among the subset of the 25% highest-ranked poses $\boldsymbol{x}$ based on the corresponding values of $C_a(\boldsymbol{x})$. The observation sampling strategy outlined in Algorithm 3 is defined in a way that uncertainty and conflict are appropriately considered while maintaining a certain degree of randomness in the observation location selection. However, it is not claimed that Algorithm 3 implements an optimal strategy. Figure 7.4 shows a set of exemplary ground-truth affordances with different numbers of observations sampled using Algorithm 3 together with the resulting joint affordance belief function in its original and binarized form.

Evidence Fusion for End-Effector Positions Figure 7.5 shows averaged F_1 scores of joint affordance belief functions for end-effector positions over increasing numbers of generated observations. The results indicate that affordance belief functions are able to resemble ground-truth affordances by fusing spatially distributed observations ω with decent accuracy.

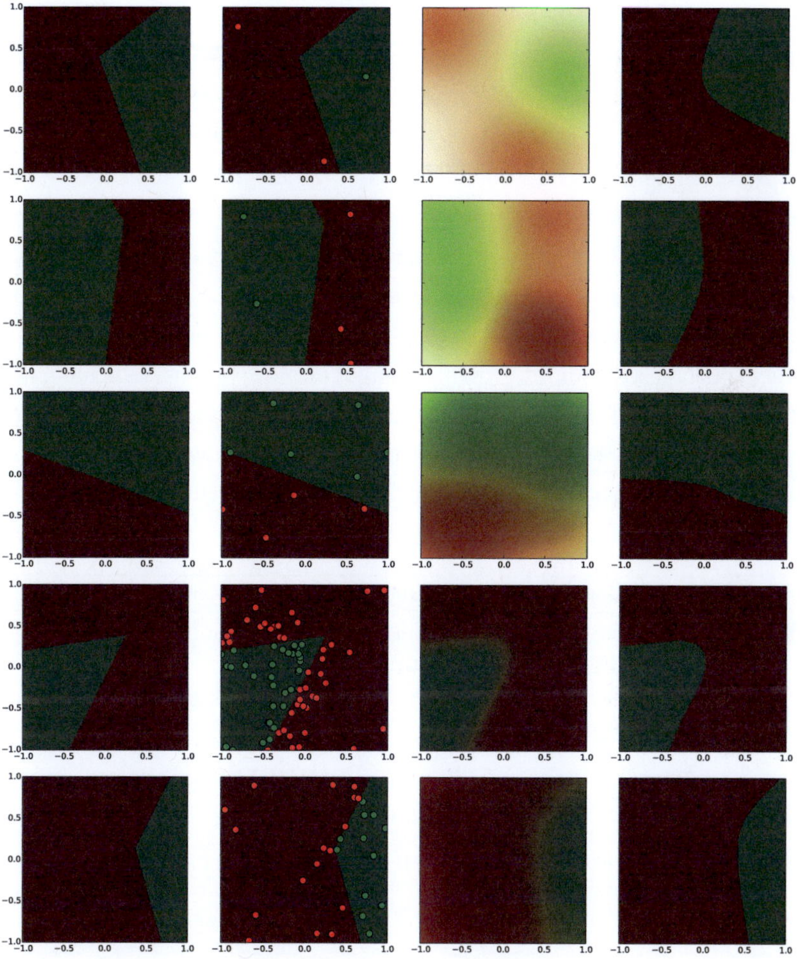

Figure 7.4: Evaluation of evidence fusion in affordance belief functions based on varying numbers of generated observations. *First column:* ground-truth affordances, *second column:* observations, *third column:* joint affordance belief functions and *fourth column:* binarized joint affordance belief functions. From top to bottom the examples receive the F_1 scores 0.84, 0.88, 0.95, 0.93 and 0.96. Joint affordance belief functions composed from fewer observations (top rows) are visualized in lighter colors, because they include higher degrees of uncertainty as joint affordance belief functions composed from large numbers of observations (bottom rows). See Figure 4.4 for further details on the visualization method.

In the experiments, an F_1 score greater than 0.8 was obtained from few observations. Although small numbers of observations do not provide enough information for an exact reconstruction of the ground-truth affordance, the evaluation shows that higher accuracy can be obtained by the fusion of more observations. The visualizations in Figure 7.4 as well as the system evaluation in Section 7.2.1 further suggest that moderate accuracy is sufficient for the purpose of whole-body affordance detection. This is particularly true as extensive observations such as visual affordance detection provide prior belief in real applications. The results show that the average uncertainty $\Theta(\mathcal{X}_a)$ decreases with the growing number of observations, indicating that the system belief converges against a state of high certainty. Further, the average conflict $\Theta(a^+) \cdot \Theta(a^-)$ moderately increases with the number of observations which is expected as the fusion of contradicting evidence causes conflict.

Algorithm 3 Generation of Validation Observation Locations

Require:
- b – Joint affordance belief function
- g – Ground-truth affordance
- S – End-effector pose space

1: **function** GENERATEOBSERVATIONLOCATION(b, g, S)
2: $\quad \Xi \leftarrow \text{sortDescending}\left((\boldsymbol{x})_{\boldsymbol{x} \in S}, \text{ key} = C_a\right)$
3: $\quad i \leftarrow \text{uniformChoice}\left(\left\{0, \dots, \lceil 0.25 \cdot |\Xi_{\text{sorted}}| \rceil\right\}\right)$
4: $\quad$ **return** Ξ_i
5: **end function**

Evidence Fusion for End-Effector Orientations A similar evaluation procedure demonstrates the effectiveness of evidence fusion in the orientational components of end-effector poses. An exemplary evaluation has been performed in the space of 2D end-effector poses $SO(2)$, employing the von Mises-Fisher distribution as explained in Section 4.3. Ground-truth affordance belief functions are randomly generated using the method outlined in Algorithm 2 and exemplarily visualized in Figure 7.6, while using the space of 2D spherical coordinates $(\theta, \phi) \in [0, \pi] \times [0, 2\pi)$ as a basis.

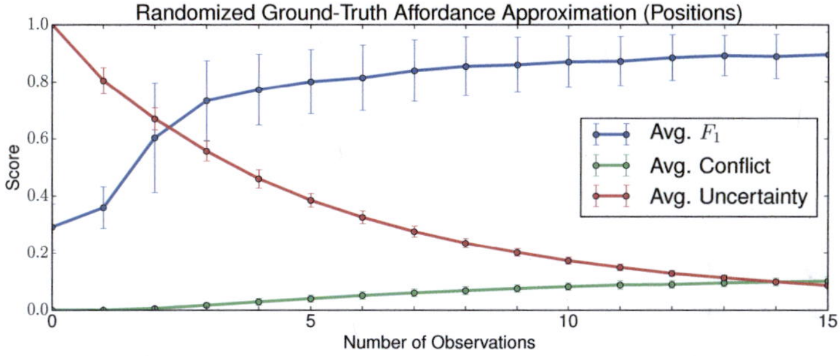

Figure 7.5: F_1-scores of joint affordance belief functions resulting from the fusion of up to 15 observations (x-axis) in a 2D position space, each averaged over 400 randomized runs (taken from Kaiser et al. 2018a, © 2018 IEEE).

Figure 7.7 shows averaged F_1 scores of the obtained joint belief functions for end-effector orientations over increasing numbers of observations. The results for the 2D orientation space are similar to those for the 2D position space shown in Figure 7.5. The results overall suggest that the iterative fusion of observations is a suitable approach for approximating ground-truth affordance belief functions. While the number of observations is not sufficient for an exact approximation, the results indicate that few observations together with prior belief from visual affordance detection can produce accurate belief about affordances.

7.2 Simulated Experiments

In this section, the proposed affordance detection and validation system is evaluated in simulated environments. The focus of experiments in this section lies on the evaluation of the system as a whole rather than the evaluation of individual system components as in the previous section.

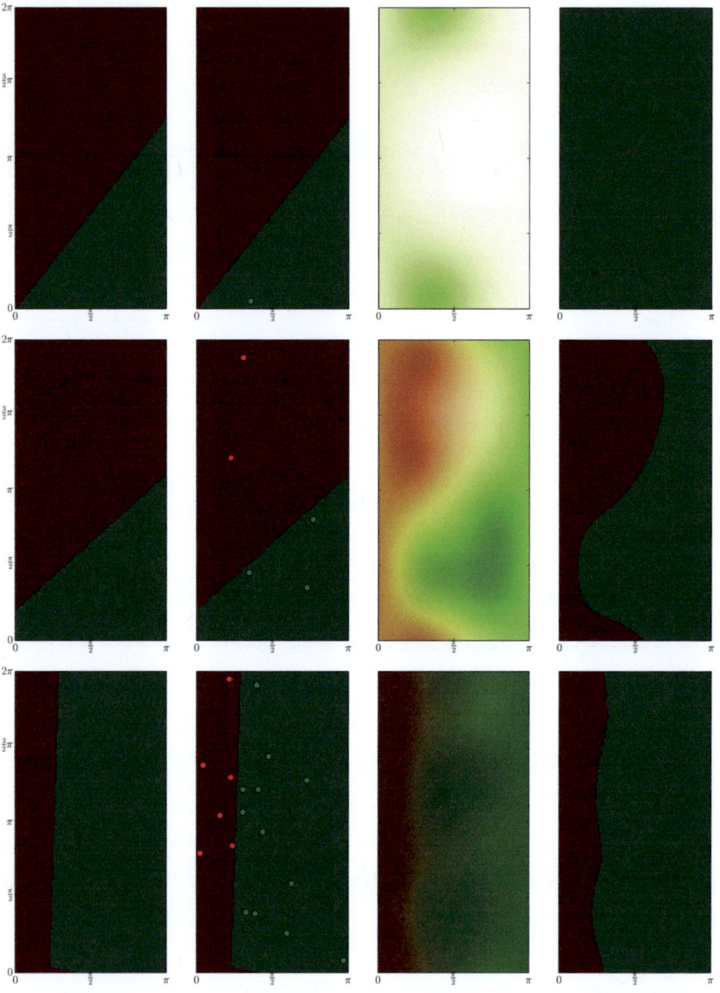

Figure 7.6: Examples for evidence fusion in affordance belief functions defined over the space $SO(2)$ of 2D orientations based on varying numbers of generated observations. *First column:* ground-truth affordances, *second column:* observations, *third column:* joint affordance belief functions and *fourth column:* binarized joint affordance belief functions. From top to bottom the shown examples receive the F_1 scores 0.24, 0.66 and 0.97.

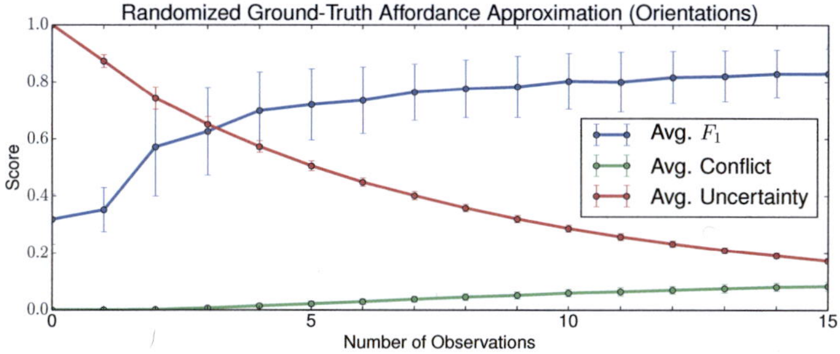

Figure 7.7: F_1-scores of joint affordance belief functions resulting from the fusion of up to 15 observations (x-axis) in a 2D orientation space, each averaged over 400 randomized runs (taken from Kaiser et al. 2018a, © 2018 IEEE).

In the following, two evaluation experiments are introduced and discussed concerning the detection and validation of *prismatic graspability* affordances with ARMAR-III in a dynamic simulation environment (Section 7.2.1) and the detection of *supportability* affordances for whole-body multi-contact pose sequence planning with ARMAR-4 in a kinematic simulation environment (Section 7.2.2).

7.2.1 Evaluation of Autonomous Affordance Detection and Validation

The principles of autonomous affordance detection and validation are evaluated using the simulated humanoid robot ARMAR-III in a sophisticated dynamic simulation environment. Evaluating the system performance in realistic applications, even when simulated environments are considered, is difficult as humanoid robotic systems are complex combinations of orthogonal, but critical subsystems. The responsibilities of these subsystems range from sensor perception and motion control to high-level planning, each of which being active research areas in the humanoid robotics community. With the intention of reducing the influence of error-prone subsystems, ARMAR-III was chosen as a passively stable platform-based humanoid robot (see Figure 1.3). In this section, the affordance detection and validation system is evaluated in the dynamic simulation of a kitchen environment using ARMAR-III.

Large portions of whole-body actions, particularly in the context of loco-manipulation tasks, require legged humanoid systems and hence exceed the capabilities of ARMAR-III. This section is an extended versions of the experimental evaluation published in Kaiser et al. (2018a). However, the focus of this evaluation lies in the visual perception and interactive validation of affordances which can be found in a kitchen environment. Figure 7.8 shows the dynamic simulation of the H^2T robot kitchen. In this simulation environment, all doors and drawers can be manipulated by the robot and simulated sensor feedback, e. g. from force-torque sensors, is available. Furthermore, simulated RGB and RGB-D camera images are generated and used as input for the H^2T perception pipeline introduced in Section 3.1.

Figure 7.8: ARMAR-III in a dynamic simulation of a kitchen environment. The simulated kitchen contains 37 joints which can be operated by the robot, e. g. the fridge door or the kitchen drawers.

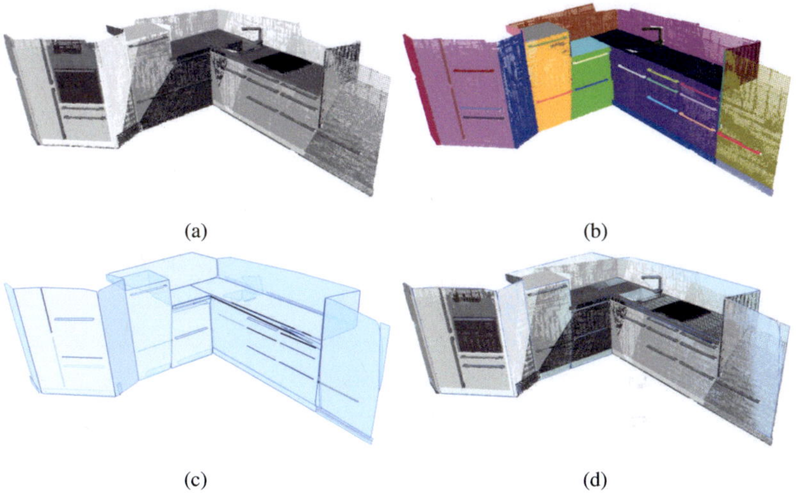

Figure 7.9: Extraction of geometric primitives in a kitchen environment: *(a)* a part of the simulated point cloud of the kitchen environment, *(b)* the manually created segmentation, *(c)* geometric primitives extracted from the segmented point cloud and *(d)* a combined view of extracted primitives with the original point cloud.

Experimental Setup and Results In this evaluation scenario, the affordance detection and validation system is evaluated in a dynamic simulation environment using the humanoid robot ARMAR-III. In the evaluation scenario, visual scene perception is simulated by passing a segmented point cloud of the kitchen environment to the H^2T perception pipeline which subsequently extracts geometric primitives and then evaluates the affordance hierarchy. Figure 7.9 visualizes the extraction of geometric primitives from the simulated kitchen point cloud based on a manually created segmentation. In Figure 7.10, the following affordance belief functions are visualized for the full kitchen environment:

- $\Theta_{\text{G-Prismatic}}$ for *prismatic graspability* (Figure 7.10c);
- $\Theta_{\text{G-Platform}}$ for *platform graspability* (Figure 7.10d);

- Θ_{Lean} for *leanability* (Figure 7.10e);
- Θ_{Support} for *supportability* (Figure 7.10f);
- Θ_{Push} for *pushability* (Figure 7.10g);
- Θ_{Pull} for *pullability* (Figure 7.10h).

Based on the visualization of $\Theta_{\text{G-Prismatic}}$ in Figure 7.10c, it can be seen that the affordance detection system assigns high belief for *prismatic graspability* to primitive edges. While this includes important elements of interaction in the kitchen, particularly the available handles, it can be seen that other areas of high belief are false positives. These end-effector poses will largely be rejected during validation experiments. This particularly applies to primitive edges which are unreachable for the robot, e. g. very low primitives, but also to connecting edges between primitives. The H^2T perception pipeline has no information about inter-primitive relations and can therefore not properly distinguish between graspable primitive edges and corners. While the robot's ability to grasp such corners is debatable, *prismatic graspability* is largely rejected for these cases during interactive affordance validation.

The affordance belief function $\Theta_{\text{G-Platform}}$ for *platform graspability* indicates predominant applicability to the inner areas of large planar primitives, making it complementary to *prismatic graspability*. Another pair of complementary affordance belief functions is *leanability* Θ_{Lean}, indicating applicability to vertical planar primitives, and *supportability* Θ_{Support}, indicating applicability to horizontal planar primitives. The visualization of *pullability* Θ_{Pull} and *pushability* Θ_{Push} shows that the affordance detection system successfully identifies the kitchen handles as interesting areas for interaction.

In the evaluation experiment, the robot generates the affordance belief function $\Theta_{\text{G-Prismatic}}$ for *prismatic graspability*, leading to the initial belief shown in Figure 7.10c. The robot then successively selects end-effector poses based on a combined measure of uncertainty and conflict (see Equation 7.7) and executes affordance-specific validation actions.

(a) Point cloud

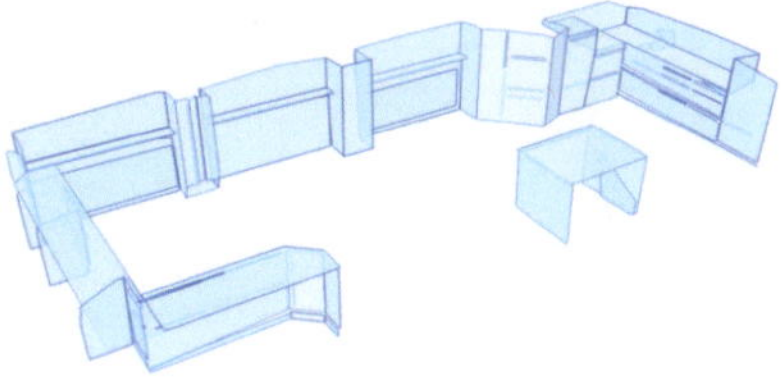

(b) Geometric primitives

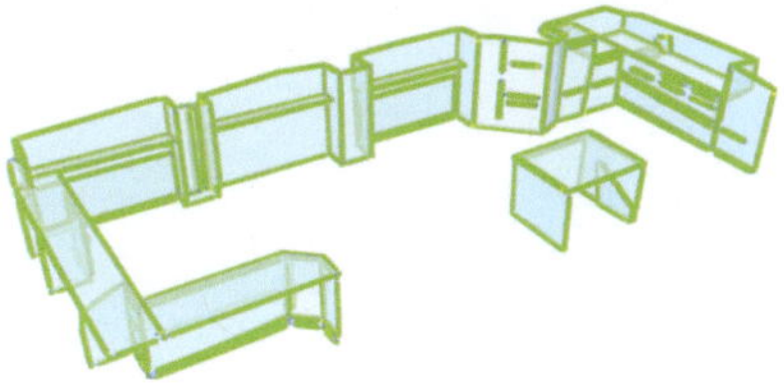

(c) $\Theta_{\text{G-Prismatic}}$

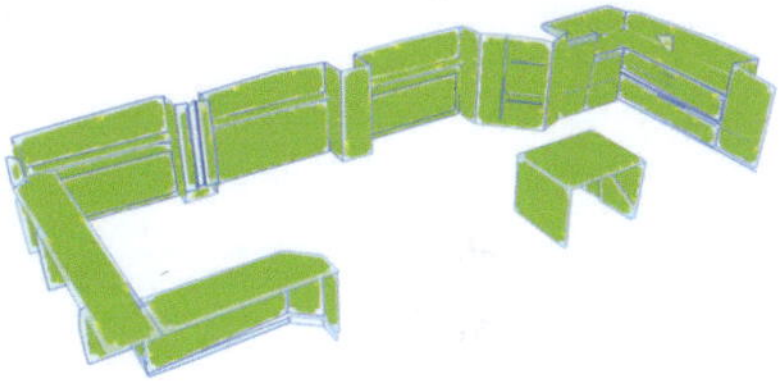

(d) $\Theta_{\text{G-Platform}}$

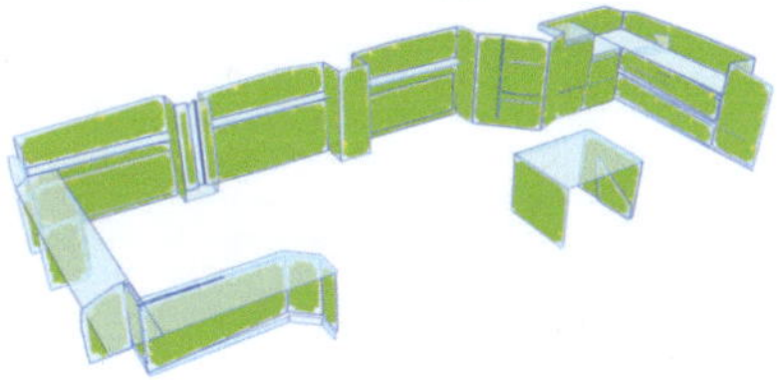

(e) Θ_{Lean}

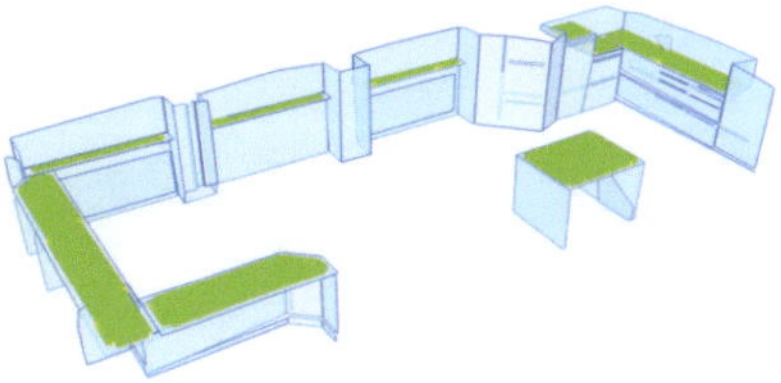

(f) Θ_{Support}

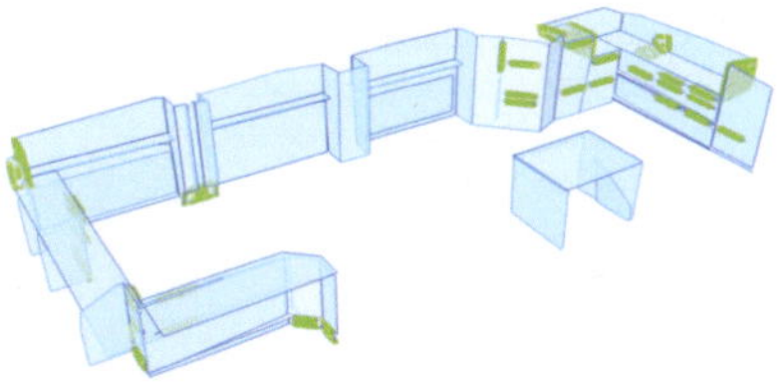

(g) Θ_{Push}

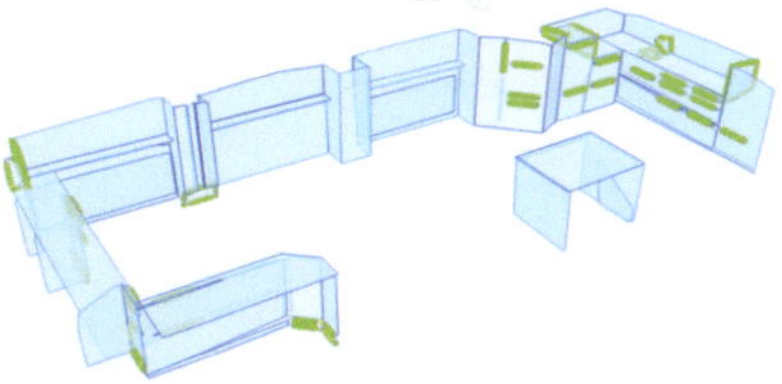

(h) Θ_{Pull}

Figure 7.10: Visualization of different affordance belief functions in the simulated kitchen environment according to the visualization scheme introduced in Figure 4.4. In the interest of a clear visualization, end-effector poses $\boldsymbol{x} \in SE(3)$ with expected probability $E(\Theta_*(\boldsymbol{x})) < 0.5$ are omitted.

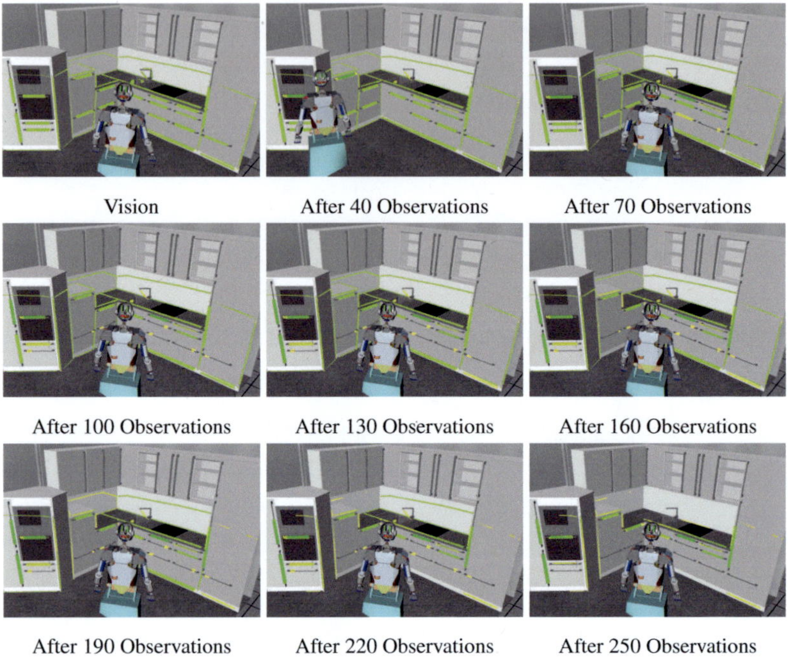

Figure 7.11: Visualization of the affordance belief function $\Theta_{\text{G-Prismatic}}$ for *prismatic graspability* in different stages of the evaluation (adapted from Kaiser et al. 2018a, © 2018 IEEE). Validation experiments predominantly reduce the amount of false positives, e. g. the handles of low drawers which are unreachable for the robot. Belief in *prismatic graspability* increases, e. g. for the vertical cupboard handles on the left side, if validation experiments succeed. Affordance belief functions are visualized according to the color scheme shown in Figure 4.4.

The results of executed validation actions are used as additional observations ω for evidence fusion. The evaluation is performed for *prismatic graspability* affordances, while the resulting joint affordance belief functions are compared to a manually created ground-truth.
The results depicted in Figure 7.11 and Figure 7.12 show that the degree of uncertainty in the affordance belief functions decreases with the number of observations. The results further demonstrate that the robot can gradually improve the initial belief from visual affordance detection which is

already relatively accurate ($F_1 > 0.6$), by performing consecutive affordance validation experiments. It needs to be noted that, although affordance validation is an important aspect of the affordance detection and validation system, validation experiments are expensive. Hence, the excessive amount of validation experiments carried out in this evaluation scenario, although providing a suitable validation of the evidence fusion formalism, does not qualify as a general strategy for affordance-based autonomy. In real applications, autonomous and shared autonomous humanoid robots are intended to perform individual validation experiments in cases of high risk or uncertainty, possibly demanded by a human pilot.

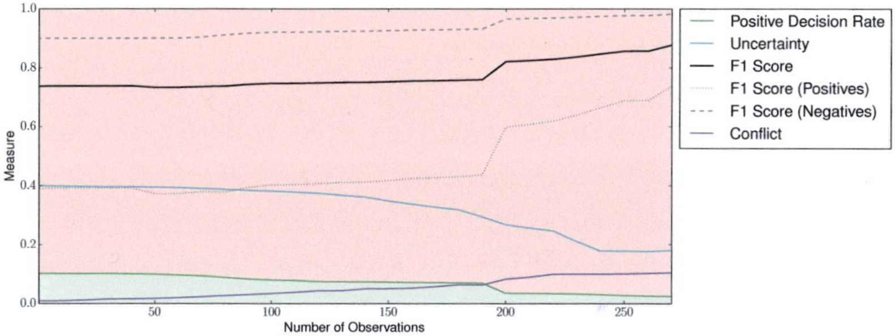

Figure 7.12: Validation of visually detected *prismatic graspability* affordances through consecutive validation experiments in a simulated kitchen environment (adapted from Kaiser et al. 2018a, © 2018 IEEE).

7.2.2 Affordance-Based Planning of Whole-Body Multi-Contact Pose Sequences

While the formalization of the affordance concept proposed in Chapter 4 is able to represent various types of affordances, the subsequently introduced affordance hierarchy described in Chapter 5 aims at the representation of whole-body affordances. Section 7.2.1 discussed a simulated experiment that evaluates the mechanisms of interactive affordance validation and evidence fusion. While the whole-body affordance hierarchy is used in the experiment, its intended focus on *loco-manipulation actions* is neglected. In this section, the whole-body multi-contact pose sequence planner from Mandery et al. (2015a, 2016) is extended in order to generate pose sequences based on affordance belief functions obtained in unknown environments. An extended version of this section is found in Kaiser et al. (2018b), where the experiment and the underlying conceptual foundations are explained. The employed multi-contact pose sequence planner uses n-gram language models learned from human observation to describe support pose transitions. The employed human motion demonstrations are taken from the large-scale *KIT Human Motion Database*[3] (Mandery et al. 2015b). It has previously been evaluated in known environments with predefined contact opportunities (Mandery et al. 2015a, 2016).

The proposed combination of whole-body affordance detection and pose sequence planning is evaluated based on a set of four exemplary hallway scenarios with different arrangements of tables (see Figure 7.13). The tables provide opportunities for supporting hand contacts along a defined locomotion path. The scenes, which are assumed to be entirely unknown to the robot, are represented as registered point clouds captured using an *ASUS Xtion Pro* sensor. In this evaluation scenario, the proposed approach is employed to plan pose sequences for walking with supporting end-effector contacts for the humanoid robot ARMAR-4. Figure 7.13 also shows the geometric primitives extracted from the scenes. All considered examples define the target locomotion trajectory as a straight path along the hallway. The trajectories are chosen such that sequences of contact and non-contact phases with the same end-effector (Scenario 1a and Scenario 2), unreachable contact opportunities (Scenario 1b), as well as sequences of simultaneous or alternating contact phases with both end-effectors (Scenario 3 and Scenario 4) are considered. In all evaluation scenarios, the locomotion is defined to start and stop in a neutral double-foot support pose.

[3] `https://motion-database.humanoids.kit.edu`

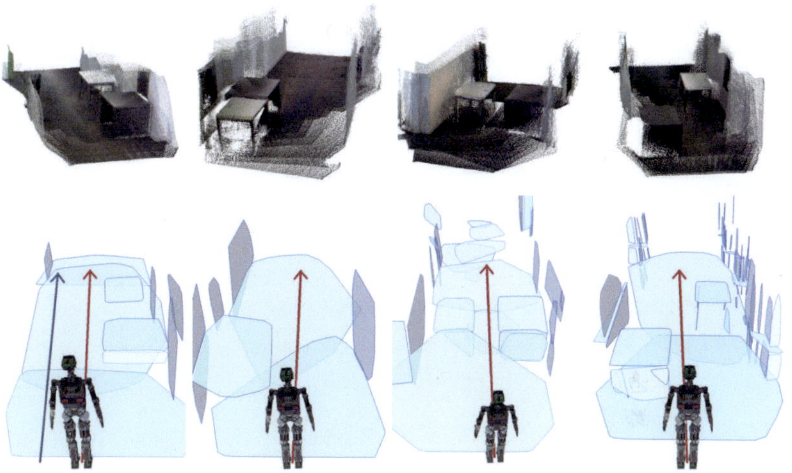

Scenario 1a/1b Scenario 2 Scenario 3 Scenario 4

Figure 7.13: *Top row:* Four evaluation scenarios for walking with support contact opportunities composed from different arrangements of tables in a hallway. The scenes are represented as registered point clouds. *Bottom row:* Visualization of geometric primitives obtained from the evaluation scenarios and the defined straight locomotion trajectories (taken from Kaiser et al. 2018b, © 2018 IEEE).

For model training, the dataset from Mandery et al. (2016) is used, consisting of 137 human motion recordings from the *KIT Whole-Body Human Motion Database*[4] (Mandery et al. 2015b). These recordings represent walking motions, in which different *supportability* affordances from handrails and tables have been used during motion demonstrations. The employed dataset is symmetric with respect to left and right hand supports. The multi-contact pose sequence planner employs a penalty term for missed contact opportunities in order to maximize contact utilization in generated solution paths.

[4] The motions can be found at `https://motion-database.humanoids.kit.edu/details/motions/<ID>` with ID $\in \{395, 396, 677, 678, 679, 681, 705, 724\}$.

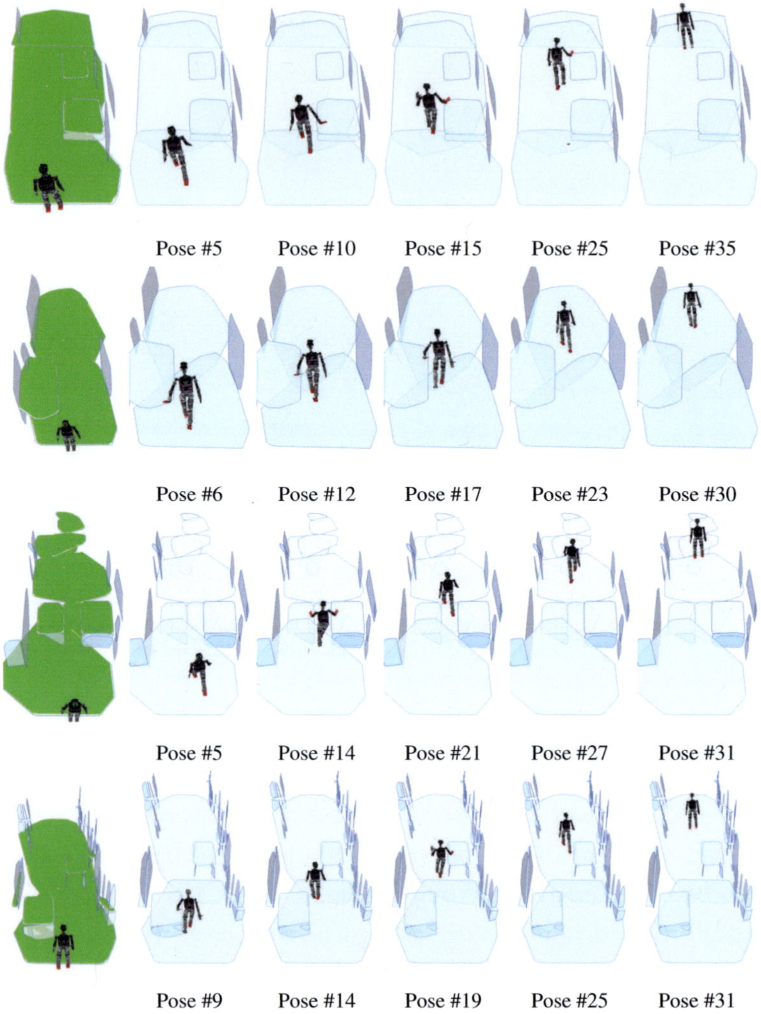

Figure 7.14: Solution paths for the humanoid robot ARMAR-4 in the evaluation scenarios 1a (*first row*), 2 (*second row*), 3 (*third row*) and 4 (*fourth row*) (taken from Kaiser et al. 2018b, © 2018 IEEE). See Figure 7.13 for descriptions of the scenario setups. The affordance belief function Θ_{Support} is visualized in the leftmost pictures in which support contact opportunities are highlighted in green color. Note that the presented solutions are sequences of whole-body poses with end-effector contact information and do not represent motion trajectories.

The proposed affordance-based pose sequence planner is able to successfully find pose sequences for ARMAR-4 with appropriate utilization of environmental support opportunities in all evaluated scenarios. The solution pose sequences generated for the evaluation scenarios 1a, 2, 3 and 4 are visualized in Figure 7.14, where selected intermediate robot poses are depicted with end-effector contact indicated by red highlighting. The detected *supportability* affordance belief functions are visualized as green areas in the respective first pictures. The examples demonstrate that the affordance-based pose sequence planner is able to produce meaningful multi-contact poses for crucial points in a desired whole-body locomotion trajectory which can be used for subdividing the subsequent problem of whole-body motion planning into multiple computationally feasible subproblems.

7.3 Real Experiments

While the results of the synthetic and simulated evaluation experiments presented in the previous sections suggest that the affordance system can be successfully deployed on autonomous and shared autonomous humanoid robots in various scenarios, the applicability to real robots still needs to be demonstrated as the differences between *simulation* and *reality* can be enormous. In this section, the affordance detection and validation system is evaluated on different humanoid robots in different realistic scenarios. This includes the detection of bimanual affordances for valve-turning with ARMAR-III (Section 7.3.1), the detection and validation of *pushability* and *liftability* affordances for path clearance with ARMAR-III (Section 7.3.2) and the execution of object-removal and valve-turning actions using the affordance-based pilot interface for shared autonomous control with WALK-MAN (Section 7.3.3).

7.3.1 Experiment I: Bimanual Valve-Turning

In the first experiment, the humanoid robot ARMAR-III is confronted with a DRC-inspired experimental setup of valve-turning. Turning an industrial valve has been defined as one of the challenges in the DRC and has therefore evolved into a popular scenario for testing humanoid robotic skills in perception and action execution. This section is an extended version of the experimental evaluation published in Kaiser et al. (2016a). The experimental setup is depicted in Figure 7.15.

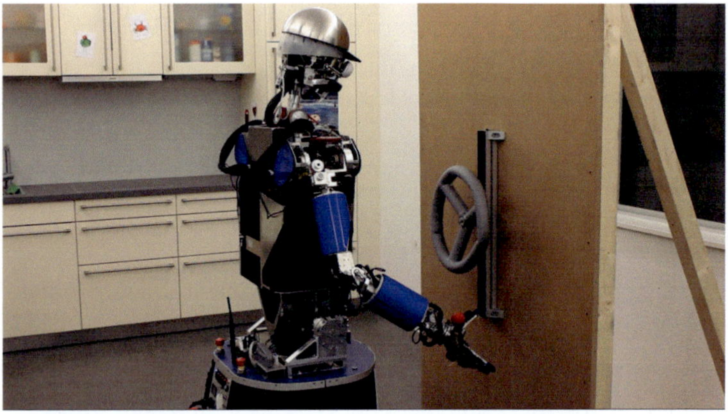

Figure 7.15: The experiment of *valve-turning* using the humanoid robot ARMAR-III. The robot is requested to autonomously perceive the unknown environment and to detect available affordances in the constructed environmental model. Affordance candidates for *bimanual turning* are then selected and a respective OAC is executed.

In the first phase of the experiment, the robot needs to perceive the unknown environment in order to construct an environmental model in terms of geometric primitives. This step employs the H^2T perception pipeline discussed in Section 3.1. Figure 7.16 shows the experimental situation together with a visualization of the robot's environmental perception. The perception pipeline successfully identifies two predominant primitives in the scene, representing the valve and the wall. Both of these primitives are planar, the primitive representing the valve however receives a high circularity score (circular$(p) \approx 1$). In this exemplary situation of valve-turning, the robot needs to autonomously detect *bimanual turnability* affordances (see Section 5.4) which are defined based on unimanual *turnability* affordances (see Section 5.3) in the affordance hierarchy.

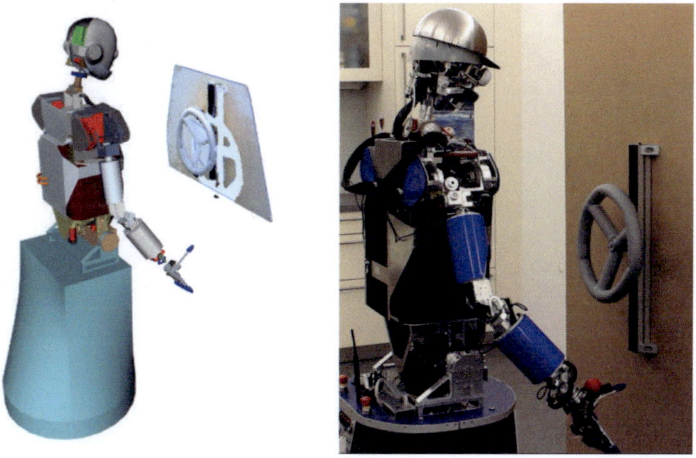

Figure 7.16: ARMAR-III perceives an unknown environment in a valve-turning scenario (taken from Kaiser et al. 2016a, © 2016 IEEE). *Left:* The robot's perceptual knowledge state. Two predominant geometric primitives are detected representing the valve and the wall, respectively. *Right:* The actual experimental situation of the robot.

See Figure 7.17 for a visualization of the hierarchical composition of the affordance belief function Θ_{Turn} for unimanual turning which requires the existence of a circular shaped primitive. In order to circumvent the problem of high-level planning (see Section 6.1), the robot is provided with a preference for automatically executing OACs related to *bimanual turnability* affordances. The affordance detection system successfully identifies the valve as turnable and proposes a *bimanual turnability* affordance. With the detection of the affordance and the generation of the associated affordance belief function $\Theta_{\text{Bi-Turn}}$, bimanual end-effector poses are automatically suggested, which are visualized as green hands in Figure 7.18.

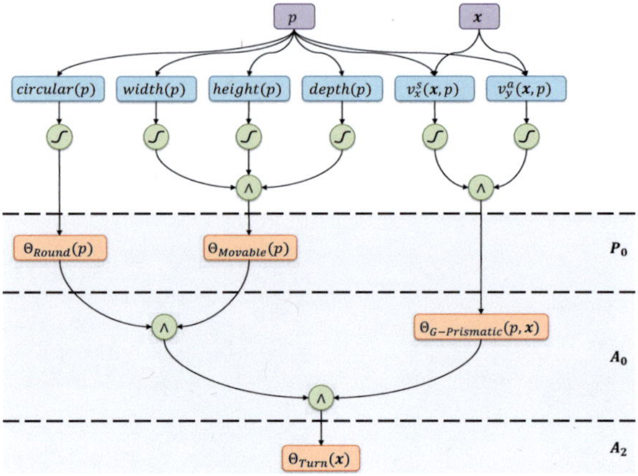

Figure 7.17: The composition of *unimanual turnability* $\Theta_{\text{Turn}}(\boldsymbol{x})$ based on *prismatic graspability* $\Theta_{\text{G-Prismatic}}(\boldsymbol{x})$ in combination with a circular shape of the primitive p expressed in Θ_{Round} and estimated primitive mobility expressed in Θ_{Movable}.

In the final step, the OAC for bimanual turning associated with the *bimanual turnability* affordance is executed based on the provided end-effector pose selection (see Figure 7.19). The execution program of the OAC for bimanual turning implements a general bimanual end-effector trajectory for the reactive turning of medium-sized objects, parameterized only by the end-effector poses provided by the affordance system. Task-specific parameterization, such as the turning angle or force thresholds, have been predefined in this scenario.

7.3.2 Experiment II: Validation of Pushability and Liftability Affordances

This section describes an experiment carried out on the humanoid robot ARMAR-III, demonstrating the detection and validation of affordance hypotheses for *pushability* and *liftability*. In the experiment ARMAR-III is facing a cluttered arrangement of different obstacles that block its way: A pipe (**O1**), a chair (**O2**) and a box (**O3**).

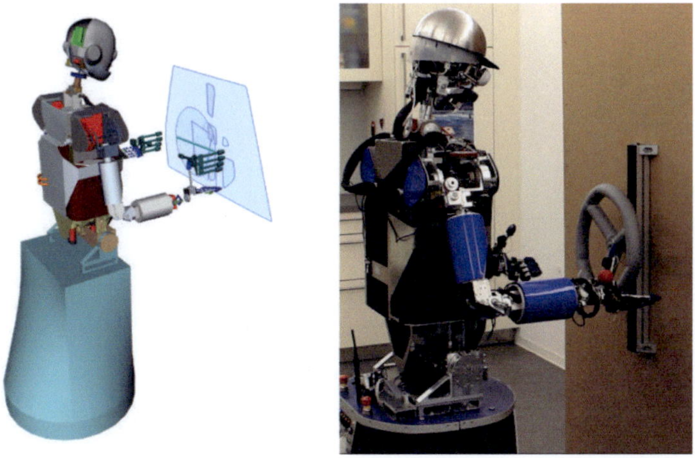

Figure 7.18: ARMAR-III detects *bimanual turnability* for the valve (taken from Kaiser et al. 2016a, © 2016 IEEE). *Left:* The robot selects the most credible hypothesis for *bimanual turnability* based on the values of the respective affordance belief function. This selection process automatically suggests suitable end-effector poses for subsequent action execution (visualized as green hands). *Right:* The actual experimental situation of the robot.

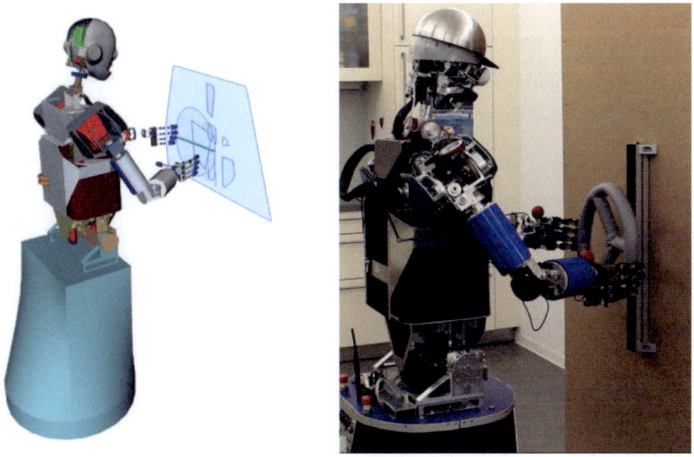

Figure 7.19: ARMAR-III bimanually turns the valve based on the detected affordances (taken from Kaiser et al. 2016a, © 2016 IEEE). *Left:* Visualization of the robot state and its perceptual knowledge. *Right:* The actual experimental situation of the robot.

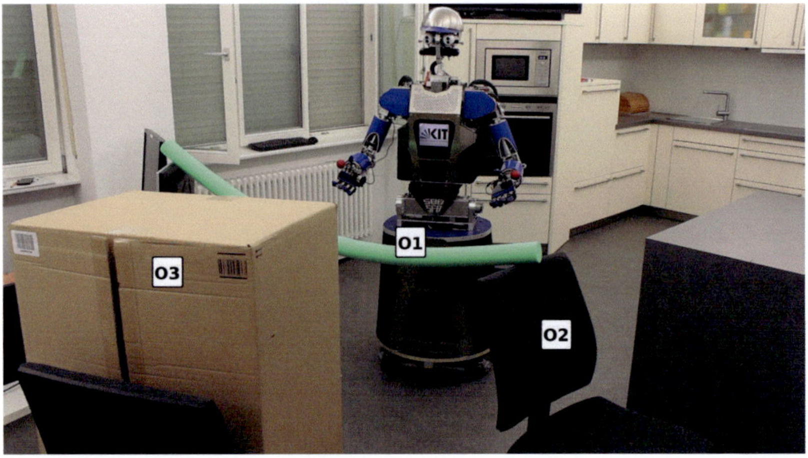

Figure 7.20: The experiment of affordance validation using the humanoid robot ARMAR-III. The robot autonomously perceives its unknown environment by registering multiple views of the scene and subsequently detects available affordances. Based on *pushability* and *liftability* affordances, the robot is requested to remove blocking objects **O1**, **O2** and **O3**. Before action execution, the robot performs validation actions for validating the generated affordance belief functions.

This section is an extended version of the experimental evaluations published in Kaiser et al. (2015a,b). The experimental setup is depicted in Figure 7.20. The robot has no a-priori knowledge on the types or locations of the employed obstacles. In order to successfully remove the objects, the robot is provided with a straightforward strategy: Iteratively move to a given initial position in front of the obstacles, capture multiple snapshots of the scene with different head orientations and detect affordances in the registered point clouds. Subsequently, pick the closest movable primitive, i. e. a primitive that is pushable or liftable, validate the attributed affordance of *pushability* or *liftability* and, in the case of a successful validation, execute a corresponding OAC for removing the obstacle. This process is repeated until no further obstacles are found.

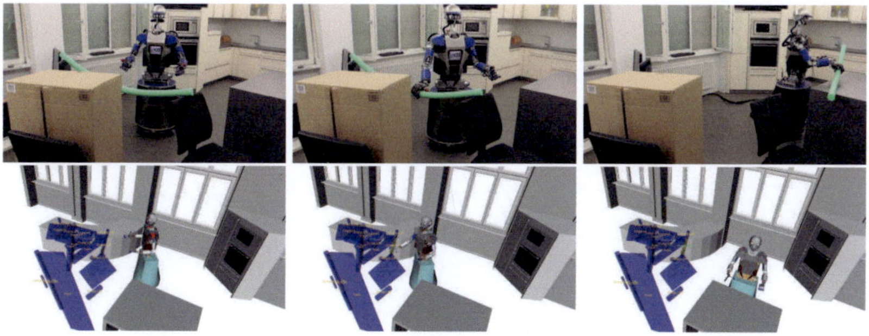

(a) Detection (b) Validation (c) Execution

Figure 7.21: *Left:* Detection of the pipe as a liftable cylindrical primitive. *Middle:* Execution of the validation OAC associated with the *liftability* affordance. *Right:* Execution of the OAC for object removal associated with the *liftability* affordance.

The Pipe (O1) Figure 7.21 shows the detection of the pipe (obstacle **O1** in Figure 7.20) as a liftable cylindrical primitive. After detection of *liftability*, the robot executes an associated validation OAC which assesses liftability by attempting a lift and monitoring the wrist forces. If the forces exceed a defined threshold, the validation is considered failed and the investigated *liftability* affordance is marked as invalid. In the case of Figure 7.21, the validation is successful and the associated OAC for object removal is successfully executed.

The Chair (O2) Figure 7.22 shows the detection of the chair (obstacle **O2** in Figure 7.20) as a pushable planar primitive. As the employed version of the H^2T perception pipeline does not reason about higher semantic structures, the chair is detected as a planar, pushable backrest. After detection of *pushability*, the robot executes an associated validation OAC which assesses pushability by attempting a push and monitoring the wrist forces. If the forces exceed a defined threshold, the validation is considered failed and the investigated *pushability* affordance is marked as invalid. In the case of Figure 7.22, the validation is successful and the associated OAC for object removal is executed.

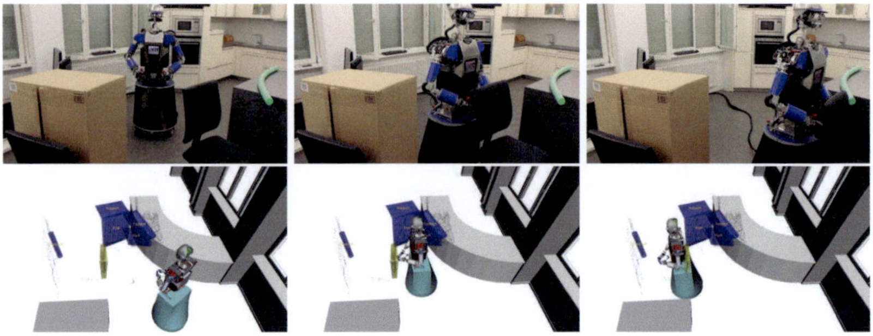

(a) Detection (b) Validation (c) Execution

Figure 7.22: *Left:* Detection of the chair as a pushable planar primitive. *Middle:* Execution of the validation OAC associated with the *pushability* affordance. *Right:* Execution of the OAC for object removal associated with the *pushability* affordance.

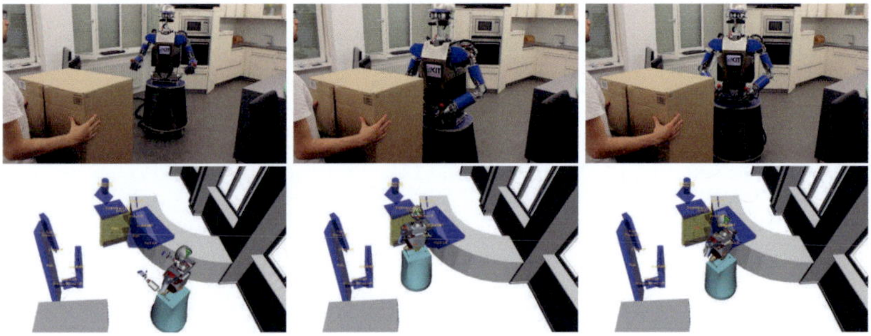

(a) Detection (b) Validation (c) Execution

Figure 7.23: *Left:* Detection of the box as a pushable planar primitive. *Middle:* Execution of the validation OAC associated with the *pushability* affordance. *Right:* The execution of the OAC for object removal associated with the *pushability* affordance is not initiated as the validation of *pushability* failed.

The Box (O3) Figure 7.23 shows the detection of the box (obstacle **O3** in Figure 7.20) as a pushable, planar primitive. As the employed version of the H^2T perception pipeline does not reason about higher semantic structures, the box is detected as one planar, pushable side. In this case, the box is manually fixed in order to artificially create a false affordance hypothesis. While executing the associated validation OAC, the robot monitors wrist forces exceeding a defined threshold, leading to the assumption of a fixed object. Hence, the validation is considered failed and the investigated *pushability* affordance is marked as invalid. In this case, no further action execution is initiated as *pushability* is refuted.

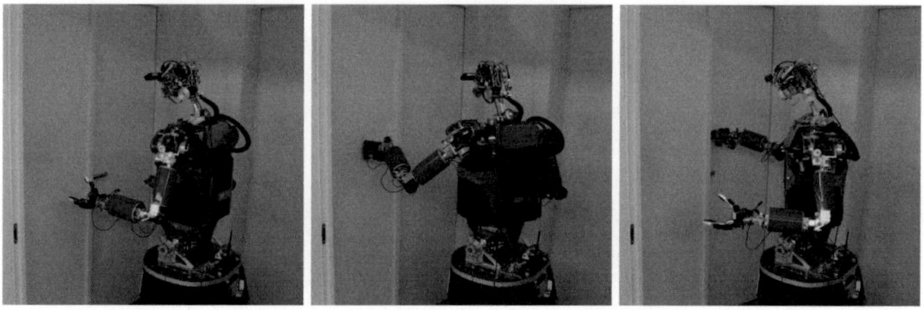

Figure 7.24: Detection and validation of *leanability* affordances for a two-sided door (taken from Kaiser et al. 2015b, © 2015 World Scientific Publishing Company). The left side of the door is locked and therefore affords leaning, while the right side of the door is unlocked and hence does not afford leaning. Based on validation strategies incorporating wrist force sensing, the robot is able to validate the initial *leanability* hypotheses.

Validation of Leanability Affordances Figure 7.24 shows a related experimental setup in which ARMAR-III validates *leanability* affordances at a two-sided door. While the left part of the door is locked, the right part is freely movable. The robot detects both parts of the door as individual planar primitives with associated *leanability* affordances and subsequently executes corresponding validation OACs.

The experiments in this section show that the autonomous detection of affordances based on the methods proposed in this thesis is feasible in application on real humanoid robots exposed to unknown environments. Multiple consecutive experiments have been performed, suggesting that the detection of geometric primitives and affordances works sufficiently reliable with real sensor data. The experiment further shows that the validation of affordance hypotheses based on simple sensory cues is possible and allows the implementation of basic autonomous behavior.

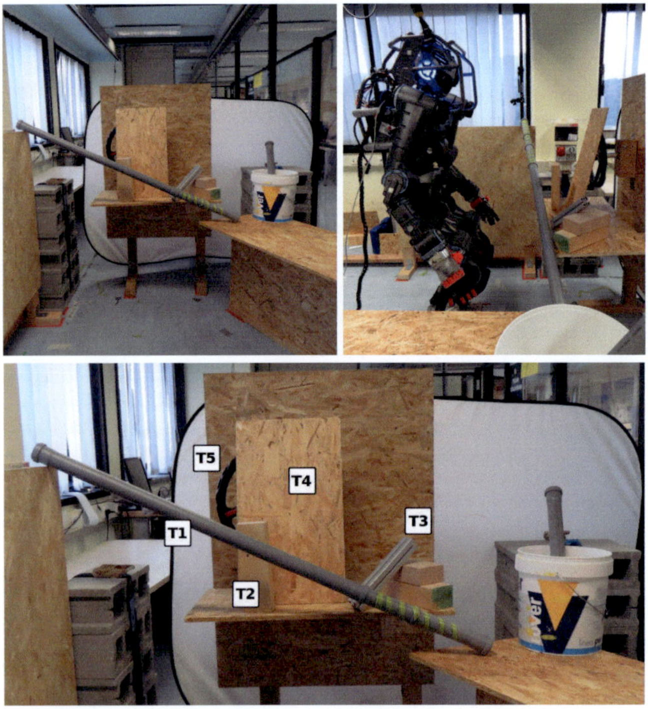

Figure 7.25: The experimental setup consists of several objects blocking the robot's access to an industrial valve (**T5**). The objects are a large, horizontal pipe (**T1**), a wooden and a metallic block (**T2** and **T3**) and a wooden board (**T4**). The experiment has been performed using the humanoid robot WALK-MAN (*top right*) (taken from Kaiser et al. 2016c, © 2016 IEEE).

7.3.3 Experiment III: Shared Autonomous Pilot Interface

In this section, the affordance-based pilot interface is experimentally evaluated in a DRC-inspired scenario targeting the removal of blocking objects and the turning of an industrial valve using the humanoid robot WALK-MAN. Figure 7.25 depicts the complete scenario setup and introduces the labels **T1** to **T5** that will be used throughout this section, referring to the individual objects in the scenario. This section is an extended version of the experimental evaluations published in Kaiser et al. (2016b,c).
The unknown environment is perceived and processed using the H^2T perception pipeline with the stereo camera system of WALK-MAN[5] and resulting affordances are presented to the pilot via the affordance-based pilot interface introduced in Section 6.2. The pilot interface allows the application of the affordance detection and validation system in a shared autonomous fashion, resulting in a more reliable and robust approach as perceptual shortcomings, e. g. segmentation errors, can be recognized and corrected by the pilot. The following sections is discuss the actions taken by the pilot in order to successfully achieve the goal defined in Figure 7.25.

T1: The Pipe In the first task, the pilot needs to remove the long pipe **T1** (see Figure 7.25). The perceptual pipeline successfully identifies the pipe as a distinct primitive and offers the pilot the option to grasp it. The object is also assigned a *liftability* affordance which is related to a number of different OACs. One of these OACs, termed *remove*, attempts to lift the object and subsequently moves and drops it in order to remove it from its disturbing position. Other OACs could implement different behavior at this point and would be offered to the pilot in the same way. See Figure 7.26 for a visualization of the pilot side of this experiment and for snapshots of the corresponding OAC execution with WALK-MAN.

[5] A *MultiSense SL* head from *Carnegie Robotics*.

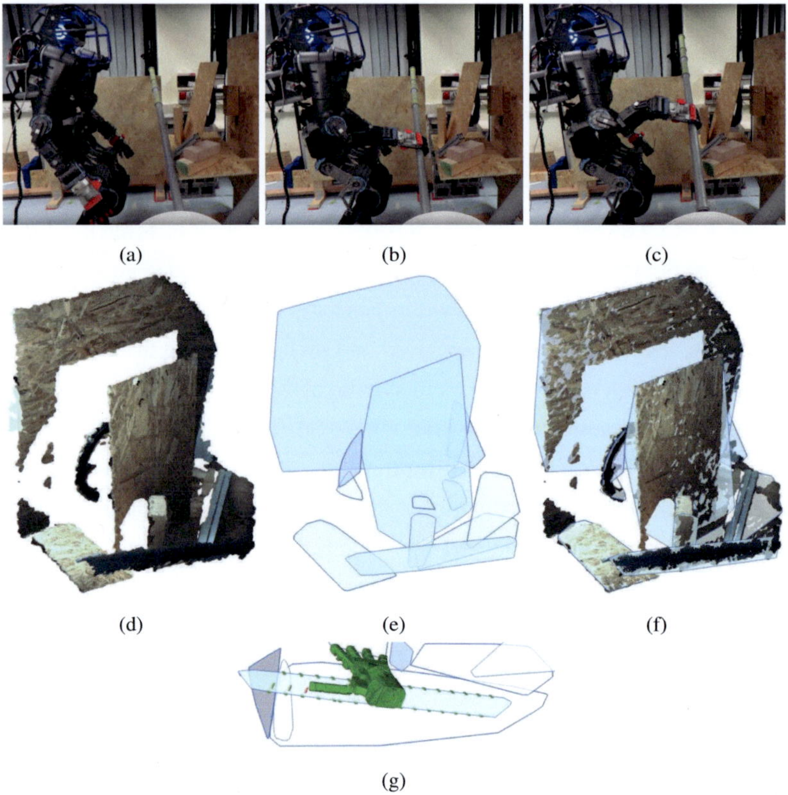

Figure 7.26: *(a)-(c):* Snapshots of the pipe removal experiment with WALK-MAN controlled using the affordance-based pilot interface introduced in Section 6.2. *(d)-(f):* Visualization of the perceptual process for the experiment. The visualizations shown are: (d) the raw point cloud obtained by stereo vision, (e) the extracted primitives and (f) the extracted primitives in a combined view with the point cloud. *(g):* Suitable unimanual end-effector pose for action execution (taken from Kaiser et al. 2016c, © 2016 IEEE)

Note that the generated affordance belief functions are not explicitly visualized in Figure 7.26 and in the following figures. However, the affordance belief functions are queried for determining the reachable end-effector poses with the highest attributed belief. In the evaluation experiments, the best end-effector pose is automatically proposed by the pilot interface based on the generated affordance belief functions. The pilot can adjust the proposed end-effector pose if needed, resulting in the final end-effector pose that is used for OAC parameterization which is indicated by the visualization of a colored robot hand in Figure 7.26g.

Figure 7.26e shows that the pipe **T1** is misleadingly detected as a planar primitive instead of a cylinder. This example shows that the affordance detection system is flexible enough to account for those perceptual inaccuracies and is still able to offer reasonable affordances and end-effector poses to the pilot (Figure 7.26g).

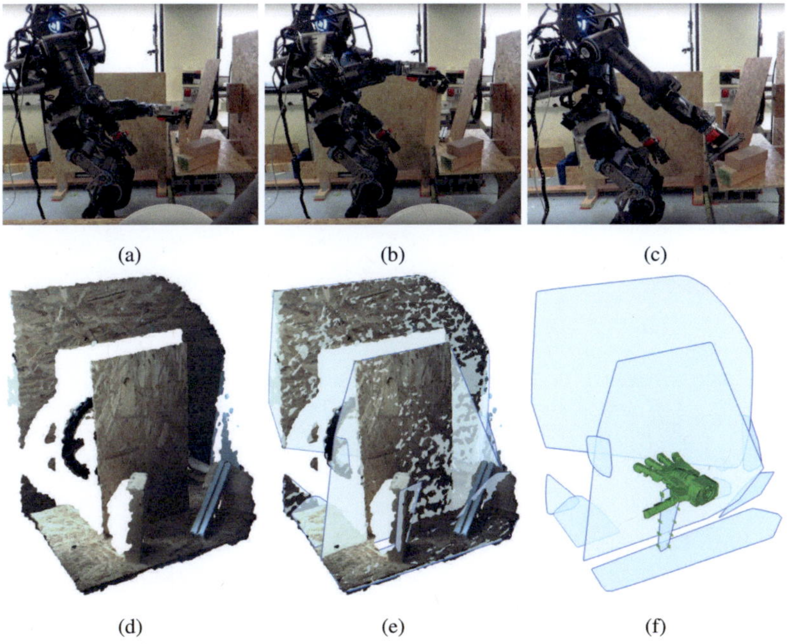

Figure 7.27: *(a)-(c):* Snapshots of the humanoid robot WALK-MAN executing a removal OAC for the block-shaped object **T2**. *(d)-(f):* The visualization of the robot perception for the pilot and the end-effector pose selected by the pilot based on the system's proposals (taken from Kaiser et al. 2016c, © 2016 IEEE)

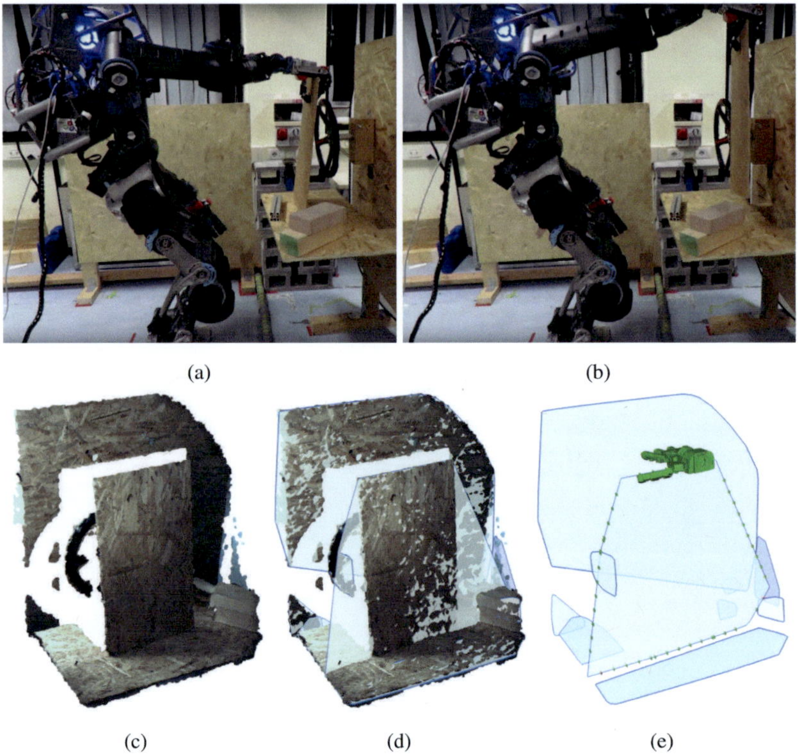

Figure 7.28: *(a) and (b):* Pictures of the humanoid robot WALK-MAN executing a removal OAC for the wooden board **T4**. *(c)-(e):* The visualization of the robot perception for the pilot and the end-effector pose selected by the pilot based on the system's proposals (taken from Kaiser et al. 2016c, © 2016 IEEE)

T2 and T3: The Blocks Subsequent to the pipe, the pilot needs to command the robot to remove the two small block-like objects **T2** and **T3** from the scene. As the employed version of the H^2T perception pipeline does not reason about higher semantic structures, block-shaped objects result in sets of planar primitives for the visible sides. In this case, the pilot can apply prismatic grasping to the slim sides of the primitives in the intention of grasping the entire object. Subsequently, the pilot executes the associated OAC for object removal to initiate the action. See Figure 7.27 for a visualization of the pilot side of this experiment and for snapshots of the corresponding OAC execution.

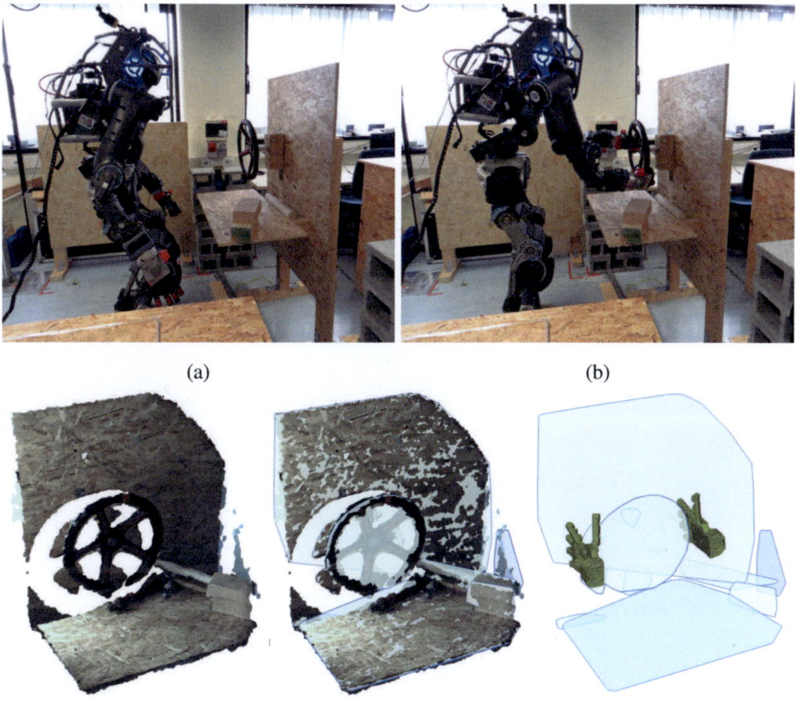

(a) (b)

(c) (d) (e)

Figure 7.29: *(a) and (b):* Snapshots of the humanoid robot WALK-MAN executing a valve-turning OAC for the industrial valve **T5**. *(c)-(e):* The visualization of the robot perception for the pilot and the end-effector poses selected by the pilot based on the system's proposals (taken from Kaiser et al. 2016c, © 2016 IEEE)

T4: The Wooden Board In the next task, a wooden board needs to be removed that is located directly in front of the valve. As shown in Figure 7.28, the board is correctly detected as a planar primitive, although the segmentation algorithms failed to properly extract its lower bound. Hence, the primitive appears larger than its actual size. Autonomous strategies for object removal might fail if they attempt to grasp the board from the sides. However, the pilot is able to recognize the unfortunate segmentation by comparing the resulting geometric primitives to the captured point cloud (see Figure 7.28d). Using the affordance-based pilot interface, the pilot can move the autonomously proposed end-effector pose for prismatic grasping towards the top side of the board which is properly reflected in the primitive. See Figure 7.28 for a visualization of the pilot side of this experiment and for snapshots of the corresponding OAC execution.

T5: The Valve In the final step, after clearing the area around the valve, the pilot is able to command the robot to bimanually turn the valve. The valve is recognized as a planar primitive with a circular shape. Based on this information, the pilot is offered a *bimanual turnability* affordance $\Theta_{\text{Bi-Turn}}$ with appropriately suggested end-effector poses for bimanual prismatic grasping. See Figure 7.29 for a visualization of the pilot side of this experiment and for snapshots of the corresponding OAC execution.

7.4 Performance Measurements

This section provides performance measurements for the different components of the H^{2}T perception pipeline including the reference implementation of the affordance detection subsystem which is proposed in this thesis. The discussions in this section are an extended versions of the system performance evaluation published in Kaiser et al. (2018a). All measurements have been generated on standard *Intel Core i7-7700* desktop quad-core processors with 3.6 GHz and 32 GB RAM. Figure 7.30 displays performance measurements for the different exemplary scenes summarized in Table 4.2. The scenes *Bar*, *Board*, *Valve* and *Kitchen Counter* refer to the evaluation scenarios discussed in Section 7.3.3 and Section 7.2.1, respectively. As explained in Table 4.2, the scene complexity, i. e. the point cloud size, varies dramatically among the evaluated scenes. Hence, different runtime characteristics are expected, particularly with respect to the large-scale scenes *Large Staircase*, *Kitchen* and *Kitchen Counter*. All input point clouds have been down-sampled first with a leaf size of 2 cm, before extracting primitives. Extracted primitives have been sampled with a spatial sampling distance of 2.5 cm and an orientational sampling distance of $\pi/8$ rad. During the performance measurements, eight affordance belief functions have been evaluated on all considered scenes: $\Theta_{\text{G-Prismatic}}$, $\Theta_{\text{G-Platform}}$, Θ_{Grasp}, Θ_{Support}, Θ_{Lean}, Θ_{Push}, Θ_{Pull} and Θ_{Turn}.

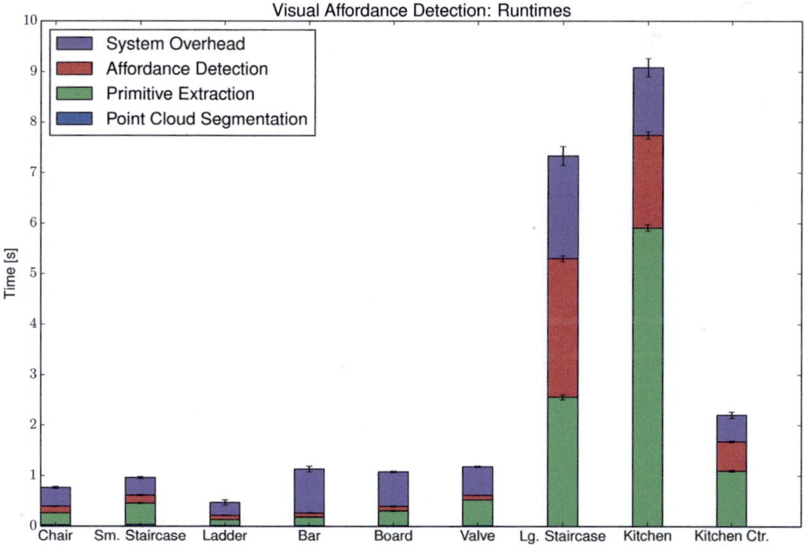

Figure 7.30: Performance measurements of the affordance detection system proposed in this thesis in different exemplary scenes. The measurements have been generated using a spatial sampling distance of 2.5 cm and an orientational sampling distance of $\pi/8$ rad, averaged over 100 measurements. Black range markers indicate the standard deviation.

The performance measurements in Figure 7.30 show that affordance detection based on the formalism of affordance belief functions is computationally feasible for realistic scene sizes. In the case of the first six scenes, which consist of single-view point clouds, the defined set of affordances is processed within 50 ms - 200 ms, making online application of the concept possible. The results further show that the initial segmentation step $\boldsymbol{S_2}$ of the H^{2}T perception pipeline as introduced in Figure 3.1 has negligible runtime compared to the primitive extraction step $\boldsymbol{S_3}$. A significant fraction of the runtime is spent with *system overhead* which refers to the time needed for transporting point clouds, geometric primitives and affordance belief functions between system components and the storage subsystem. The detection of affordances in the large-scale evaluation scenarios *Large Staircase*, *Kitchen* and *Kitchen Counter* show similar runtime distributions while taking significantly longer in general which is expected due to the increased scene complexity.

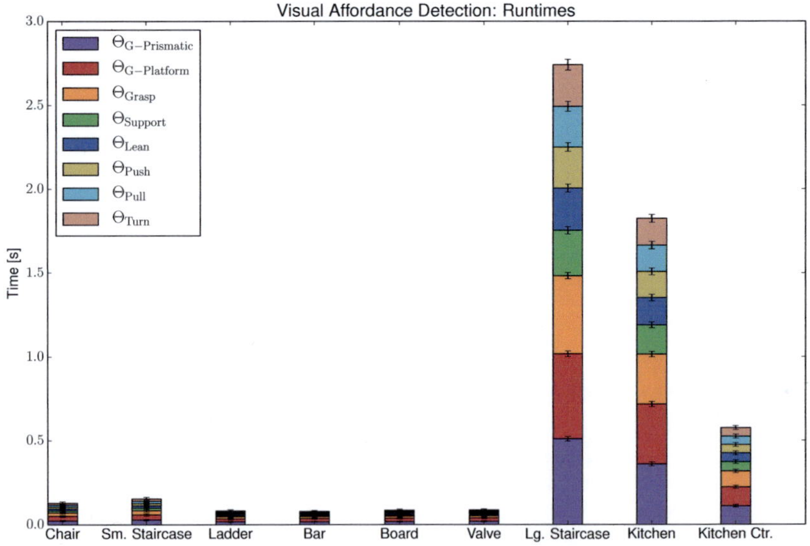

Figure 7.31: Performance measurements of the affordance detection process, i. e. the evaluation of hierarchically defined affordance belief functions, for different affordances in different exemplary scenarios. The measurements have been generated using a spatial sampling distance of 2.5 cm and an orientational sampling distance of $\pi/8$ rad, averaged over 100 measurements. Black range markers indicate the standard deviation.

The results presented in Figure 7.31 show that the evaluation of different affordance belief functions have approximately the same runtime characteristics, independent of the affordance level in the hierarchy. The reason for this is that affordance detection is efficiently implemented in a way that avoids re-evaluation of affordances that have been evaluated before. Hence, higher-level affordances that include evidence from lower-level affordances reuse already computed evidences. The lowest-level affordances $\Theta_{\text{G-Prismatic}}$ and $\Theta_{\text{G-Platform}}$ show a slightly higher runtime than other affordances which can be justified with their relatively complex implementation (see Table A.2).

7.5 Summary and Review

In this chapter the theoretic contributions of this thesis, i. e. the formalization of affordance belief functions and the principles of evidence fusion, have been evaluated in synthetic, simulated and real experiments. Section 7.1 focused on the evaluation of the principle of evidence fusion in affordance belief functions, both in the spaces of end-effector positions and orientations. For this purpose, joint affordance belief functions obtained via the fusion of consecutive observations have been compared to randomly generated ground-truth affordances. The evaluation shows that the methods for evidence fusion introduced in Section 4.3 provide a feasible solution for fusing affordance-related evidence into a consistent system belief. With increasing numbers of fused observations, the joint belief functions produce increasingly accurate representations of ground-truth affordances. This finding emphasizes the applicability of affordance belief functions and allows the further evaluation in a dynamic simulation environment and on real humanoid robots.

In Section 7.2.1, the affordance detection and validation system based on the formalism of affordance belief functions is evaluated in a dynamically simulated kitchen environment. The environmental perception is simulated using a manually segmented artificial point cloud of the simulated environment. The affordance detection system subsequently extracts geometric primitives and identifies *prismatic graspability* affordances. Due to the definition of $\Theta_{\text{G-Prismatic}}$, the visual affordance detection system produces a significant number of false positives, making the affordances subject to validation experiments. In the dynamically simulated environment, the humanoid robot ARMAR-III autonomously performs validation experiments and iteratively obtains an accurate belief about the existence of *prismatic graspability* affordances in the scene.

Section 7.2.2 evaluated the combination of the affordance detection system with the whole-body multi-contact pose sequence planner from Mandery et al. (2015a) which provides an initial step towards whole-body multi-contact motion trajectory planning in a contacts-before-motion approach. Affordance belief functions Θ_{Support} for *supportability* are queried in the search path extension step of the approach, in order to determine the availability of contact opportunities for the humanoid robot ARMAR-4 in a kinematic simulation environment. The evaluation shows that affordance belief functions generated by the affordance detection system are suitable for supporting the application of multi-contact pose sequence planning in unknown environments. The original approach from Mandery et al. (2015a) has previously been evaluated in known environments with predefined support contact opportunities.

Section 7.3 investigated the applicability of the affordance detection and validation system to real humanoid robots in real evaluation environments. The step from simulated environments to real robotic hardware is critical to demonstrate the applicability of the concepts to real scenarios which are not as well-behaved as simulation environments. The affordance-based pilot interface for shared autonomous control of humanoid robots introduced in Section 6.2 has been employed in this evaluation on the humanoid robots ARMAR-III and WALK-MAN. Evaluation experiments include the detection and utilization of *bimanual turnability* affordances in a valve-turning scenario inspired by the DRC (Section 7.3.1), the autonomous detection and validation of *pushability* and *liftability* affordances for clearing cluttered object arrangements (Section 7.3.2) and the shared autonomous removal of blocking objects in a cluttered valve-turning scenario (Section 7.3.3). The experiments on real humanoid robots suggest the feasibility and applicability of the concept of affordance detection and the affordance-based pilot interface to realistic problems.

In a final evaluation, performance measurements of the affordance detection system have been provided for the different exemplary scenes used throughout the thesis. The results show that affordance detection based on affordance belief functions can be efficiently implemented for reasonably scaled environments. Although the reference implementation used for the provided measurements already exhibits decent performance, further optimization, e. g. through GPU-based implementations, seems possible.

8 Conclusion

The goal of this thesis was the development of an affordance detection and validation system for humanoid robots, its implementation and its evaluation in simulation, as well as on real humanoid robots in realistic scenarios. The developed computational model for affordances was used for defining a hierarchy of whole-body affordances which describe possibilities for whole-body actions. The planning and execution of whole-body actions has been a key element of the *DARPA Robotics Challenge* where impressive whole-body loco-manipulation skills have been demonstrated in scenarios inspired by robotic disaster response. However, the teams predominantly implemented task-specific solutions to action possibility perception. The proposed affordance detection system was developed in the motivation of providing the foundation for a more generic approach towards the perception of whole-body action possibilities, i. e. whole-body affordances.

8.1 Scientific Contributions of the Thesis

With respect to the goals formulated in Section 1.1, the main contributions of this thesis can be summarized as follows.

Computational Formalization of Affordances The computational formalization of the affordance concept proposed in Chapter 4 is inspired by the idea that whole-body actions are predominantly based upon elementary power grasping contacts between end-effectors and environmental structures. Hence, affordances have been formalized as *affordance belief functions* defined over the space of end-effector poses. The formal definition of affordance belief functions allows the representation of affordance-related evidence by means of the *Dempster-Shafer Theory*. It further provides the formal means for consistently fusing affordance-related evidence from different sources such as visual affordance detection and haptic validation experiments. Section 4.7 and Section 7.4 demonstrate that the proposed computational affordance model lays the foundation for a computationally feasible approach towards affordance-driven action execution in real world scenarios.

Hierarchy of Whole-Body Affordances The formalization of affordances as belief functions over the space of end-effector poses allows the application of the *Theory of Subjective Logic*, as introduced in Section 4.4, in order to combine belief functions for different affordances by logic operators. This formalism allows the hierarchical composition of affordance belief functions. Starting from the hypothesis that whole-body affordances are based on fundamental power grasping affordances, Chapter 5 proposes a *hierarchy of whole-body affordances* which allows the propagation of affordance-related evidence from lower-level affordances, such as *graspability* to higher-level affordances, such as *liftability* or *turnability*. While the hierarchy of whole-body affordances is subject to revision and completion, it allows the implementation of effective mechanisms for visual affordance detection based on the H^2T perception pipeline introduced in Section 3.1.

Affordance-Based Autonomous and Shared-Autonomous Control The hierarchical formalization of affordances as described in Chapter 4 and Chapter 5 lays the foundation for effective affordance detection and validation mechanisms. As affordance belief functions are defined over the end-effector pose space, detected affordances inherently provide information for parameterizing action execution skills. Hence, the proposed mechanisms for affordance detection and validation establish a link between perception and action and therefore qualify for the integration in autonomous or shared autonomous control strategies for humanoid robots in unknown environments. While autonomous control is certainly the long-term goal, Chapter 6 suggests that fundamental problems in robotics and artificial intelligence, such as autonomous task and action planning, need to be addressed before implementing autonomous affordance-based control modes for humanoid robots. Hence, Chapter 6 focuses on affordance-based shared autonomous control which implements the cooperative operation of a humanoid robot based on detected affordances. The robot is controlled by a human pilot on an abstract level, by selecting among detected affordances and action execution skills, as well as by supervising autonomous skill parameterization and action execution. Section 6.2 discusses the implementation of an affordance-based pilot interface within the robot software environment *ArmarX*. While the pilot interface is subject to improvement in terms of user experience, it serves as a reference implementation for affordance-based shared autonomy on multiple simulated and real humanoid robots and consequently allows the experimental evaluation carried out in Chapter 7.

Evaluation of the Affordance Detection and Validation System In Chapter 7, the computational model for affordances and the corresponding affordance detection and validation system, for which a reference implementation has been created within the robot software environment ArmarX, has been evaluated in multiple synthetic, simulated and real experiments. First, in Section 7.1, the principle concept of evidence fusion has been investigated in synthetic experiments based on randomly generated ground-truth affordances, suggesting that the proposed formalisms for evidence fusion are viable and can sufficiently well approximate the ground-truth by iterative fusion of observations. In Section 7.2.1, the entire affordance system ranging from visual affordance detection to the execution of affordance validation experiments and the subsequent fusion of obtained evidence is evaluated for *prismatic graspability* affordances in a dynamic simulation environment using the humanoid robot ARMAR-III. The simulated experiments performed in this environment indicate that continuous affordance validation and evidence fusion lets the system belief converge against the ground-truth assumption. The experiment further shows that the proposed affordance system establishes a viable link between perception and action and that visual affordance detection which has been performed based on manual point cloud segmentation, already provides a sufficiently accurate approximation to the ground-truth. Section 7.2.2 evaluated the conceptual combination of the affordance detection system with a whole-body multi-contact pose sequence planner, approaching the problem of planning multi-contact pose sequences in loco-manipulation scenarios. Furthermore, Section 7.3 summarizes the results of multiple experiments on actual humanoid robots in realistic exemplary environments which have been assumed to be entirely unknown to the robot. The experiments have been carried out on the humanoid robots ARMAR-III and WALK-MAN demonstrating the ability of the concept to generalize among robot platforms and experimental setups. The experiment shown in Section 7.3.3 has been reliably and successfully performed in a semi-public demonstration in the context of the WALK-MAN project review in Genoa, Italy.

8.2 Discussion and Future Work

In Chapter 7, the affordance system proposed in this thesis has proven to provide a viable, promising and computationally feasible way for robotic action perception. Inspired by the tasks of the DARPA Robotics Challenge, which represent the state-of-the-art in the field, the affordance system was developed as an approach towards a more general solution to the perception of possibilities for whole-body actions targeting unknown environments. It needs to be noted that the DRC contained highly complex and integrated tasks, such as the utility vehicle egress (see Table 2.1), which are not captured in the proposed system. Furthermore, the prototypical implementation of the affordance system proposed in this thesis does not qualify for application in challenges such as the DRC. However, the affordance system advances the state-of-the-art in this area and provides the foundation for a more general approach to the detection of whole-body affordances in tasks and challenges similar to those from the DRC. The affordance detection and validation system as proposed in this thesis lays the foundation for a variety of interesting extensions which are left to be investigated in future work.

Efficient implementation of affordances for multiple end-effectors The combination of multiple end-effectors is particularly important in humanoid robotics as four distinct end-effectors are commonly available and as important groups of actions, e. g. walking or bimanual manipulation, require environmental contact of multiple end-effectors. Section 4.6 shows a natural way for extending the formalism of affordance belief functions to multiple end-effectors. However, as the proposed approach extends the definition space of affordance belief functions to the Cartesian product of end-effector poses, it has a strong impact on the overall efficiency. While bimanual affordance detection is feasible, as demonstrated in Section 7.3.1, it comes at much higher costs compared to unimanual affordance detection. One aspect of future work is the question if the computational costs of affordance belief functions for multiple end-effectors can be reduced, e. g. by using data structures that condense homogeneous areas of affordance belief functions into few samples.

Consistent integration of robot experience and human expert knowledge Chapter 4 identifies the consistent fusion of affordance-related evidence as one of the driving motivations behind the proposed formalization of the affordance concept. While any type of evidence that is expressible in terms of affordance belief functions can be processed by the proposed formalization, only two types of evidence have been considered in this thesis: visual affordance detection and interactive affordance validation experiments. It is an open and interesting question how to properly formalize additional sources of evidence to be included in the affordance system, such as experience from previous experiments or human expert knowledge.

Implementation of affordance-based action and task planning The detection of action possibilities as investigated in this thesis serves the sole purpose of providing adequate information for subsequent action planning and execution. While the affordance system developed in this thesis provides rudimentary information for action parameterization as discussed in Chapter 6, complex actions that go beyond the level of simple execution skills require sophisticated parameterization which cannot be solely produced based on affordances. Section 3.3 introduces the concept of Object-Action Complexes (OACs) which are used in this thesis for linking affordances with action execution skills. However, OACs provide further information, particularly links to symbolic planning domains and success measures based on the execution history, that can be used by high-level planning components to generate complex and robust execution strategies. The link between affordances and OACs therefore appears as a promising approach towards affordance-based action and task planning.

Extension to further affordances and applications Chapter 7 showed and evaluated different applications of the affordance system in simulation as well as on real humanoid robots. However, one exciting aspect of the proposed system is its intended use in unknown environments allowing the straight-forward evaluation in novel scenes and use-cases. Furthermore, the affordance system itself is robot-agnostic. Hence, a major part of future work will be the application of the developed methods to further environments, use-cases and robotic platforms. The whole-body affordances hierarchy introduced in Chapter 5 has been developed with the explicit intention of being extended and refined in novel scenarios and applications.

A Appendix

A.1 Von Mises-Fisher Distribution in SO(3)

The method for spatial generalization of observations introduced in Section 4.3.2 employs a combination of two distribution functions which are further reviewed in this section. For a given observation pose $\boldsymbol{x} \in SE(3)$, the translational components $\mathrm{t}(\boldsymbol{x}) \in \mathbb{R}^3$ are spatially generalized by applying a multivariate normal distribution $\mathcal{N}$:

$$\mathcal{N}(\boldsymbol{x};\boldsymbol{\mu},\boldsymbol{\Sigma}) = \frac{1}{|2\pi\boldsymbol{\Sigma}|}\exp\left(-\frac{1}{2}(\boldsymbol{x}-\boldsymbol{\mu})^T\boldsymbol{\Sigma}^{-1}(\boldsymbol{x}-\boldsymbol{\mu})\right). \tag{A.1}$$

The distribution is parameterized by the mean vector $\boldsymbol{\mu} \in \mathbb{R}^3$ and the covariance matrix $\boldsymbol{\Sigma} \in \mathbb{R}^{3\times 3}$. While the translational components can be spatially generalized by a standard normal distribution, the periodic nature of $SO(3)$ needs to be considered when generalizing the orientational components. According to Sudderth (2006), the natural analogy of the normal distribution for circular data is the *wrapped normal distribution*[1] $\mathcal{N}_w$:

$$\mathcal{N}_w(\theta;\mu,\sigma^2) = \frac{1}{\sqrt{2\pi\sigma^2}}\sum_{k=-\infty}^{\infty}\exp\left(\frac{-(\theta-\mu+2\pi k)^2}{2\sigma^2}\right). \tag{A.2}$$

This univariate distribution is parameterized by the mean $\mu \in \mathbb{R}$ and the variance $\sigma^2 \in \mathbb{R}^+$. A mathematically simpler and more convenient option

[1] Also called *folded normal distribution*

is the *von Mises distribution* $\mathcal{M}$ which closely approximates the wrapped normal distribution as:

$$\mathcal{M}(\theta;\mu,\kappa) = \frac{1}{2\pi I_0(\kappa)} \exp\left(\kappa \cos(\theta-\mu)\right). \tag{A.3}$$

with the zero-order *Bessel function* $I_0(\kappa)$. The parameters μ and $\frac{1}{\kappa}$ refer to the parameters μ and σ^2 of the wrapped normal distribution. Following Sudderth (2006), the univariate von Mises distribution shown above can be generalized to points $\boldsymbol{r} \in S^3$ on the three-dimensional unit sphere:

$$\mathcal{M}(\boldsymbol{r};\boldsymbol{\mu},\kappa) = \frac{\kappa}{2I_1(\kappa)} \exp(\kappa \boldsymbol{\mu}^T \boldsymbol{r}). \tag{A.4}$$

This distribution is called *von Mises-Fisher distribution*. The interested reader is referred to Sudderth (2006) for further details. The combination of a multivariate normal distribution $\mathcal{N}$ and a von Mises-Fisher distribution $\mathcal{M}$ as outlined in Section 4.3.2 allows the spatial and orientational generalization of observations for end-effector poses $\boldsymbol{x} \in SE(3)$. Note that both distributions are normalized to a maximum value of 1 for the considerations in Section 4.3.2. Hence, more formally, the proportional functions $\mathcal{N}_1$ and $\mathcal{M}_1$ are used:

$$\begin{aligned}\mathcal{N}_1(\boldsymbol{x};\boldsymbol{\mu},\boldsymbol{\Sigma}) &= \exp\left(-\frac{1}{2}(\boldsymbol{x}-\boldsymbol{\mu})^T\boldsymbol{\Sigma}^{-1}(\boldsymbol{x}-\boldsymbol{\mu})\right)\\ \mathcal{M}_1(\boldsymbol{r};\boldsymbol{\mu},\kappa) &= \frac{1}{\exp(\kappa)} \exp(\kappa \boldsymbol{\mu}^T \boldsymbol{r}).\end{aligned} \tag{A.5}$$

Figure A.1 shows exemplary plots of $\mathcal{N}_1$ and $\mathcal{M}_1$ for different values of the standard deviation σ, visualizing the wrapped shape of the von Mises-Fisher distribution in the one-dimensional case. Figure A.2 shows a visualization of a von Mises-Fisher distribution on the two-dimensional unit sphere S^2.

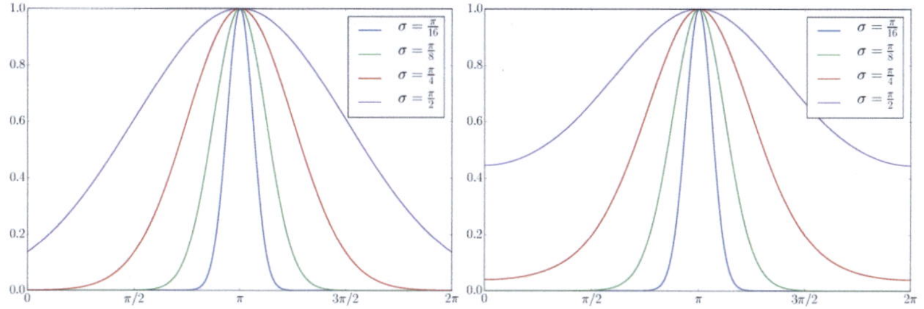

Figure A.1: Visualizations of the distribution functions $\mathcal{N}_1$, which is proportional to a normal distribution (*left*), and $\mathcal{M}_1$, which is proportional to a von Mises distribution (*right*), with varying standard deviations σ (for $\mathcal{M}_1$: $\sigma = \frac{1}{\sqrt{\kappa}}$).

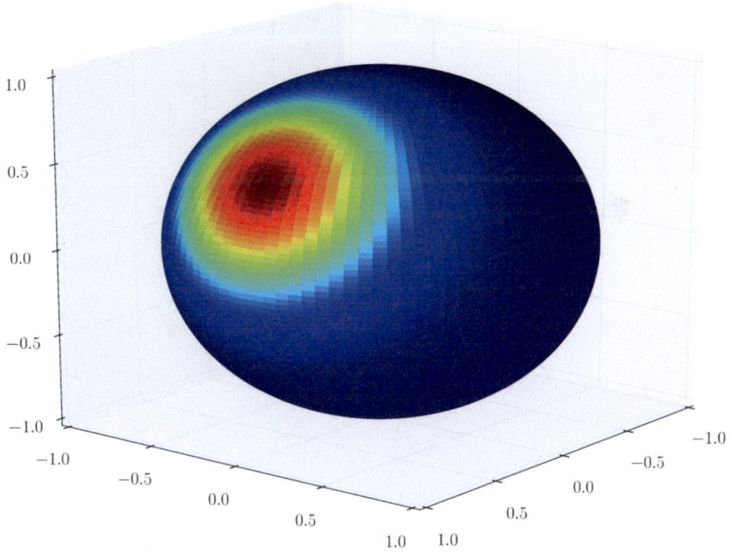

Figure A.2: Visualization of a von Mises-Fisher distribution with $\sigma = \frac{\pi}{8}$ (i. e. $\kappa = \sqrt{8/\pi}$) for the two-dimensional unit sphere S^2.

A.2 Proof of Iterative Evidence Fusion

This section provides a proof for the claim of iterative evidence fusion formulated in Section 4.3.1. The claim states that affordance-related evidence expressed as basic belief assignments in the sense of the Dempster-Shafer theory can be iteratively combined. This is an important precondition for the process of affordance validation as proposed in Section 4.3 which produces affordance-related evidence in an iterative process. The evidence generated during affordance validation needs to be consistently fused with the existing system belief. More formally, the claim of iterative evidence fusion is expressed in the following theorem.

Theorem. *Let $\mathcal{X}$ be a hypothesis space and $m_1, \dots, m_N$ be basic belief assignments over the associated space of hypothesis combinations $2^{\mathcal{X}}$. Then it holds that:*

$$\bigoplus_{i=1}^{N} m_i = m_1 \oplus \cdots \oplus m_N. \tag{A.6}$$

Proof. Due to the associativity of Dempster's combination rule (Sentz et al. 2002), the right hand side of Equation A.6 is well defined and can be written as:

$$m_1 \oplus \cdots \oplus m_N = \big((m_1 \oplus m_2) \oplus m_3\big) \cdots \oplus m_N. \tag{A.7}$$

Furthermore, the trivial base case for $n = 2$ holds by definition:

$$\bigoplus_{i=1}^{2} m_i = m_1 \oplus m_2. \tag{A.8}$$

Let $A \in 2^{\mathcal{X}}$ be a hypothesis. If $A = \emptyset$, then Equation A.6 is trivially true as the result of Dempster's rule of combination is a basic belief assignment which by definition assigns a probability mass of 0 to the empty hypothesis. If $A \neq \emptyset$, then we conclude for $N \in \mathbb{N}^{\geq 3}$:

$$\left(\left(\bigoplus_{i=1}^{N-1} m_i\right) \oplus m_N\right)(A) \overset{(Eq.\ 4.18)}{=} \frac{1}{1-K_*} \sum_{A_* \cap A_N = A} m_N(A_N) \left(\bigoplus_{i=1}^{N-1} m_i\right)(A_*), \tag{A.9}$$

while the implicit notation $A_* \cap A_N = A$ for the summation set, adopted from Equation 4.18, is interpreted as:

$$\left\{(A_*, A_N) \in \mathcal{X}^2 \,\middle|\, A_* \cap A_N = A\right\}. \tag{A.10}$$

The indices of hypotheses A_i and conflict factors K_i refer to the index of the associated basic belief assignment m_i in the $(n-1)$-ary combination, while A_* and K_* refer to the binary combination of the result of the $(n-1)$-ary combination and m_N.

$$\begin{aligned}
(Eq.\,A.9) &\overset{(Eq.\,4.18)}{=} \frac{1}{(1-K_*)(1-K_{N-1})} \sum_{A_* \cap A_N = A} m_N(A_N) \sum_{\bigcap_{j=1}^{N-1} A_j = A_*} \prod_{k=1}^{N-1} m_k(A_k) \\
&= \frac{1}{(1-K_*)(1-K_{N-1})} \sum_{A_* \cap A_N = A} \sum_{\bigcap_{j=1}^{N-1} A_j = A_*} \prod_{k=1}^{N} m_k(A_k) \\
&= \underbrace{\frac{1}{(1-K_*)(1-K_{N-1})}}_{(*)} \sum_{\bigcap_{j=1}^{N} A_j = A} \prod_{k=1}^{N} m_k(A_k).
\end{aligned} \tag{A.11}$$

The combination of the conflict factors K_* and K_{N-1} in $(*)$ can be processed as follows:

$$\begin{aligned}
(*) &= \left((1-K_*)(1-K_{N-1})\right)^{-1} \\
&\overset{(Eq.\ 4.19)}{=} \left(\left(1-\sum_{A_*\cap A_N=\emptyset} m_N(A_N)\cdot\left(\bigoplus_{i=1}^{N-1} m_i\right)(A_*)\right)\cdot(1-K_{N-1})\right)^{-1} \\
&= \left(\left(1-\frac{1}{1-K_{N-1}}\sum_{\substack{A_*\cap A_N=\emptyset\\ A_*\neq\emptyset}} m_N(A_N)\sum_{\bigcap_{j=1}^{N-1}A_j=A_*}\prod_{k=1}^{N-1} m_k(A_k)\right)\cdot(1-K_{N-1})\right)^{-1} \\
&= \left(1-\left(K_{N-1}+\sum_{\substack{A_*\cap A_N=\emptyset\\ A_*\neq\emptyset}}\sum_{\bigcap_{j=1}^{N-1}A_j=A_*}\prod_{k=1}^{N} m_k(A_k)\right)\right)^{-1} \\
&= \left(1-\left(K_{N-1}+\sum_{\substack{\bigcap_{j=1}^{N}A_j=\emptyset\\ \bigcap_{j=1}^{N-1}A_j\neq\emptyset}}\prod_{k=1}^{N} m_k(A_k)\right)\right)^{-1} \qquad \text{(A.12)} \\
&\overset{(Eq.\ 4.19)}{=} \left(1-\left(\sum_{\bigcap_{j=1}^{N-1}A_j=\emptyset}\prod_{k=1}^{N-1} m_k(A_k)+\sum_{\substack{\bigcap_{j=1}^{N}A_j=\emptyset\\ \bigcap_{j=1}^{N-1}A_j\neq\emptyset}}\prod_{k=1}^{N} m_k(A_k)\right)\right)^{-1} \\
&\overset{(**)}{=} \left(1-\left(\sum_{A_N\in 2^X} m_N(A_N)\sum_{\bigcap_{j=1}^{N-1}A_j=\emptyset}\prod_{k=1}^{N-1} m_k(A_k)+\sum_{\substack{\bigcap_{j=1}^{N}A_j=\emptyset\\ \bigcap_{j=1}^{N-1}A_j\neq\emptyset}}\prod_{k=1}^{N} m_k(A_k)\right)\right)^{-1} \\
&= \left(1-\left(\sum_{\substack{\bigcap_{j=1}^{N}A_j=\emptyset\\ \bigcap_{j=1}^{N-1}A_j=\emptyset}}\prod_{k=1}^{N} m_k(A_k)+\sum_{\substack{\bigcap_{j=1}^{N}A_j=\emptyset\\ \bigcap_{j=1}^{N-1}A_j\neq\emptyset}}\prod_{k=1}^{N} m_k(A_k)\right)\right)^{-1} = \frac{1}{1-K_N}.
\end{aligned}$$

In $(**)$ it is implicitly used that m_N is a basic belief assignment and therefore $\sum_{A_N\in 2^X} m_N(A_N) = 1$. Finally, it follows that:

$$(Eq.\ A.11) \overset{(Eq.\ A.12)}{=} \frac{1}{1-K_N}\sum_{\bigcap_{j=1}^{N}A_j=A}\prod_{k=1}^{N} m_k(A_k) \overset{(Eq.\ 4.18)}{=} \left(\bigoplus_{i=1}^{N} m_i\right)(A). \qquad \text{(A.13)}$$

□

A.3 Body Scalings

The hierarchical definition of affordance belief functions discussed in Chapter 5 allows the inclusion of body-scaled parameters in order to relate the perception of affordances to physical properties of the robot embodiment. This section contains the body-scaled parameters β_L, β_B, β_A, β_F and β_{sh} for the humanoid robots ARMAR-III, ARMAR-IV and WALK-MAN, as well as their human equivalents. The hand measures for the human embodiment refer to the hand of an average male adult as defined in Garrett (1971). Furthermore, the shoulder length is given for an assumed body height of 180 cm according to the relative description in Winter (1990).

Table A.1: Body-scaled parameters for an average human and the humanoid robots ARMAR-III, ARMAR-4 and WALK-MAN (adapted from Kaiser et al. 2016a, © 2016 IEEE).

Parameter	**Sym.**	**Human**	**ARMAR-III**	**ARMAR-4**	**WALK-MAN**
Hand Length	β_L	19.71 cm	17.0 cm	16.0 cm	23.0 cm
Hand Breadth	β_B	8.97 cm	10.0 cm	6.5 cm	13.0 cm
Hand Aperture	β_A	12.42 cm	13.0 cm	10.0 cm	10.0 cm
Forehand Len.[2]	β_F	8.56 cm	9.5 cm	8.5 cm	11.0 cm
Shoulder Len.	β_{Sh}	46.44 cm	40.0 cm	40.0 cm	81.5 cm

A.4 Complete Whole-Body Affordance Hierarchy

The hierarchy of whole-body affordances was introduced in Section 5.3 and Section 5.4 layer for layer in multiple tables. In Table A.2, the entire

[2] The middle finger length measured in Garrett (1971) was used here for approximating β_F for the average human embodiment.

hierarchy is provided as a whole for reference. A preliminary version of the complete whole-body affordance hierarchy has been published in Kaiser et al. (2016a).

A.5 Software

The H^2T perception pipeline introduced in Section 3.1, as well as the software library *Spoac* for symbolic planning based on Object-Action Complexes are part of the robot software environment *ArmarX* which is in development at the H^2T. ArmarX is open source software and can be obtained from:

`https://gitlab.com/ArmarX`

Further information and documentation is found under:

`https://armarx.humanoids.kit.edu`

While the affordance-based pilot interface and the robot demonstrations have been developed in ArmarX, the reference implementation of the affordance detection component based on the formalisms introduced in this thesis has no mandatory dependencies to ArmarX. The *AffordanceKit* is open source software and can be obtained independently of ArmarX under:

`https://gitlab.com/h2t/affordance-kit`

Table A.2: The complete whole-body affordance hierarchy

Layer	Symbol	Composition of Belief Function
$\boldsymbol{P}_0$	$\Theta_{\text{Vertical}}(p)$	$\Theta_{\text{up}(p)\approx_\varepsilon 0}(p)$
	$\Theta_{\text{Horizontal}}(p)$	$\Theta_{\text{up}(p)\approx_\varepsilon \pi}(p)$
	$\Theta_{\text{Round}}(p)$	$\Theta_{\text{circular}(p)\approx_\varepsilon 1}(p)$
	$\Theta_{\text{Movable}}(p)$	$\Theta_{\text{width}(p)<\lambda_1}(p) \wedge \Theta_{\text{height}(p)<\lambda_1}(p) \wedge \Theta_{\text{depth}(p)<\lambda_1}(p)$
	$\Theta_{\text{Fixed}}(p)$	$\Theta_{\text{width}(p)>\lambda_1}(p) \vee \Theta_{\text{height}(p)>\lambda_1}(p) \vee \Theta_{\text{depth}(p)>\lambda_1}(p)$
$\boldsymbol{A}_0$	$\Theta_{\text{G-Platform}}(p, \boldsymbol{x})$	$\Theta_{v_x^s(\boldsymbol{x},p,\beta_F)>\beta_B}(\boldsymbol{x}) \wedge \Theta_{v_y^s(\boldsymbol{x},p,\beta_F)>\beta_L}(\boldsymbol{x})$
	$\Theta_{\text{G-Prismatic}}(p, \boldsymbol{x})$	$\Theta_{v_x^s(\boldsymbol{x},p,\beta_F)>\beta_B}(\boldsymbol{x}) \wedge \Theta_{v_y^a(\boldsymbol{x},p,\beta_F)<\beta_A}(\boldsymbol{x})$
$\boldsymbol{A}_1$	$\Theta_{\text{Grasp}}(p, \boldsymbol{x})$	$\Theta_{\text{G-Platform}}(p, \boldsymbol{x}) \vee \Theta_{\text{G-Prismatic}}(p, \boldsymbol{x})$
$\boldsymbol{A}_2$	$\Theta_{\text{Support}}(p, \boldsymbol{x})$	$\Theta_{\text{G-Platform}}(p, \boldsymbol{x}) \wedge \Theta_{\text{Fixed}}(p) \wedge \Theta_{\text{Horizontal}}(p)$
	$\Theta_{\text{Lean}}(p, \boldsymbol{x})$	$\Theta_{\text{G-Platform}}(p, \boldsymbol{x}) \wedge \Theta_{\text{Fixed}}(p) \wedge \Theta_{\text{Vertical}}(p)$
	$\Theta_{\text{Hold}}(p, \boldsymbol{x})$	$\Theta_{\text{G-Prismatic}}(p, \boldsymbol{x}) \wedge \Theta_{\text{Fixed}}(p)$
	$\Theta_{\text{Lift}}(p, \boldsymbol{x})$	$\Theta_{\text{G-Prismatic}}(p, \boldsymbol{x}) \wedge \Theta_{\text{Movable}}(p)$
	$\Theta_{\text{Push}}(p, \boldsymbol{x})$	$\Theta_{\text{Grasp}}(p, \boldsymbol{x}) \wedge \Theta_{\text{Movable}}(p)$
	$\Theta_{\text{Pull}}(p, \boldsymbol{x})$	$\Theta_{\text{G-Prismatic}}(p, \boldsymbol{x}) \wedge \Theta_{\text{Movable}}(p)$
	$\Theta_{\text{Turn}}(\boldsymbol{x})$	$\Theta_{\text{G-Prismatic}}(p, \boldsymbol{x}) \wedge \Theta_{\text{Round}}(p)$
$\boldsymbol{P}_1$	$\Theta_{\text{Vertical}}(\boldsymbol{x}_1, \boldsymbol{x}_2)$	$\Theta_{\text{up}(\boldsymbol{x}_1,\boldsymbol{x}_2)\approx_\varepsilon 0}(\boldsymbol{x}_1, \boldsymbol{x}_2)$
	$\Theta_{\text{Horizontal}}(\boldsymbol{x}_1, \boldsymbol{x}_2)$	$\Theta_{\text{up}(\boldsymbol{x}_1,\boldsymbol{x}_2)\approx_\varepsilon \pi}(\boldsymbol{x}_1, \boldsymbol{x}_2)$
	$\Theta_{\text{Feasible}}(\boldsymbol{x}_1, \boldsymbol{x}_2)$	$\Theta_{d(\boldsymbol{x}_1,\boldsymbol{x}_2)>\beta_L}(\boldsymbol{x}_1, \boldsymbol{x}_2) \wedge \Theta_{d(\boldsymbol{x}_1,\boldsymbol{x}_2)<\beta_{\text{Sh}}}(\boldsymbol{x}_1, \boldsymbol{x}_2)$
	$\Theta_{\text{Aligned}}(\boldsymbol{x}_1, \boldsymbol{x}_2)$	$\Theta_{\alpha(\boldsymbol{x}_1,\boldsymbol{x}_2)\approx_\varepsilon 0}(\boldsymbol{x}_1, \boldsymbol{x}_2)$
	$\Theta_{\text{Opposed}}(\boldsymbol{x}_1, \boldsymbol{x}_2)$	$\Theta_{\alpha(\boldsymbol{x}_1,\boldsymbol{x}_2)\approx_\varepsilon \pi}(\boldsymbol{x}_1, \boldsymbol{x}_2)$
$\boldsymbol{A}_3$	$\Theta_{\text{Bi-G-Platform}}(p, \boldsymbol{x}_1, \boldsymbol{x}_2)$	$\Theta_{\text{G-Platform}}(p, \boldsymbol{x}_1) \wedge \Theta_{\text{G-Platform}}(p, \boldsymbol{x}_2) \wedge \Theta_{\text{Feasible}}(\boldsymbol{x}_1, \boldsymbol{x}_2)$
	$\Theta_{\text{Bi-G-Prismatic}}(p, \boldsymbol{x}_1, \boldsymbol{x}_2)$	$\Theta_{\text{G-Prismatic}}(p, \boldsymbol{x}_1) \wedge \Theta_{\text{G-Prismatic}}(p, \boldsymbol{x}_2) \wedge \Theta_{\text{Feasible}}(\boldsymbol{x}_1, \boldsymbol{x}_2)$
$\boldsymbol{A}_4$	$\Theta_{\text{Bi-Grasp}}(p, \boldsymbol{x}_1, \boldsymbol{x}_2)$	$\Theta_{\text{Bi-G-Platform}}(p, \boldsymbol{x}_1, \boldsymbol{x}_2) \vee \Theta_{\text{Bi-G-Prismatic}}(p, \boldsymbol{x}_1, \boldsymbol{x}_2)$
$\boldsymbol{A}_5$	$\Theta_{\text{Bi-G-Aligned}}(p, \boldsymbol{x}_1, \boldsymbol{x}_2)$	$\Theta_{\text{Bi-Grasp}}(p, \boldsymbol{x}_1, \boldsymbol{x}_2) \wedge \Theta_{\text{Aligned}}(\boldsymbol{x}_1, \boldsymbol{x}_2)$
	$\Theta_{\text{Bi-G-Opposed}}(p, \boldsymbol{x}_1, \boldsymbol{x}_2)$	$\Theta_{\text{Bi-Grasp}}(p, \boldsymbol{x}_1, \boldsymbol{x}_2) \wedge \Theta_{\text{Opposed}}(\boldsymbol{x}_1, \boldsymbol{x}_2)$
	$\Theta_{\text{Bi-G-Aligned-Platform}}(p, \boldsymbol{x}_1, \boldsymbol{x}_2)$	$\Theta_{\text{Bi-G-Platform}}(p, \boldsymbol{x}_1, \boldsymbol{x}_2) \wedge \Theta_{\text{Aligned}}(\boldsymbol{x}_1, \boldsymbol{x}_2)$
	$\Theta_{\text{Bi-G-Aligned-Prismatic}}(p, \boldsymbol{x}_1, \boldsymbol{x}_2)$	$\Theta_{\text{Bi-G-Prismatic}}(p, \boldsymbol{x}_1, \boldsymbol{x}_2) \wedge \Theta_{\text{Aligned}}(\boldsymbol{x}_1, \boldsymbol{x}_2)$
	$\Theta_{\text{Bi-G-Opposed-Platform}}(p, \boldsymbol{x}_1, \boldsymbol{x}_2)$	$\Theta_{\text{Bi-G-Platform}}(p, \boldsymbol{x}_1, \boldsymbol{x}_2) \wedge \Theta_{\text{Opposed}}(\boldsymbol{x}_1, \boldsymbol{x}_2)$
	$\Theta_{\text{Bi-G-Opposed-Prismatic}}(p, \boldsymbol{x}_1, \boldsymbol{x}_2)$	$\Theta_{\text{Bi-G-Prismatic}}(p, \boldsymbol{x}_1, \boldsymbol{x}_2) \wedge \Theta_{\text{Opposed}}(\boldsymbol{x}_1, \boldsymbol{x}_2)$
$\boldsymbol{A}_6$	$\Theta_{\text{Bi-Support}}(p, \boldsymbol{x}_1, \boldsymbol{x}_2)$	$\Theta_{\text{Bi-G-Platform}}(p, \boldsymbol{x}_1, \boldsymbol{x}_2) \wedge \Theta_{\text{Fixed}}(p) \wedge \Theta_{\text{Horizontal}}(p)$
	$\Theta_{\text{Bi-Lean}}(p, \boldsymbol{x}_1, \boldsymbol{x}_2)$	$\Theta_{\text{Bi-G-Platform}}(p, \boldsymbol{x}_1, \boldsymbol{x}_2) \wedge \Theta_{\text{Fixed}}(p) \wedge \Theta_{\text{Vertical}}(p)$
	$\Theta_{\text{Bi-Hold}}(p, \boldsymbol{x}_1, \boldsymbol{x}_2)$	$\Theta_{\text{Bi-G-Prismatic}}(p, \boldsymbol{x}_1, \boldsymbol{x}_2) \wedge \Theta_{\text{Hold}}(p, \boldsymbol{x}_1) \wedge \Theta_{\text{Hold}}(p, \boldsymbol{x}_2)$
	$\Theta_{\text{Bi-Lift}}(p, \boldsymbol{x}_1, \boldsymbol{x}_2)$	$\Theta_{\text{Bi-G-Prismatic}}(p, \boldsymbol{x}_1, \boldsymbol{x}_2) \wedge \Theta_{\text{Lift}}(p, \boldsymbol{x}_1) \wedge \Theta_{\text{Lift}}(p, \boldsymbol{x}_2)$
	$\Theta_{\text{Bi-Push}}(p, \boldsymbol{x}_1, \boldsymbol{x}_2)$	$\Theta_{\text{Bi-G-Aligned}}(p, \boldsymbol{x}_1, \boldsymbol{x}_2) \wedge \Theta_{\text{Push}}(\boldsymbol{x}_1) \wedge \Theta_{\text{Push}}(\boldsymbol{x}_2)$
	$\Theta_{\text{Bi-Pull}}(p, \boldsymbol{x}_1, \boldsymbol{x}_2)$	$\Theta_{\text{Bi-G-Aligned-Prismatic}}(p, \boldsymbol{x}_1, \boldsymbol{x}_2) \wedge \Theta_{\text{Pull}}(\boldsymbol{x}_1) \wedge \Theta_{\text{Pull}}(\boldsymbol{x}_2)$
	$\Theta_{\text{Bi-Turn}}(p, \boldsymbol{x}_1, \boldsymbol{x}_2)$	$\Theta_{\text{Bi-G-Opposed-Prismatic}}(p, \boldsymbol{x}_1, \boldsymbol{x}_2) \wedge \Theta_{\text{Round}}(p)$

List of Figures

List of Tables

List of Algorithms

Acronyms

BN	Bayesian Network
CNN	Convolutional Neural Network
DARPA	Defence Advanced Research Project Agency
DRC	DARPA Robotics Challenge
DST	Dempster-Shafer Theory
H^2T	High-Performance Humanoid Technologies
LOA	Level of Automation
OAC	Object-Action Complex
RANSAC	Random Sample Consensus
RGB	Red-Green-Blue
RGB-D	Red-Green-Blue-Depth
SIFT	Scale-Invariant Feature Transform
SLAM	Simultaneous Localization and Mapping
SVM	Support Vector Machine
WALK-MAN	Whole-body Adaptive Locomotion and Manipulation

Bibliography

K. E. Adolph and K. S. Kretch (2015), „Gibson's Theory of Perceptual Learning", *International Encyclopedia of the Social and Behavioral Sciences*, vol. 10, no. 2, pp. 127–134.

B. Akgün, N. Dağ, T. Bilal, İ. Atıl, and E. Şahin (2009), „Unsupervised Learning of Affordance Relations on a Humanoid Robot", *IEEE International Symposium on Computer and Information Sciences (ISCIS)*, pp. 254–259.

A. Aldoma, F. Tombari, and M. Vincze (2012), „Supervised Learning of Hidden and Non-Hidden 0-order Affordances and Detection in Real Scenes", *IEEE International Conference on Robotics and Automation (ICRA)*, pp. 1732–1739.

E. Ambrosini and M. Costantini (2013), „Handles lost in non-reachable space", *Experimental Brain Research*, vol. 229, pp. 197–202.

A. Antunes, L. Jamone, G. Saponaro, A. Bernardino, and R. Ventura (2016), „From Human Instructions to Robot Actions: Formulation of Goals, Affordances and Probabilistic Planning", *IEEE International Conference on Robotics and Automation (ICRA)*, pp. 5449–5454.

R. C. Arkin (1998), *Behavior-based Robotics*, MIT Press.

T. Asfour, K. Regenstein, P. Azad, J. Schröder, A. Bierbaum, N. Vahrenkamp, and R. Dillmann (2006), „ARMAR-III: An Integrated Humanoid Platform for Sensory-Motor Control“, *IEEE/RAS International Conference on Humanoid Robots (Humanoids)*, pp. 169–175.

T. Asfour, J. Schill, H. Peters, C. Klas, J. Bücker, C. Sander, S. Schulz, A. Kargov, T. Werner, and V. Bartenbach (2013), „ARMAR-4: A 63 DOF Torque Controlled Humanoid Robot“, *IEEE/RAS International Conference on Humanoid Robots (Humanoids)*, pp. 390–396.

C. G. Atkeson, B. P. Babu, N. Banerjee, D. Berenson, C. P. Bove, X. Cui, M. DeDonato, R. Du, S. Feng, P. Franklin, M. Gennert, J. P. Graff, P. He, A. Jaeger, J. Kim, K. Knoedler, L. Li, C. Liu, X. Long, T. Padir, F. Polido, G. G. Tighe, and X. Xinjilefu (2015), „NO FALLS, NO RESETS: Reliable Humanoid Behavior in the DARPA Robotics Challenge“, *IEEE/RAS International Conference on Humanoid Robots (Humanoids)*, pp. 623–630.

J. Baleia, P. Santana, and J. Barata (2015), „On Exploiting Haptic Cues for Self-Supervised Learning of Depth-Based Robot Navigation Affordances“, *Journal of Intelligent & Robotic Systems*, vol. 80, no. 3, pp. 455–474.

C. Barck-Holst, M. Ralph, F. Holmar, and D. Kragic (2009), „Learning Grasping Affordance Using Probabilistic and Ontological Approaches“, *IEEE International Conference on Advanced Robotics (ICAR)*, pp. 1–6.

M. Beynon, B. Curry, and P. Morgan (2000), „The Dempster–Shafer theory of evidence: an alternative approach to multicriteria decision modelling“, *Omega*, vol. 28, no. 1, pp. 37–50.

A. Bierbaum, M. Rambow, T. Asfour, and R. Dillmann (2009), „Grasp Affordances from Multi-Fingered Tactile Exploration using Dynamic Potential Fields“, *IEEE/RAS International Conference on Humanoid Robots (Humanoids)*, pp. 168–174.

P. Birkenkampf, D. Leidner, and C. Borst (2014), „A Knowledge-Driven Shared Autonomy Human-Robot Interface for Tablet Computes“, *IEEE/RAS International Conference on Humanoid Robots (Humanoids)*, pp. 152–159.

J. Bohg, A. Morales, T. Asfour, and D. Kragic (2014), „Data-Driven Grasp Synthesis - A Survey“, *IEEE Transactions on Robotics*, vol. 30, no. 2, pp. 289–309.

V. Braitenberg (1986), *Vehicles: Experiments in Synthetic Psychology*, MIT Press.

R. A. Brooks (1986), „A Robust Layered Control System for a Mobile Robot“, *IEEE Journal on Robotics and Automation*, vol. 2, no. 1, pp. 14–23.

R. A. Brooks (1990), „Elephants Don't Play Chess“, *Robotics and Autonomous Systems*, vol. 6, no. 1, pp. 3–15.

D. N. Bub and M. E. J. Masson (2010), „Grasping Beer Mugs: On the Dynamics of Alignment Effects Induced by Handled Objects“, *Journal of Experimental Psychology: Human Perception and Performance*, vol. 36, no. 2, pp. 341–358.

I. M. Bullock, J. Z. Zheng, S. De La Rosa, C. Guertler, and A. M. Dollar (2013), „Grasp Frequency and Usage in Daily Household and Machine Shop Tasks“, *IEEE Transactions on Haptics*, vol. 6, no. 3, pp. 296–308.

M. Çakmak, M. R. Doğar, E. Uğur, and E. Şahin (2007), „Affordances as a Framework for Robot Control“, *International Conference on Epigenetic Robotics (EpiRob)*.

H. Çelikkanat, G. Orhan, and S. Kalkan (2015), „A Probabilistic Concept Web on a Humanoid Robot“, *IEEE Transactions on Autonomous Mental Development*, vol. 7, no. 2, pp. 92–106.

A. Chemero (2003), „An Outline of a Theory of Affordances", *Ecological Psychology*, vol. 15, no. 2, pp. 181–195.

V. Chu, B. Akgün, and A. L. Thomaz (2016a), „Learning Haptic Affordances from Demonstration and Human-Guided Exploration", *IEEE Haptics Symposium (HAPTICS)*, pp. 119–125.

V. Chu, T. Fitzgerald, and A. L. Thomaz (2016b), „Learning Object Affordances by Leveraging the Combination of Human-Guidance and Self-Exploration", *IEEE/ACM International Conference on Human Robot Interaction*, pp. 221–228.

T. Collett (1977), „Stereopsis in toads", *Nature*, vol. 267, pp. 349–351.

M. Costantini, E. Ambrosini, G. Tieri, C. Sinigaglia, and G. Committeri (2010), „Where does an object trigger an action? An investigation about affordances in space", *Experimental Brain Research*, vol. 207, pp. 95–103.

M. R. Cutkosky (1989), „On Grasp Choice, Grasp Models, and the Design of Hands for Manufacturing Tasks", *IEEE Transactions on Robotics and Automation*, vol. 5, no. 3, pp. 269–279.

N. Dağ, İ. Atıl, S. Kalkan, and E. Şahin (2010), „Learning Affordances for Categorizing Objects and Their Properties", *IEEE International Conference on Pattern Recognition (ICPR)*, pp. 3089–3092.

C. de Granville, J. Southerland, and A. H. Fagg (2006), „Learning Grasp Affordances Through Human Demonstration", *IEEE International Conference on Development and Learning (ICDL)*.

M. DeDonato, F. Polido, K. Knoedler, B. P. W. Babu, N. Banerjee, C. P. Bove, X. Cui, R. Du, P. Franklin, J. P. Graff, P. He, A. Jaeger, L. Li, D. Berenson, M. A. Gennert, S. Feng, C. Liu, X. Xinjilefu, J. Kim, C. G. Atkeson, X. Long, and T. Padır (2017), „Team WPI-CMU: Achieving

Reliable Humanoid Behavior in the DARPA Robotics Challenge“, *Journal of Field Robotics*, vol. 34, no. 2, pp. 381–399.

A. Dehban, L. Jamone, A. R. Kampff, and J. Santos-Victor (2016), „Denoising Auto-encoders for Learning of Objects and Tools Affordances in Continuous Space“, *IEEE International Conference on Robotics and Automation (ICRA)*, pp. 4866–4871.

A. P. Dempster (1967), „Upper and Lower Probabilities Induced by a Multi-valued Mapping“, *The Annals of Mathematical Statistics*, vol. 38, no. 2, pp. 325–339.

C. Desai and D. Ramanan (2013), „Predicting Functional Regions of Objects“, *IEEE Conference on Computer Vision and Pattern Recognition (CVPR) Workshops*, pp. 968–975.

R. Detry, E. Başeski, M. Popović, Y. Touati, N. Krüger, O. Kroemer, J. Peters, and J. Piater (2009), „Learning object-specific grasp affordance densities“, *IEEE International Conference on Development and Learning (ICDL)*, pp. 1–7.

R. Detry, D. Kraft, A. G. Buch, N. Krüger, and J. Piater (2010), „Refining Grasp Affordance Models by Experience“, *IEEE International Conference on Robotics and Automation (ICRA)*, pp. 2287–2293.

R. Detry, D. Kraft, O. Kroemer, L. Bodenhagen, J. Peters, N. Krüger, and J. Piater (2011), „Learning Grasp Affordance Densities“, *Paladyn*, vol. 2, no. 1.

T.-T. Do, A. Nguyen, I. Reid, D. G. Caldwell, and N. G. Tsagarakis (2017), „AffordanceNet: An End-to-End Deep Learning Approach for Object Affordance Detection“, *arXiv:1709.07326 [cs.CV]*, arXiv: 1709.07326.

M. R. Doğar, M. Çakmak, E. Uğur, and E. Şahin (2007), „From Primitive Behaviors to Goal-Directed Behavior Using Affordances“, *IEEE/RSJ Inter-*

national Conference on Intelligent Robots and Systems (IROS), pp. 729–734.

M. R. Doğar, E. Uğur, E. Şahin, and M. Çakmak (2008), „Using Learned Affordances for Robotic Behavior Development“, *IEEE International Conference on Robotics and Automation (ICRA)*, pp. 3802–3807.

D. G. Dotov, L. Nie, and M. M. de Witt (2012), „Understanding affordances: history and contemporary development of Gibson's central concept“, *AVANT*, vol. 3, no. 2, pp. 28–39.

DRC-Teams (2015), *What Happened at the DARPA Robotics Challenge?*, URL: `http://www.cs.cmu.edu/~cga/drc/events/`.

A. P. Duchon, W. H. Warren, and L. P. Kaelbling (1998), „Ecological Robotics“, *Adaptive Behavior*, vol. 6, no. 3, pp. 473–507.

V. Dutta and T. Zielinska (2016), „Predicting the Intention of Human Activities for Real-Time Human-Robot Interaction (HRI)“, *International Conference on Social Robotics*, vol. 9979, Lecture Notes in Computer Science, Cham: Springer, pp. 723–734.

M. R. Endsley and D. B. Kaber (1999), „Level of automation effects on performance, situation awareness and workload in a dynamic control task“, *Ergonomics*, vol. 42, no. 3, pp. 462–492.

E. Erdemir, C. B. Frankel, K. Kawamura, S. M. Gordon, S. Thornton, and B. Ulutas (2008), „Towards a Cognitive Robot that Uses Internal Rehearsal to Learn Affordance Relations“, *IEEE/RSJ International Conference on Intelligent Robots and Systems (IROS)*, pp. 2016–2021.

B. R. Fajen, M. A. Riley, and M. T. Turvey (2008), „Information, affordances, and the control of action in sport“, *International Journal of Sport Psychology*, vol. 40, pp. 79–107.

M. Fallon, S. Kuindersma, S. Karumanchi, M. Antone, T. Schneider, H. Dai, C. Pérez D'Arpino, R. Deits, M. DiCicco, D. Fourie, T. Koolen, P. Marion, M. Posa, A. Valenzuela, K.-T. Yu, J. Shah, K. Iagnemma, R. Tedrake, and S. Teller (2015a), „An Architecture for Online Affordance-based Perception and Whole-body Planning", *Journal of Field Robotics*, vol. 32, no. 2, pp. 229–254.

M. Fallon, P. Marion, R. Deits, T. Whelan, M. Antone, J. McDonald, and R. Tedrake (2015b), „Continuous Humanoid Locomotion over Uneven Terrain using Stereo Fusion", *IEEE/RAS International Conference on Humanoid Robots (Humanoids)*, pp. 881–888.

M. A. Fischler and R. C. Bolles (1981), „Random Sample Consensus: A Paradigm for Model Fitting with Applications to Image Analysis and Automated Cartography", *Communications of the ACM*, vol. 24, no. 6, pp. 381–395.

P. Fitzpatrick and G. Metta (2003a), „Grounding Vision through Experimental Manipulation", *Philosophical Transactions: Mathematical, Physical and Engineering Sciences*, vol. 361, no. 1811, pp. 2165–2185.

P. Fitzpatrick, G. Metta, L. Natale, S. Rao, and G. Sandini (2003b), „Learning About Objects Through Action - Initial Steps Towards Artificial Cognition", *IEEE International Conference on Robotics and Automation (ICRA)*, pp. 3140–3145.

G. Fritz, L. Paletta, M. Kumar, G. Dorffner, R. Breithaupt, and E. Rome (2006), „Visual Learning of Affordance Based Cues", *International Conference on Simulation of Adaptive Behavior (SAB)*, pp. 52–64.

J. W. Garrett (1971), „The Adult Human Hand: Some Anthropometric and Biomechanical Considerations", *Human Factors*, vol. 13, no. 2, pp. 117–131.

A. Giagkos, D. Lewkowicz, P. Shaw, S. Kumar, M. Lee, and Q. Shen (2017), „Perception of Localized Features during Robotic Sensorimotor Development“, *IEEE Transactions on Cognitive and Developmental Systems*, vol. 9, no. 2, pp. 127–140.

E. J. Gibson (1992), „How to think about perceptual learning: Twenty-five years later.“, *Cognition: Conceptual and methodological issues*, pp. 215–239.

E. J. Gibson, G. Riccio, M. A. Schmuckler, T. A. Stoffregen, D. Rosenberg, and J. Taormina (1987), „Detection of the traversability of surfaces by crawling and walking infants“, *Journal of Experimental Psychology: Human Perception and Performance*, vol. 13, no. 4, pp. 533–544.

J. J. Gibson (1966), *The senses considered as perceptual systems*, Boston: Houghton Mifflin.

J. J. Gibson (1986), *The Ecological Approach to Visual Perception*, original work published in 1979, New Jersey, USA: Lawrence Erlbaum Associates.

A. Gonçalves, J. Abrantes, G. Saponaro, L. Jamone, and A. Bernardino (2014a), „Learning Intermediate Object Affordances: Towards the Development of a Tool Concept“, *IEEE International Conference on Developmental Learning and Epigenetic Robotics*, pp. 474–480.

A. Gonçalves, G. Saponaro, L. Jamone, and A. Bernardino (2014b), „Learning Visual Affordances of Objects and Tools through Autonomous Robot Exploration“, *IEEE International Conference on Autonomous Robot Systems and Competitions (ICARSC)*, pp. 128–133.

M. Grotz, P. Kaiser, E. E. Aksoy, F. Paus, and T. Asfour (2017), „Graph-Based Visual Semantic Perception for Humanoid Robots“, *IEEE/RAS International Conference on Humanoid Robots (Humanoids)*.

S. Hart (2009), „An Intrinsic Reward for Affordance Exploration“, *IEEE International Conference on Development and Learning (ICDL)*, pp. 1–6.

S. Hart, P. Dinh, and K. Hambuchen (2015), „The Affordance Template ROS Package for Robot Task Programming“, *IEEE International Conference on Robotics and Automation (ICRA)*, pp. 6227–6234.

S. Hart and R. Grupen (2011), „Learning Generalizable Control Programs“, *IEEE Transactions on Autonomous Mental Development*, vol. 3, no. 3, pp. 216–231.

S. Hart, R. Grupen, and D. Jensen (2005), „A Relational Representation for Procedural Task Knowledge“, *AAAI National Conference on Artificial Intelligence*, pp. 1280–1285.

T. E. Horton, A. Chakraborty, and R. S. Amant (2012), „Affordances for robots: a brief survey“, *AVANT*, vol. 3, no. 2, pp. 70–84.

D. Ingle and J. Cook (1977), „The Effect of Viewing Distance Upon Size Preference of Frogs for Prey“, *Vision Research*, vol. 17, pp. 1009–1013.

International Federation of Robotics (2016a), *Executive Summary World Robotics 2016 Industrial Robots*.

International Federation of Robotics (2016b), *Executive Summary World Robotics 2016 Service Robots*.

R. Jain and T. Inamura (2013), „Bayesian learning of tool affordances based on generalization of functional feature to estimate effects of unseen tools“, *Artificial Life and Robotics*, vol. 18, pp. 95–103.

L. Jamone, E. Uğur, A. Cangelosi, L. Fadiga, A. Bernardino, J. Piater, and J. Santos-Victor (2016), „Affordances in psychology, neuroscience and robotics: a survey“, *IEEE Transactions on Cognitive and Developmental Systems*.

Y. Jiang, H. Koppula, and A. Saxena (2013), „Hallucinated Humans as the Hidden Context for Labeling 3D Scenes“, *IEEE Conference on Computer Vision and Pattern Recognition (CVPR)*, pp. 2993–3000.

M. Johnson, B. Shrewsbury, S. Bertrand, T. Wu, D. Duran, M. Floyd, P. Abeles, D. Stephen, N. Mertins, A. Lesman, J. Carff, W. Rifenburgh, P. Kaveti, W. Straatman, J. Smith, M. Griffioen, B. Layton, T. de Boer, T. Koolen, P. Neuhaus, and J. Pratt (2015), „Team IHMC's Lessons Learned from the DARPA Robotics Challenge Trials“, *Journal of Field Robotics (JFR)*, vol. 32, no. 2, pp. 192–208.

K. S. Jones (2003), „What Is an Affordance?“, *Ecological Psychology*, vol. 15, no. 2, pp. 107–114.

A. Jøsang (2001), „A Logic for Uncertain Probabilities“, *International Journal of Uncertainty, Fuzziness and Knowledge-Based Systems*, vol. 9, no. 3, pp. 279–311.

P. Kaiser, E. E. Aksoy, M. Grotz, and T. Asfour (2016a), „Towards a Hierarchy of Loco-Manipulation Affordances“, *IEEE/RSJ International Conference on Intelligent Robots and Systems (IROS)*, pp. 2839–2846.

P. Kaiser, E. E. Aksoy, M. Grotz, D. Kanoulas, N. G. Tsagarakis, and T. Asfour (2016b), „Experimental Evaluation of a Perceptual Pipeline for Hierarchical Affordance Extraction“, *International Symposium on Experimental Robotics*, vol. 1, Springer Proceedings in Advanced Robotics (SPAR), Springer International Publishing, pp. 136–146.

P. Kaiser and T. Asfour (2018a), „Autonomous Detection and Experimental Validation of Affordances“, *IEEE Robotics and Automation Letters (RA-L)*.

P. Kaiser, D. Gonzalez-Aguirre, F. Schültje, J. Borràs, N. Vahrenkamp, and T. Asfour (2014a), „Extracting Whole-Body Affordances from Multimodal

Exploration“, *IEEE/RAS International Conference on Humanoid Robots (Humanoids)*, pp. 1036–1043.

P. Kaiser, M. Grotz, E. E. Aksoy, M. Do, N. Vahrenkamp, and T. Asfour (2015a), „Validation of Whole-Body Loco-Manipulation Affordances for Pushability and Liftability“, *IEEE/RAS International Conference on Humanoid Robots (Humanoids)*, pp. 920–927.

P. Kaiser, D. Kanoulas, M. Grotz, L. Muratore, A. Rocchi, E. Mingo Hoffman, N. G. Tsagarakis, and T. Asfour (2016c), „An Affordance-Based Pilot Interface for High-Level Control of Humanoid Robots in Supervised Autonomy“, *IEEE/RAS International Conference on Humanoid Robots (Humanoids)*, pp. 621–628.

P. Kaiser, M. Lewis, R. P. A. Petrick, T. Asfour, and M. Steedman (2014b), „Extracting Common Sense Knowledge from Text for Robot Planning“, *IEEE International Conference on Robotics and Automation (ICRA)*, pp. 3749–3756.

P. Kaiser, C. Mandery, A. Boltres, and T. Asfour (2018b), „Affordance-Based Multi-Contact Whole-Body Pose Sequence Planning for Humanoid Robots in Unknown Environments“, *IEEE International Conference on Robotics and Automation (ICRA)*.

P. Kaiser, N. Vahrenkamp, F. Schültje, J. Borràs, and T. Asfour (2015b), „Extraction of Whole-Body Affordances for Loco-Manipulation Tasks“, *International Journal of Humanoid Robotics*, vol. 12, no. 3.

D. Kanoulas, J. Lee, D. G. Caldwell, and N. G. Tsagarakis (2017), „Visual Grasp Affordance Localization in Point Clouds using Curved Contact Patches“, *International Journal of Humanoid Robotics (IJHR)*, vol. 14, no. 1, p. 1650028.

S. Karumanchi, K. Edelberg, I. Baldwin, J. Nash, J. Reid, C. Bergh, J. Leichty, K. Carpenter, M. Shekels, M. Gildner, D. Newill-Smith, J. Carlton, J. Koehler, T. Dobreva, M. Frost, P. Hebert, J. Borders, J. Ma, B. Douillard, P. Backes, B. Kennedy, B. Satzinger, C. Lau, K. Byl, K. Shankar, and J. Burdick (2017), „Team RoboSimian: Semi-autonomous Mobile Manipulation at the 2015 DARPA Robotics Challenge Finals“, *Journal of Field Robotics (JFR)*, vol. 34, no. 2, pp. 305–332.

D. Katz, A. Venkatraman, M. Kazemi, J. A. Bagnell, and A. Stentz (2014), „Perceiving, Learning, and Exploiting Object Affordances for Autonomous Pile Manipulation“, *Autonomous Robots*, vol. 37, no. 4, pp. 369–382.

D. I. Kim and G. S. Sukhatme (2014), „Semantic Labeling of 3D Point Clouds with Object Affordance for Robot Manipulation“, *IEEE International Conference on Robotics and Automation (ICRA)*, pp. 5578–5584.

D. I. Kim and G. S. Sukhatme (2015), „Interactive Affordance Map Building for a Robotic Task“, *IEEE/RSJ International Conference on Intelligent Robots and Systems (IROS)*, pp. 4581–4586.

D. Kim, J. Sun, S. M. Oh, J. M. Rehg, and A. F. Bobick (2006), „Traversability Classification using Unsupervised On-line Visual Learning for Outdoor Robot Navigation“, *IEEE International Conference on Robotics and Automation (ICRA)*, pp. 518–525.

S. Kim, M. Kim, J. Lee, S. Hwang, J. Chae, B. Park, H. Cho, J. Sim, J. Jung, H. Lee, S. Shin, M. Kim, W. Choi, Y. Lee, S. Park, J. Oh, Y. Lee, S. Lee, M. Lee, S. Yi, K.-S. K. C. Chang, N. Kwak, and J. Park (2017), „Team SNU's Control Strategies for Enhancing a Robot's Capability: Lessons from the 2015 DARPA Robotics Challenge Finals“, *Journal of Field Robotics (JFR)*, vol. 34, no. 2, pp. 359–380.

J. Kinsella-Shaw, B. Shaw, and M. T. Turvey (1992), „Perceiving "Walk-on-able" Slopes“, *Ecological Psychology*, vol. 4, no. 4, pp. 223–239.

H. Kjellström, J. Romero, and D. Kragić (2011), „Visual object-action recognition: Inferring object affordances from human demonstration“, *Computer Vision and Image Understanding*, vol. 115, no. 1, pp. 81–90.

W. Köhler (1925), *The Mentality of Apes*, New York: Harcourt Brace and World.

H. S. Koppula and A. Saxena (2013), „Anticipating Human Activities using Object Affordances for Reactive Robotic Response“, Robotics: Science and Systems (RSS).

H. S. Koppula and A. Saxena (2014), „Physically-Grounded Spatio-Temporal Object Affordances“, European Conference on Computer Vision (ECCV).

H. S. Koppula and A. Saxena (2016), „Anticipating Human Activities using Object Affordances for Reactive Robotic Response“, *IEEE Transactions on Pattern Analysis and Machine Intelligence*, vol. 38, no. 1, pp. 14–29.

I. Kostavelis, L. Nalpantidis, and A. Gasteratos (2012), „Collision risk assessment for autonomous robots by offline traversability learning“, *Robotics and Autonomous Systems*, vol. 60, no. 11, pp. 1367–1376.

D. Kraft, N. Pugeault, E. Başeski, M. Popović, D. Kragić, S. Kalkan, F. Wörgötter, and N. Krüger (2008), „Birth of the Object: Detection of Objectness and Extraction of Object Shape through Object Action Complexes“, *International Journal of Humanoid Robotics (IJHR)*, vol. 5, no. 2, pp. 247–265.

O. Kroemer and G. S. Sukhatme (2016), „Learning Spatial Preconditions of Manipulation Skills using Random Forests“, *IEEE/RAS International Conference on Humanoid Robots (Humanoids)*, pp. 676–683.

O. Kroemer, E. Uğur, E. Oztop, and J. Peters (2012), „A Kernel-based Approach to Direct Action Perception“, IEEE International Conference on Robotics and Automation (ICRA), pp. 2605–2610.

E. Krotkov, D. Hackett, L. Jackel, M. Perschbacher, J. Pippine, J. Strauss, G. Pratt, and C. Orlowski (2017), „The DARPA Robotics Challenge Finals: Results and Perspectives“, *Journal of Field Robotics (JFR)*, vol. 34, no. 2, pp. 229–240.

N. Krüger, C. Geib, J. Piater, R. Petrick, M. Steedman, F. Wörgötter, A. Ude, T. Asfour, D. Kraft, D. Omrčen, A. Agostini, and R. Dillmann (2011), „Object-Action Complexes: Grounded abstractions of sensory-motor processes“, *Robotics and Autonomous Systems*, vol. 59, no. 10, pp. 740–757.

M. Labbé and F. Michaud (2014), „Online Global Loop Closure Detection for Large-Scale Multi-Session Graph-Based SLAM“, *IEEE/RSJ International Conference on Intelligent Robots and Systems (IROS)*, pp. 2661–2666.

S. R. Lakani, A. J. Rodríguez-Sánchez, and J. Piater (2017), „Can Affordances Guide Object Decomposition into Semantically Meaningful Parts?“, *IEEE Winter Conference on Applications of Computer Vision (WACV)*, pp. 82–90.

I. Lenz, H. Lee, and A. Saxena (2015), „Deep learning for detecting robotic grasps“, *International Journal of Robotics Research (IJRR)*, vol. 34, no. 4, pp. 705–724.

J. Y. Lettvin, H. R. Maturana, W. S. McCulloch, and W. H. Pitts (1959), „What the Frog's Eye Tells the Frog's Brain“, *Proceedings of the IRE*, vol. 47, no. 11, pp. 1940–1951.

M. A. Lewis, H.-K. Lee, and A. Patla (2005), „Foot Placement Selection Using Non-geometric Visual Properties“, *International Journal of Robotics Research (IJRR)*, vol. 24, no. 7, pp. 553–561.

H. Liu and P. Singh (2004), „ConceptNet — a practical commonsense reasoning tool-kit“, *BT Technology Journal*, vol. 22, no. 4, pp. 211–226.

Y. Liu and G. Nejat (2013), „Robotic Urban Search and Rescue: A Survey from the Control Perspective“, *Journal of Intelligent & Robotic Systems*, vol. 72, no. 2, pp. 147–165.

A. Lock and T. Collett (1979), „A Toad's Devious Approach to Its Prey: A Study of Some Complex Uses of Depth Vision“, *Journal of Comparative Physiology*, vol. 131, pp. 179–189.

M. Lopes, F. S. Melo, and L. Montesano (2007), „Affordance-based imitation learning in robots“, IEEE/RSJ International Conference on Intelligent Robots and Systems (IROS), pp. 1015–1021.

T. Lüddecke and F. Wörgötter (2016), „Scene Affordance: Inferring Actions from Household Scenes“, *Workshop on Action and Anticipation for Visual Learning*, European Conference on Computer Vision (ECCV).

T. Lüddecke and F. Wörgötter (2017), „Learning to Label Affordances from Simulated and Real Data“, *arXiv:1709.08872 [cs.CV]*.

K. F. MacDorman (2000), „Responding to Affordances: Learning and Projecting a Sensorimotor Mapping“, *IEEE International Conference on Robotics and Automation (ICRA)*, pp. 3253–3259.

C. Mandery, J. Borràs, M. Jöchner, and T. Asfour (2015a), „Analyzing Whole-Body Pose Transitions in Multi-Contact Motions“, *IEEE/RAS International Conference on Humanoid Robots (Humanoids)*, pp. 1020–1027.

C. Mandery, J. Borràs, M. Jöchner, and T. Asfour (2016), „Using Language Models to Generate Whole-Body Multi-Contact Motions“, *IEEE/RSJ International Conference on Intelligent Robots and Systems (IROS)*, pp. 5411–5418.

C. Mandery, Ö. Terlemez, M. Do, N. Vahrenkamp, and T. Asfour (2015b), „The KIT Whole-Body Human Motion Database“, *IEEE International Conference on Advanced Robotics (ICAR)*, pp. 329–336.

T. Mar, V. Tikhanoff, G. Metta, and L. Natale (2015), „Self-supervised learning of grasp dependent tool affordances on the iCub Humanoid robot", *IEEE International Conference on Robotics and Automation (ICRA)*, pp. 3200–3206.

T. Mar, V. Tikhanoff, and L. Natale (2017), „What can I do with this tool? Self-supervised learning of tool affordances from their 3D geometry.", *IEEE Transactions on Cognitive and Developmental Systems*.

L. S. Mark (1987), „Eyeheight-Scaled Information About Affordances: A Study of Sitting and Stair Climbing", *Journal of Experimental Psychology: Human Perception and Performance*, vol. 13, no. 3, pp. 361–370.

J. McGrenere and W. Ho (2000), „Affordances: Clarifying and Evolving a Concept", *Graphics Interface*, pp. 179–186.

S. McMahon, N. Sünderhauf, B. Upcroft, and M. Milford (2017), „Multi-modal Trip Hazard Affordance Detection On Construction Sites", *IEEE Robotics and Automation Letters*, vol. 3, no. 1.

G. Metta and P. Fitzpatrick (2003), „Better Vision Through Manipulation", *Adaptive Behavior*, vol. 11, no. 2, pp. 109–128.

C. F. Michaels (2003), „Affordances: Four Points of Debate", *Ecological Psychology*, vol. 15, no. 2, pp. 135–148.

G. A. Miller (1995), „WordNet: A Lexical Database for English", *Communications of the ACM*, vol. 38, no. 11, pp. 39–41.

H. Min, C. Yi, R. Luo, J. Zhu, and S. Bi (2016), „Affordance Research in Developmental Robotics: A Survey", *IEEE Transactions on Cognitive and Developmental Systems*, vol. 8, no. 4, pp. 237–255.

B. Moldovan and L. De Raedt (2014), „Occluded Object Search by Relational Affordances“, *IEEE International Conference on Robotics and Automation (ICRA)*, pp. 169–174.

B. Moldovan, P. Moreno, D. Nitti, J. Santos-Victor, and L. De Raedt (2017), „Relational affordances for multiple-object manipulation“, *Autonomous Robots*.

B. Moldovan, P. Moreno, and M. van Otterlo (2013), „On the Use of Probabilistic Relational Affordance Models for Sequential Manipulation Tasks in Robotics“, *IEEE International Conference on Robotics and Automation (ICRA)*, pp. 1050–4729.

B. Moldovan, P. Moreno, M. van Otterlo, J. Santos-Victor, and L. De Raedt (2012), „Learning Relational Affordance Models for Robots in Multi-Object Manipulation Tasks“, *IEEE International Conference on Robotics and Automation (ICRA)*, pp. 4373–4378.

L. Montesano and M. Lopes (2009), „Learning grasping affordances from local visual descriptors“, *IEEE International Conference on Development and Learning (ICDL)*, pp. 1–6.

L. Montesano, M. Lopes, A. Bernardino, and J. Santos-Victor (2007a), „Affordances, development and imitation“, *IEEE International Conference on Development and Learning (ICDL)*, pp. 270–275.

L. Montesano, M. Lopes, A. Bernardino, and J. Santos-Victor (2007b), „Modeling Affordances using Bayesian networks“, IEEE/RSJ International Conference on Intelligent Robots and Systems (IROS), pp. 4102–4107.

L. Montesano, M. Lopes, A. Bernardino, and J. Santos-Victor (2008), „Learning Object Affordances: From Sensory-Motor Coordination to Imitation“, *IEEE Transactions on Robotics*, vol. 24, no. 1, pp. 15–26.

R. R. Murphy (1999), „Case Studies of Applying Gibson's Ecological Approach to Mobile Robots“, *IEEE Transactions on Systems, Man, and Cybernetics*, vol. 29, no. 1, pp. 105–111.

R. R. Murphy (2015), „Meta-analysis of Autonomy at the DARPA Robotics Challenge Trials“, *Journal of Field Robotics*, vol. 32, no. 2, pp. 189–191.

W. Mustafa, M. Wächter, S. Szedmak, A. Agostini, D. Kraft, T. Asfour, J. Piater, F. Wörgötter, and N. Krüger (2016), „Affordance Estimation For Vision-Based Object Replacement on a Humanoid Robot“, *International Symposium on Robotics (ISR)*, pp. 1–9.

A. Myers, C. L. Teo, C. Fermüller, and Y. Aloimonos (2015), „Affordance Detection of Tool Parts from Geometric Features“, *IEEE International Conference on Robotics and Automation (ICRA)*, pp. 1374–1381.

A. Nguyen, D. Kanoulas, D. G. Caldwell, and N. G. Tsagarakis (2016), „Detecting Object Affordances with Convolutional Neural Networks“, *IEEE/RSJ International Conference on Intelligent Robots and Systems (IROS)*, pp. 2765–2770.

P. Osório, A. Bernardino, R. Martinez-Cantin, and J. Santos-Victor (2010), „Gaussian Mixture Models for Affordance Learning using Bayesian Networks“, *IEEE/RSJ International Conference on Intelligent Robots and Systems (IROS)*, pp. 4432–4437.

S. Oßwald, A. Görög, A. Hornung, and M. Bennewitz (2011a), „Autonomous Climbing of Spiral Staircases with Humanoids“, *IEEE/RSJ International Conference on Intelligent Robots and Systems (IROS)*, pp. 4844–4849.

S. Oßwald, J.-S. Gutmann, A. Hornung, and M. Bennewitz (2011b), „From 3D Point Clouds to Climbing Stairs: A Comparison of Plane Segmentation Approaches for Humanoids“, *IEEE/RAS International Conference on Humanoid Robots (Humanoids)*, pp. 93–98.

E. Ovchinnikova, M. Wächter, V. Wittenbeck, and T. Asfour (2015), „Multi-Purpose Natural Language Understanding Linked to Sensorimotor Experience in Humanoid Robots“, *IEEE/RAS International Conference on Humanoid Robots (Humanoids)*, pp. 365–372.

A. Paikan, D. Schiebener, M. Wächter, T. Asfour, G. Metta, and L. Natale (2015), „Transferring Object Grasping Knowledge and Skill Across Different Robotic Platforms“, *IEEE International Conference on Advanced Robotics (ICAR)*, pp. 498–503.

L. Paletta, G. Fritz, F. Kintzler, J. Irran, and G. Dorffner (2007), „Learning to Perceive Affordances in a Framework of Developmental Embodied Cognition“, *IEEE International Conference on Development and Learning (ICDL)*, pp. 110–115.

T. T. Pham, M. Eich, I. Reid, and G. Wyeth (2016), „Geometrically Consistent Plane Extraction for Dense Indoor 3D Maps Segmentation“, *IEEE/RSJ International Conference on Intelligent Robots and Systems (IROS)*, pp. 4199–4204.

J. Piater, S. Jodogne, R. Detry, D. Kraft, N. Krüger, O. Kroemer, and J. Peters (2011), „Learning visual representations for perception-action systems“, *The International Journal of Robotics Research (IJRR)*, vol. 30, no. 3, pp. 294–307.

L. Porzi, S. R. Bulò, A. Penate-Sanchez, E. Ricci, and F. Moreno-Noguer (2017), „Learning Depth-aware Deep Representations for Robotic Perception“, *IEEE Robotics and Automation Letters (RA-L)*, vol. 2, no. 2, pp. 468–475.

G. Pratt and J. Manzo (2013), „The DARPA Robotics Challenge“, *IEEE Robotics & Automation Magazine*, vol. 20, no. 2, pp. 10–12.

A. Price, S. Balakirsky, A. Bobick, and H. Christensen (2016), „Affordance-Feasible Planning with Manipulator Wrench Spaces“, *IEEE International Conference on Robotics and Automation (ICRA)*, pp. 3979–3986.

W. Pryor, Y.-C. Lin, and D. Berenson (2016), „Integrated Affordance Detection and Humanoid Locomotion Planning“, *IEEE/RAS International Conference on Humanoid Robots (Humanoids)*, pp. 125–131.

B. Ridge, A. Leonardis, A. Ude, M. Deniša, and D. Skočaj (2015), „Self-Supervised Online Learning of Basic Object Push Affordances“, *International Journal of Advanced Robotic Systems*, vol. 12, no. 3.

B. Ridge and A. Ude (2013), „Action-Grounded Push Affordance Bootstrapping of Unknown Objects“, *IEEE/RSJ International Conference on Intelligent Robots and Systems (IROS)*, pp. 2791–2798.

A. Romay, S. Kohlbrecher, D. C. Conner, and O. von Stryk (2015), „Achieving Versatile Manipulation Tasks with Unknown Objects by Supervised Humanoid Robots based on Object Templates“, *IEEE/RAS International Conference on Humanoid Robots (Humanoids)*, pp. 249–255.

A. Romay, S. Kohlbrecher, A. Stumpf, O. von Stryk, S. Maniatopoulos, H. Kress-Gazit, P. Schillinger, and D. C. Conner (2017), „Collaborative Autonomy between High-level Behaviors and Human Operators for Remote Manipulation Tasks using Different Humanoid Robots“, *Journal of Field Robotics (JFR)*, vol. 34, no. 2, pp. 333–358.

A. Roy and S. Todorovic (2016), „A Multi-scale CNN for Affordance Segmentation in RGB Images“, *European Conference on Computer Vision (ECCV)*, pp. 186–201.

M. Rudolph, M. Mühlig, M. Gienger, and H.-J. Böhme (2010), „Learning the Consequences of Actions: Representing Effects as Feature Changes“, *Inter-*

national Conference on Emerging Security Technologies (EST), pp. 124–129.

E. Ruiz and W. Mayol-Cuevas (2017), „Geometric Affordances from a Single Example via the Interaction Tensor", *arXiv:1703.10584 [cs.CV].*

R. B. Rusu and S. Cousins (2011), „3D is here: Point Cloud Library (PCL)", *IEEE International Conference on Robotics and Automation (ICRA)*, pp. 1–4.

E. Şahin, M. Çakmak, M. R. Doğar, E. Uğur, and G. Üçoluk (2007), „To Afford or Not to Afford: A New Formalization of Affordances Toward Affordance-Based Robot Control", *Adaptive Behavior*, vol. 15, no. 4, pp. 447–472.

V. Sarathy and M. Scheutz (2016), „Beyond Grasping - Perceiving Affordances Across Various Stages of Cognitive Development", *IEEE International Conference on Developmental Learning and Epigenetic Robotics*, pp. 180–185.

J. Sawatzky, A. Srikantha, and J. Gall (2017), „Weakly Supervised Affordance Detection", *IEEE Conference on Computer Vision and Pattern Recognition (CVPR)*, pp. 2795–2804.

M. Schwarz, T. Rodehutskors, D. Droeschel, M. Beul, M. Schreiber, N. Araslanov, I. Ivanov, C. Lenz, J. Razlaw, S. Schüller, D. Schwarz, A. Topalidou-Kyniazopoulou, and S. Behnke (2017), „NimbRo Rescue: Solving Disaster-response Tasks with the Mobile Manipulation Robot Momaro", *Journal of Field Robotics (JFR)*, vol. 34, no. 2, pp. 400–425.

K. Sentz and S. Ferson (2002), *Combination of Evidence in Dempster-Shafer Theory*, SAND2002-0835, Sandia National Laboratories.

G. Shafer (1976), „A Mathematical Theory of Evidence", Princeton University Press.

T. B. Sheridan and W. L. Verplank (1978), *Human and Computer Control of Undersea Teleoperators*, Man-Machine Systems Lab, Massachusetts Institute of Technology (MIT).

J. Sinapov and A. Stoytchev (2007), „Learning and Generalization of Behavior-Grounded Tool Affordances“, *IEEE International Conference on Development and Learning (ICDL)*, pp. 19–24.

J. Sinapov and A. Stoytchev (2008), „Detecting the Functional Similarities Between Tools Using a Hierarchical Representation of Outcomes“, *IEEE International Conference on Development and Learning (ICDL)*, pp. 91–96.

M. Sokolova and G. Lapalme (2009), „A systematic analysis of performance measures for classification tasks“, *Information Processing and Management*, vol. 45, no. 4, pp. 427–437.

H. O. Song, M. Fritz, D. Goehring, and T. Darrell (2016), „Learning to Detect Visual Grasp Affordance“, *IEEE Transactions on Automation Science and Engineering*, vol. 13, no. 2, pp. 798–809.

M. Stark, P. Lies, M. Zillich, J. Wyatt, and B. Schiele (2008), „Functional Object Class Detection Based on Learned Affordance Cues“, *Computer Vision Systems*, Lecture Notes in Computer Science 5008, Berlin, Heidelberg: Springer, pp. 435–444.

M. Steedman (2002a), „Formalizing Affordance“, *Proceedings of the Cognitive Science Society*.

M. Steedman (2002b), „Plans, Affordances and Combinatory Grammar“, *Linguistics and Philosophy*, vol. 25, no. 5, pp. 723–753.

S. C. Stein, F. Wörgötter, M. Schoeler, J. Papon, and T. Kulvicius (2014), „Convexity based object partitioning for robot applications“, *IEEE International Conference on Robotics and Automation (ICRA)*, pp. 3213–3220.

T. A. Stoffregen (2003), „Affordances as Properties of the Animal-Environment System“, *Ecological Psychology*, vol. 15, no. 2, pp. 115–134.

A. Stoytchev (2005), „Behavior-Grounded Representation of Tool Affordances“, *IEEE International Conference on Robotics and Automation (ICRA)*, pp. 3060–3065.

A. Stoytchev (2008), „Learning the Affordances of Tools Using a Behavior-Grounded Approach“, *Towards Affordance-Based Robot Control*, Lecture Notes in Computer Science 4760, Berlin, Heidelberg: Springer.

F. Stramandinoli, V. Tikhanoff, U. Pattacini, and F. Nori (2015), „A Bayesian Approach Towards Affordance Learning in Artificial Agents“, *IEEE International Conference on Development and Learning and on Epigenetic Robotics*, pp. 298–299.

F. Stramandinoli, V. Tikhanoff, U. Pattacini, and F. Nori (2017), „Heteroscedastic Regression and Active Learning for Modeling Affordances in Humanoids“, *IEEE Transactions on Cognitive and Developmental Systems*.

E. B. Sudderth (2006), „Graphical Models for Visual Object Recognition and Tracking“, PhD thesis, Massachusetts Institute of Technology.

J. Sun, J. L. Moore, A. Bobick, and J. M. Rehg (2010), „Learning Visual Object Categories for Robot Affordance Prediction“, *International Journal of Robotics Research (IJRR)*, vol. 29, no. 2, pp. 174–197.

J. D. Sweeney and R. Grupen (2007), „A Model of Shared Grasp Affordances from Demonstration“, *IEEE/RAS International Conference on Humanoid Robots (Humanoids)*, pp. 27–35.

S. Szedmak, E. Uğur, and J. Piater (2014), „Knowledge Propagation and Relation Learning for Predicting Action Effects", *IEEE/RSJ International Conference on Intelligent Robots and Systems (IROS)*, pp. 623–629.

A. ten Pas and R. Platt (2016), „Localizing Handle-like Grasp Affordances in 3D Point Clouds", *Experimental Robotics*, Springer Tracts in Advanced Robotics 109, Springer, pp. 623–638.

M. Tenorth and M. Beetz (2013), „KnowRob: A knowledge processing infrastructure for cognition-enabled robots", *The International Journal of Robotics Research*, vol. 32, no. 5, pp. 566–590.

S. Thill, D. Caligiore, A. M. Borghi, T. Ziemke, and G. Baldassarre (2013), „Theories and computational models of affordance and mirror systems: An integrative review", *Neuroscience and Biobehavioral Reviews*, vol. 37, no. 3, pp. 491–521.

V. Tikhanoff, U. Pattacini, L. Natale, and G. Metta (2013), „Exploring affordances and tool use on the iCub", *IEEE/RAS International Conference on Humanoid Robots (Humanoids)*, pp. 130–137.

N. G. Tsagarakis, D. G. Caldwell, F. Negrello, W. Choi, L. Baccelliere, V. Loc, J. Noorden, L. Muratore, A. Margan, A. Cardellino, L. Natale, E. Mingo Hoffman, H. Dallali, N. Kashiri, J. Malzahn, J. Lee, P. Kryczka, D. Kanoulas, M. Garabini, M. Catalano, M. Ferrati, V. Varrichio, L. Pallottino, C. Pavan, A. Bicchi, A. Settimi, A. Rocchi, and A. Ajoudani (2017), „WALK-MAN: A High-Performance Humanoid Platform for Realistic Environments", *Journal of Field Robotics (JFR)*, vol. 34, no. 7, pp. 1225–1259.

M. T. Turvey (1992), „Affordances and Prospective Control: An Outline of the Ontology", *Ecological Psychology*, vol. 4, no. 3, pp. 173–187.

E. Uğur, M. R. Doğar, M. Çakmak, and E. Şahin (2007), „The learning and use of traversability affordance using range images on a mobile robot“, *IEEE International Conference on Robotics and Automation (ICRA)*, pp. 1721–1726.

E. Uğur, E. Oztop, and E. Şahin (2011a), „Goal emulation and planning in perceptual space using learned affordances“, *Robotics and Autonomous Systems*, vol. 59, no. 7, pp. 580–595.

E. Uğur, E. Oztop, and E. Şahin (2011b), „Going beyond the perception of affordances: Learning how to actualize them through behavioral parameters“, *IEEE International Conference on Robotics and Automation (ICRA)*, pp. 4768–4773.

E. Uğur and J. Piater (2015a), „Bottom-Up Learning of Object Categories, Action Effects and Logical Rules: From Continuous Manipulative Exploration to Symbolic Planning“, IEEE International Conference on Robotics and Automation (ICRA), pp. 119–139.

E. Uğur and J. Piater (2015b), „Refining discovered symbols with multi-step interaction experience“, *IEEE/RAS International Conference on Humanoid Robots (Humanoids)*, pp. 1007–1012.

E. Uğur and E. Şahin (2010), „Traversability: A Case Study for Learning and Perceiving Affordances in Robots“, *Adaptive Behavior*, vol. 18, no. 3, pp. 258–284.

E. Uğur, E. Şahin, and O. Erhan (2012), „Self-discovery of motor primitives and learning grasp affordances“, IEEE/RSJ International Conference on Intelligent Robots and Systems (IROS), pp. 3260–3267.

E. Uğur, S. Szedmak, and J. Piater (2014), „Bootstrapping paired-object affordance learning with learned single-affordance features“, International

Conference on Development and Learning and on Epigenetic Robotics, pp. 468–473.

N. Vahrenkamp, M. Wächter, M. Kröhnert, K. Welke, and T. Asfour (2015), „The Robot Software Framework ArmarX", *it - Information Technology*, vol. 57, no. 2, pp. 99–111.

K. M. Varadarajan and M. Vincze (2012a), „AfNet: The Affordance Network", *Asian Conference on Computer Vision*, pp. 512–523.

K. M. Varadarajan and M. Vincze (2012b), „AfRob: The Affordance Network Ontology for Robots", *IEEE/RSJ International Conference on Intelligent Robots and Systems (IROS)*, pp. 1343–1350.

M. Vergara, J. Sancho-Bru, V. Gracia-Ibáñez, and A. Pérez-González (2014), „An introductory study of common grasps used by adults during performance of activities of daily living", *Journal of Hand Therapy*, vol. 27, pp. 225–234.

M. Wächter, S. Ottenhaus, M. Kröhnert, N. Vahrenkamp, and T. Asfour (2016), „The ArmarX Statechart Concept: Graphical Programming of Robot Behavior", *Frontiers in Robotics and AI*, vol. 3.

M. Waibel, M. Beetz, J. Civera, R. D'Andrea, J. Elfring, D. Gálvez-López, K. Häussermann, R. Janssen, J. Montiel, A. Perzylo, B. Schießle, M. Tenorth, O. Zweigle, and R. van de Molengraft (2011), „RoboEarth", *IEEE Robotics & Automation Magazine*, vol. 18, no. 2, pp. 69–82.

W. H. Warren (1984), „Perceiving Affordances: Visual Guidance of Stair Climbing", *Journal of Experimental Psychology*, vol. 10, no. 5, pp. 683–703.

W. H. Warren and S. Whang (1987), „Visual Guidance of Walking Through Apertures: Body-Scaled Information for Affordances", *Journal of Experi-*

mental Psychology: Human Perception and Performance, vol. 13, no. 3, pp. 371–383.

A. Werner, B. Henze, D. A. Rodriguez, J. Gabaret, O. Porges, and M. A. Roa (2016), „Multi-Contact Planning and Control for a Torque-Controlled Humanoid Robot“, *IEEE/RSJ International Conference on Intelligent Robots and Systems (IROS)*, pp. 5708–5715.

D. A. Winter (1990), „Biomechanics and Motor Control of Human Movement“, New York: John Wiley & Sons.

F. Wörgötter, A. Agostini, N. Krüger, N. Shylo, and B. Porr (2009), „Cognitive agents - a procedural perspective relying on the predictability of Object-Action-Complexes (OACs)“, *Robotics and Autonomous Systems*, vol. 57, pp. 420–432.

C. Ye, Y. Yang, R. Mao, C. Fermüller, and Y. Aloimonos (2017), „What Can I Do Around Here? Deep Functional Scene Understanding for Cognitive Robots“, *IEEE International Conference on Robotics and Automation (ICRA)*, pp. 4604–4611.

P. Zech, S. Haller, S. R. Lakani, B. Ridge, E. Uğur, and J. Piater (2017), „Computational models of affordance in robotics: a taxonomy and systematic classification“, *Adaptive Behavior*, vol. 25, no. 5, pp. 235–271.

Y. Zhu, A. Fathi, and L. Fei-Fei (2014), „Reasoning about Object Affordances in a Knowledge Base Representation“, *European Conference on Computer Vision (ECCV)*, pp. 408–424.

M. Zucker, S. Joo, M. X. Grey, C. Rasmussen, E. Huang, M. Stilman, and A. Bobick (2015), „A General-purpose System for Teleoperation of the DRC-HUBO Humanoid Robot“, *Journal of Field Robotics (JFR)*, vol. 32, no. 3, pp. 336–351.